Advance Praise for

The Power of Servant-Leadership

"*The Power of Servant-Leadership* is an extraordinary collection of Robert Greenleaf's finest and most mature essays on servant-leadership, spirit, and wholeness. Today there is a growing worldwide movement of people and organizations— deeply committed to servant-leadership—who have been inspired by Greenleaf's earlier writings. Beautifully enriched by Peter Vaill's Foreword, Jim Shannon's Afterword, and Larry Spears's Introduction, *The Power of Servant-Leadership* is a wonderful and unexpected gift to the world. It is destined to become a classic."

> **Max DePree**, *author of* Leading Without Power
> *and* Leadership is an Art

"No one in the past 30 years has had a more profound impact on thinking about leadership than Robert Greenleaf. If we sought an objective measure of the quality of leadership available to society, there would be none better than the number of people reading and studying Robert Greenleaf's writings."

> **Peter M. Senge**, *author of* The Fifth Discipline

"It is wonderful to have access to Greenleaf's visionary thought in *The Power of Servant-Leadership*. Every time I read him, I am both humbled and awed. Nearly thirty years ago he wrote clearly and forcefully about the issues that still challenge us today. It is time to act on his visions, and this volume is a great help for stepping into the future that Greenleaf describes so eloquently."

> **Margaret J. Wheatley**, *author of* Leadership and
> the New Science, *co-author of* A Simpler Way

"The most difficult steps, Greenleaf has written, that any developing servant-leader must take, is to begin the personal journey toward wholeness and self-discovery. This new collection of essays, written with exceptional depth and grace, offer Robert Greenleaf's most powerful insights about this journey. Anyone interested in the most subtle yet most important aspects of the emerging leadership paradigm must read this book."

Joseph Jaworski, *author of* Synchronicity

"In my area of work, I've found that the concept of servant-leadership is crucial to advance governing boards beyond their current primitive state. *The Power of Servant-Leadership* assembles Greenleaf's groundbreaking observations in an accessible and concentrated form for today's busy readers."

John Carver, *author of* Boards That Make a Difference

"The writings of Robert Greenleaf grow as the reader matures in leadership and understanding of the cultural transformation taking place around us. The essays in *The Power of Servant-Leadership* take on new meaning with each reading and are well worth continuing reflection. We first met Greenleaf in 1978. Each year since, we have grown to discover fresh dimensions within his writing and thought. Like special mentors, these penetrating essays will continue to guide you like the wise words alive in your memory when needed."

Ann McGee-Cooper and Duane Trammell, *co-authors of* You Don't Have To Go Home From Work Exhausted!

"Bob Greenleaf was the first author on leadership to emphasize that human institutions mean far more than results or success or profits. He believed that we exist in order to cooperate with others to achieve purposes beyond ourselves, for some greater collective good. These splendidly thoughtful essays elaborate on that theme. I've read each of them over the past 20 or so years, and it's about time they've been published in one place. A blessing for all of us."

> **Warren Bennis**, *Distinguished Professor,*
> *Marshall School of Business at the University of Southern California,*
> *author of* Organizing Genius

"We are greatly encouraged to know that the servant-leadership movement will have access to these inspiring and important writings of Robert Greenleaf. These are reflective and burnished works. For many who have had their lives affected by Greenleaf, they will be a promise fulfilled. For those who will be introduced to servant-leadership through these essays, the experience will be a welcoming introduction."

> **Dr. John C. Burkhardt**, *Program Director, Leadership*
> *and Higher Education, W.K. Kellogg Foundation*

"Robert Greenleaf's unique voice speaks to what, in the end, matters most in the life of a leader—how *others* have grown and prospered. Though conceived and composed years ago, Greenleaf is profoundly modern, and with the mature wisdom of experience he guides us to the essence of our current search for meaning and purpose. *The Power of Servant-Leadership* is an extraordinary collection of a master's work, and Greenleaf's voice will resonate in your soul long after you have read the last word."

> **Jim Kouzes**, *Chairman and CEO, TPG/Learning Systems,*
> *co-author of* The Leadership Challenge and Credibility

"I am honored to add my voice to those in praise of *The Power of Servant-Leadership* . Even though it has been many years since Robert Greenleaf first gave the world his compelling insights, there has never been a time when we needed servant-leadership more than we need it now. Who knows how long business will be suffering the destructive residue of a generation of gunslinger superstar CEOs who, in their excessively narrow definition of "stockholder value," have created workplaces of fear and anxiety? The only salvation of the workplace as a source of personal meaning and purpose is to develop and reinforce manager-leaders who will embrace the values of Robert Greenleaf. I hope that this book will be a powerful tool in that effort."

James A. Autry, *author,* Love & Profit
and Confessions of an Accidental Businessman

"Management thought has always been captivated by innovation, always looking for a quick fix in five or seven lessons. The overconfidence such neophilia generates is already beginning to produce a reaction—the friendly critics of capitalism from George Soros to Charles Handy signal growing dissatisfaction with superficial formulas. Robert Greenleaf is not about formulas; Greenleaf is about wisdom. Wisdom is a rare and precious thing, perhaps too precious for best-seller lists, too demanding for people in search of easy answers. For people willing to think about organizational life and culture, Greenleaf is indispensable."

Robert L. Payton, *author,* Philanthropy:
Voluntary Action for the Public Good

"That Robert Greenleaf wrote the essays on leadership in this beautiful collection some years ago hardly vitiates their importance. Today they are more relevant—and more accepted by thoughtful leaders—than ever before. Using words ranging from E. B. White's commentary on the "gift of language" to the warning in Proverbs that "where there is no vision, the people perish," the author articulates profound ideas that, in this rapid-fire age of global technology, are more critical to effective leadership than ever before. Yes, the leader is—must also be—the servant. Mr. Greenleaf, far before his time, got it just right."

> *John Bogle, Chairman, The Vanguard Group;*
> *author,* Bogle on Mutual Funds

"With so many publications now directing leaders to look beyond enterprise gains to find meaning and wholeness, it is most timely to revisit Robert Greenleaf's servant-leadership ideas in *The Power of Servant-Leadership.* Progressive leaders are compelled to build sustainable value, social accountability, trust and integrity in the workplace, and purpose and character in the corporation. Greenleaf's writings are sure to focus such leaders' endeavors on the heart and soul of the organization: its own people.

> *Kendrick B. Melrose, Chairman and CEO, The Toro Company;*
> *author,* Making the Grass Greener on Your Side

"At last, these timeless essays by Robert Greenleaf gathered in a single volume. Buy one for yourself, and one for each of your children and grandchildren. They will thank you even as we thank this great servant-leader."

> *Frances Hesselbein, President, The Drucker Foundation; co-editor,*
> The Community of the Future, The Leader of the Future,
> The Organization of the Future

The Power of Servant-Leadership

Also Edited by Larry C. Spears

Insights on Leadership: Service, Stewardship, Spirit and Servant-Leadership, 1998

On Becoming a Servant-Leader (with Don M. Frick), 1996

Seeker and Servant (with Anne T. Fraker), 1996

Reflections on Leadership: How Robert K. Greenleaf's Theory of Servant-Leadership Influenced Today's Top Management Thinkers, 1995

As Contributing Author

Stone Soup for the World, edited by Marianne Larned, 1998

Leadership in a New Era, edited by John Renesch, 1994

The Power of Servant-Leadership

ESSAYS BY ROBERT K. GREENLEAF

EDITED BY LARRY C. SPEARS

Foreword by Peter B. Vaill

Afterword by James P. Shannon

Berrett-Koehler Publishers, Inc.
San Francisco

02-437

Berrett-Koehler Publishers, Inc.
450 Sansome Street, Suite 1200
San Francisco, CA 94111-3320
Tel: 415-288-0260   Fax: 415-362-2512
www.bkpub.com

Ordering information
Individual sales. Berrett-Koehler publications are available through most bookstores. They can also be ordered direct from Berrett-Koehler at the address above.

Quantity sales. Special discounts are available on quantity purchases by corporations, associations, and others. For details, write to the "Special Sales Department" at the Berrett-Koehler address above.

Orders for college textbook/course adoption use. Please contact Berrett-Koehler Publishers at the address above.

Orders by U.S. trade bookstores and wholesalers. Please contact Publishers Group West, 1700 Fourth Street, Berkeley, CA 94710; 510-528-1444; 1-800-788-3123; Fax 510-528-3444.

Printed in the United States of America

Printed on acid-free and recycled paper that is composed of 50% recovered fiber, including 10% postconsumer waste.

Library of Congress Cataloging-in-Publication Data
Greenleaf, Robert K.
    The power of servant-leadership: essays / by Robert K. Greenleaf ; edited and intro-duction by Larry C. Spears ; foreword by Peter B. Vaill ; afterword by James P. Shannon.
        p.   cm.
    Includes bibliographical references and index.
    ISBN 1-57675-035-3 (alk. paper)
    1. Leadership.   2. Associations, institutions, etc.   3. Christian leadership.
    4. Service (Theology).   I. Spears, Larry C., 1955– .   II. Title.
HM141.G687   1998
303.3´4—dc21   98-24143
                                                                                    CIP

First printing: August 1998
01   10 9 8 7 6 5

Text design by Detta Penna

Table of Contents

About the Author

Robert K. Greenleaf spent most of his organizational life in the field of management research, development, and education at AT&T. Just before his retirement as director of management research there, he held a joint appointment as visiting lecturer of the Massachusetts Institute of Technology's Sloan School of Management and at the

Harvard Business School. In addition, he held teaching positions at both Dartmouth College and the University of Virginia.

His consultancies included Ohio University; MIT; the Ford Foundation; the R.K. Mellon Foundation; Lilly Endowment, Inc.; and the American Foundation for Management Research.

As a consultant to universities, businesses, foundations, and churches during the tumultuous 1960s and 1970s, his eclectic and wide-ranging curiosity, reading, and contemplation provided an unusual background for observing these institutions.

As a lifelong student of organization—that is, how things get done—he distilled these observations in a series of essays on the theme of "the servant as leader," the objective of which is to stimulate thought and action for building a better, more caring society.

Robert K. Greenleaf, who died in 1990, is the author of four other books in addition to *The Power of Servant-Leadership*. They are: *On Becoming a Servant-Leader* (1996), *Seeker and Servant* (1996), *Teacher as Servant* (1979), and *Servant-Leadership* (1977).

Foreword

PETER B. VAILL, UNIVERSITY OF ST. THOMAS

In a favorite book of meditations, John Thom, a 19th-century clergy-man, is quoted as follows:

> The real corrupters of society may be, not the corrupt, but those who have held back the righteous leaven, the salt that has Lost its savor, the innocent who have not even the moral courage to show what they think of the effrontery of impurity, the serious, who yet timidly succeed before some loud-voiced scoffer—the heart trembling all over with religious sensibilities that yet suffers itself through false shame to be beaten down into outward and practical acquiescence by some rude and worldly nature. (Tileston, 1934, p. 221)

Bob Greenleaf could have written this paragraph. He might have been a little more informal about the matter. He would have been careful not to sound holier than thou as he spoke of the lack of moral courage and "hearts trembling with false shame." I do think, though, that these last essays of his reveal over and over, in dozens of ways, the courage the paragraph calls for. Greenleaf would have smiled at the realization that his work indeed can be seen as the "righteous leaven" for his favorite subject: organizations and how things get done in them.

I feel privileged to be able to introduce this collection. I don't begin to think I understand these essays in their true depth and implications, but repeatedly as I have read through them and reflected on them, I find myself saying, "Yes, he's right and what he's saying is terribly important." His deceptively casual writing style draws me into thinking along with him. I am sure other readers have the same experience with his thought that I do—of finding him saying something that is just about in so many words what has occurred to one independently. Yet I never find him derivative or simply rehashing. Instead I, at least, find myself wondering why I haven't been more insistent about the point Greenleaf is making, why I haven't taken the idea and made it the righteous leaven of my work. His is both a familiar voice and an original one.

Greenleaf has what we may call a "big idea." It is the idea of the servant as leader, and many of these essays are his last explorations of the extraordinary implications of that notion. The big idea is that leadership, in the final analysis, must be about service. That is the only way it can both sustain itself as leadership and truly offer to its colleagues and "followers" the benefits of its insights and its energy. Greenleaf's idea resolves one of the oldest paradoxes of the leadership field: how can a leader be both concerned about the "task" and mindful of the "social," "concerned for production and concerned for people," "effective" in getting work done and "efficient" in not causing all kinds of human problems in the process? Every leadership theory tries in one way or another to deal with both of these "dimensions." The big idea about service—Greenleaf probably would not like this description—is that it is both an attitudinal and behavioral concept. It combines a concern for getting things done with attention to the needs of those who are getting things done. There are not two functions; there is only one—servanthood.

Greenleaf's challenge is to make a worldly and pressured—and somewhat distracted, exhausted, and frightened—society of leaders and potential leaders believe it. These essays are the last we shall see of him speaking his truth as plainly and insistently as he can.

In the next few paragraphs, I want to say a few more things about the big idea. Then I will close with a few more reflections about Greenleaf the man.

There are five themes in Greenleaf's way of talking about "the servant as leader" that strike me as quite significant. They are as follows: (1) the grammar of the phrase itself; (2) Greenleaf's commitment to practice; (3) the importance of mission; (4) the nature and role of "persuasion"; and (5) his idea about a "theology of institutions." These five themes appear repeatedly throughout his writings, yet, except for his discussion of mission, Greenleaf himself is frequently so offhand and low-keyed in the way he talks that the significance of the idea may be missed.

1.   The grammar of "the servant as leader." As the reader is no doubt aware, Greenleaf's idea is frequently abbreviated to "servant-leadership," or "servant leadership." For purposes of economy and simplicity, it is probably necessary to abbreviate Greenleaf's phrase in this fashion. But the danger is that a key feature of his big idea will be thereby lost. In the phrase "the servant as leader" (which after all was Greenleaf's title for the original seminal essay), the subject is the servant or service; the predicate is the leader. His phrase is an application of the philosophy of service to the practice of leadership.

As is apparent in various writings in the present volume, service was the most important thing for Greenleaf. He frequently takes the time to ground the phrase in biblical references and connect it to the deepest yearnings of the human spirit. To be sure, Greenleaf is deeply concerned about leadership, but his concern is that it is being practiced (and theorized about) without reference to service. For Greenleaf, service is the moral dimension of prime importance, not just for leadership but for life. It is service he fears has been lost sight of, not leadership. To put it compactly, I think Greenleaf is saying that leadership is a special case of service; he is not saying that service is a special case of leadership.

This distinction is important because we live in a period when there is an almost frantic casting about by leaders and leadership thinkers for answers to the profound dilemmas of leadership in our turbulent and unpredictable world. Some will take up Greenleaf's notion and test it for the extent to which it "solves their leadership problem." The "servant as leader" idea does not solve the leadership problem in the sense that leaders and scholars might hope. If anything, it will frustrate and annoy such seekers. Soon we will hear them saying, "Servant-leadership? Oh yeah, right, we tried that." But this misunderstands Greenleaf's challenge. As I understand him, he is not asking, "What service can you render as a leader?" but rather "What leadership can you exercise as a servant?"

2. Greenleaf's commitment to practice. Repeatedly in these essays, Greenleaf reminds us that he is writing about the servant as leader as a student of how things get done in organizations. He wants us to look concretely at the way the actions and attitudes of service can transform relations among concrete human beings. His short answer to the question, I think, would be, "In the long run, things get done among human beings, including within organizations, by people serving one another." That is what his experience has taught him, and for which he thinks there is overwhelming confirmatory evidence throughout human history.

Greenleaf's interest in practice has several dimensions that, taken together, give him quite a different outlook from most other contemporary writers on leadership. For one thing, he knows how complex any process of action is in an organization. His repeated references to his own business experience as well as to his many extensive contacts with other organizations make clear that he has no illusions about how unstable and dicey organizational action can be. His commitment to action is also seen in his consistent attention to the process by which his ideas can be implemented. Just about when I, as a reader, am thinking, "Sounds good, but how are you going to do that?" it turns out that Greenleaf has been asking himself the same question; and so he proceeds to offer a few thoughts about how what he is talking about can happen.

Another feature of his commitment to practice is his concern for the process by which more servant-leaders can be produced. Yes, he wants men and women in positions of influence to consider his ideas, but he is equally concerned with increasing the sheer number of younger men and women who will be helped to develop as servant-leaders.

This concern leads him to challenge educational institutions in exactly the way that they (as a professor, I should say "we") need to be challenged: we in higher education know that only by accident are we producing visionary young men and women who aspire to leadership, to the extent we are producing them at all. We don't like to admit it. Greenleaf has found us out.

Finally, his concern for practice focuses him on the *way* that any organization works. It is clear in this book that in the later years of his life, as well as at AT&T, he moved among the high and the mighty of society's major institutions: universities, businesses, foundations, and the like. As he quietly but firmly repeats his interest in how things get done, it is as if he were saying, "I know all of you are terribly important people who feel that what your organizations do is terribly important in society. But my angle of vision has taught me something about the way your institutions work and don't work that perhaps you are unaware of." We live in an age of "content experts" who know all about moon landings and heart transplants and giga-sized databases and global markets and transformations of the biosphere—and many of them are leading or aspire to lead institutions concerned with those things. Greenleaf is a process expert, and he has been thinking about phenomena that often get lost in the swirl of events that our organizational leaders are so good at triggering.

3. The importance of mission. One can hardly read a page of these essays without encountering Greenleaf's deep beliefs about the importance of mission in organizations. He, of course, is not the only or the first writer on organizations to declare the importance of mission. But as we reflect along with him in his various discussions of missions, I encourage us to keep in mind a deep conundrum—one that I think Greenleaf himself is quite aware of. The question is, Where does a sense of mission come from? The power and importance of mission, once articulated, is unquestionable. But how does it happen? What is the process by which a deep sense of an organization's reason to be gets into the collective psyche of its members? Greenleaf realizes what a tough question this is. He also realizes that a convenient answer is that some charismatic individual steps forward and articulates a mission full-blown—and there are even places in these essays where Greenleaf seems to be personally attracted to this "Great Man" model of leadership.

But I think he knows better. Without denying that a single individual can occasionally say or do something that has the requisite galvanizing effect, Greenleaf knows that servanthood is not about stepping forward and taking charge. Rather, I think he understands that there has to be such a thing as service to the mission-formulation and articulation process itself. That is different from doing people's thinking and feeling for them. Greenleaf's servant-leader is a servant of the organization's learning process, I think. About that, the servant-leader is tough-minded and unflinching. Ways must be found whereby organization members can come together on a dream.

4. The nature and role of persuasion. Greenleaf is particularly eloquent about the role of *persuasion* in servant-leadership. He uses the term in its everyday sense, and I think he would not be impressed with what the academic world has done with the concept. Nor would he accept a cynical view of persuasion that equates it to manipulation or slick rhetoric.

There is healthy and honest persuasion. I think Greenleaf wants us to envision ordinary conversation between people where at least one, but hopefully many or most, are trying to say things to each other and do things for each other that are in service of a common dream or sense of mission that they share. "Persuasion" is the process of one person co-creating to another or others what he or she thinks pursuit of the mission entails, including statements about the meaning of the mission and/or the need for new attention to its meaning. The service is in the thought, the creativity, the information, the experience, and the energetic vision the co-creator feels. I have seen these conversations many times. They occur all the time in excellent organizations—what in a series of studies some years ago I called "high performing systems." In these conversations committed people are doing everything they can to help each other. Greenleaf doesn't see why a more widespread philosophy of service to a mission or a dream can't occur almost anywhere. My own studies and experience convince me he is quite right: there is no type of organized human activity where mutual service to a common vision and the energetic reminding of each other of what is involved (i.e., persuasion) cannot happen.

5. A theology of institutions. I find Greenleaf's speculations on the idea of a theology of institutions or organizations one of the most interesting and original notions in his writings. While quick to state that he is not a theologian, and therefore does not know what is required for a body of ideas to be a worked-out theology, he nonetheless seems very sure that such a theology is needed and should be possible. He does not see why, if there can be a theology of persons, there cannot be a theology of organizations.

He is not talking about theocracy, not about top-down governance and control by theocratic principles and doctrines. He is far too independent a thinker and a man for that. No, I think he wants us to reflect on what the fundamental nature of a human organization is; how we regard it. Is it a pure invention for secular purposes? Just a vehicle, at bottom an ad hoc arrangement with no claim to a deeper significance and justification for its existence? My guess is that Greenleaf perceives intuitively that the mission or vision or dream has a quality beyond its verbal, secular content. He would like to see us work out what this quality is, and his hunch is that when we do we will find ourselves reflecting on the relation of this dream to the spiritual worldviews that we are already familiar with for persons. My main point, though, is to invite the reader to reflect deeply on these comments of Greenleaf's about a theology of institutions. They may turn out to be among his most original and significant insights.

A Final Word

Most of the essays in this volume have been previously published in pamphlet form by the Greenleaf Center for Servant-Leadership. At the back of most of these pamphlets is a brief biography of Greenleaf and a photograph of him taken apparently late in life. This photograph of Greenleaf may have a significance in his life or for those close to him that I am not aware of. Inquiries at the Center did not result in any particular stories about the photo or the reasons for its use.

Yet I consider it so extraordinary an image—one that stimulates thoughts and feelings in me that are pertinent to the spirit of these essays and to this Foreword. The picture is almost a direct frontal of his head and shoulders, open-collared and informal. He is turned very slightly to his left from the camera and the effect is to place the left half of his face almost completely in shadow while the right side remains fully illuminated. His silky white hair lies smoothly on the right side of his head but is invisible on the left. The head is tilted just slightly upward and the mouth is set in a patient composed line—not preparing to speak, but not relaxed either. Even though half-lit, the nose is strong and suggests that in profile he might have been distinctly "hawklike." It is a striking picture, and made the more so by one final feature: it is dramatically off-center. Greenleaf's head and shoulders occupy the right half of the picture, but the left half is blank space. This left half is strongly illuminated at the bottom and shades to black at the top, but is completely empty. Most of us, on pulling such a snapshot out of the envelope in the supermarket parking lot, would immediately judge the picture to be not worth saving because it is so off-center. The longer I look at this picture the more I am stimulated to think about Greenleaf as a person. There is a darkness running through his writings. He is writing about terribly complex problems which contain the potential for some very bad outcomes—and he knows it. Yet he is not wringing his hands, not paralyzed with alarm. The mouth is composed; the eyes are sharply engaged, but kindly (this judgment about the eyes being one that a friend of mine independently described the same way). The shadow down the middle of the face with the wispy white hair and the off-center placement make me feel as if I am sitting there talking to him, perhaps in the evening with late light coming horizontally through the window onto half of his face as he sits talking to me.

The slight uptilt to the head, the direct gaze, and the mouth that has said a lot and could say more but does not at the moment feel the need, combine in a sort of friendly but quizzical challenge. "I am coming from both darkness and light," says the face, "both out of problems and possibilities. I may even be a little off-center myself in my understanding of these things. But tell me: are you going to do anything about them?" Am I—are we—indeed?

References

Tileston, M. *Daily Strength for Daily Needs.* New York: Putnam, 1934. (Originally published in 1884)

Preface

The Power of Servant-Leadership is an extraordinary collection of Robert K. Greenleaf's mature and final writings on the concept of servant-leadership. Servant-leadership, itself, is an important part of the emerging leadership and management paradigm for the 21st century. Today, there is a growing movement of people and organizations that have been influenced by servant-leadership. *The Power of Servant-Leadership* offers Robert Greenleaf's own insights on the interrelated subjects of serving and leading, wholeness and spirit.

In 1970, retired AT&T executive Robert K. Greenleaf coined the term *servant-leadership* to describe a kind of leadership that he felt was largely missing from organizations. It was Greenleaf's belief that leadership ought to be based on serving the needs of others and on helping those who are served to become "healthier, wiser, freer, more autonomous, more likely themselves to become servants." Over the next 20 years, Greenleaf wrote a series of highly influential books and essays, which have helped lead the way for the emerging model in leadership and management. *The Power of Servant-Leadership* is intended to stimulate and inspire many people in their practice of a more caring, serving kind of leadership.

For those readers who may already be familiar with Greenleaf's classic book, *Servant Leadership* (1977, Paulist Press), *The Power of Servant-Leadership* represents, in many ways, a true sequel. For others, this book will serve as a good introduction to the concept and practice of servant-leadership and to the insightful ideas of Robert K. Greenleaf.

The Power of Servant-Leadership is a collection of eight essays by Robert Greenleaf, most of which were originally published as separate pamphlets by The Greenleaf Center. Because of their pamphlet format, these essays have not been previously available in bookstores or libraries, and they have had a far too limited readership. Many of the essays contained in this book were published during a ten-year period from 1977 to 1987. They include some of Greenleaf's most original, powerful, and final works. Many of them reflect Greenleaf's own continual refinement of the servant-as-leader concept; several others focus on the related issues of spirit, commitment to vision, and seeing things whole.

As an aid to the reader, the following is a brief, thumbnail description of each of the eight Greenleaf essays included in this volume.

"Servant: Retrospect and Prospect"

This is a reflection on ten years of working with the ferment that the publication of "The Servant as Leader" generated. Mind-sets that enforce rigidity in our society and frustrate reformers are identified in universities, health professions, churches, institutions, and businesses. Greenleaf addresses the creation of liberating visions that are required to surmount these mind-sets.

"Education and Maturity"
The meaning of maturity is explored as a lifelong journey of developing one's own unique potential into personal significance and character, while recognizing the relationship between using work as a means of fulfillment and conformity as an essential element of effective society.

"The Leadership Crisis"
This thought-provoking essay suggests why the institutions of our day, and our society in general, are all suffering from a leadership crisis. Greenleaf suggests a solution to this dilemma by defining three kinds of power, their uses, and their limitations. He also describes the necessary role of a "great dream," or vision, and the effective use of persuasive power in the life of an institution.

"Have You a Dream Deferred?"
By redefining responsibility for growth and constructive influence, an opportunity to build a new ethic challenges those who seek to reach their potential in serving the public interest. Focus is placed on the qualities of a lifestyle of distinction.

"The Servant as Religious Leader"
From the perspective of organization (how things get done), rather than as a scholar or theologian, this essay addresses the phenomenon of "spirit" on which all leadership is so dependent that it may never be capsulized. The central theme is: Work! Do something! Work to increase the number of spiritual leaders (not just in churches, but everywhere) who are capable of holding their own against the forces of destruction and indifference.

"Seminary as Servant"

Seminaries of all denominations are identified, along with some foundations, as standing in a strategic position to generate a much-needed liberating and prophetic vision. They are seen as having the opportunity to choose a greater vision of service to society than that to which most aspire. *Seminary as Servant* is addressed to those who would take the risks of leadership to move the seminary from where it is to the greater place it might be.

"My Debt to E. B. White"

This lively essay traces the influence of author E. B. White on Greenleaf's thinking over a period of 55 years. He concludes that two of White's abilities—"seeing things whole" and "the gift of language to express what he saw"—were key to his power as a writer. The lifelong personal development these insights stimulated in the author sings through this essay in quotations and examples.

"Old Age: The Ultimate Test of Spirit"

Here a gathering of personal reflections from 83 years of living, working, thinking, and learning weaves a definition of *spirit* as "the driving force behind the motive to serve," and defines the test of old age as the time to assess one's active life and to achieve serenity from knowing that one has served. Greenleaf identifies those significant people, events, and things that helped him—and that may help others—learn to live wholly in the moment of "now" and to pay attention to the things that make life more rewarding. One of the very last pieces written by Robert Greenleaf, "Old Age: The Ultimate Test of Spirit" contains great wisdom. This essay of depth and grace ranks alongside the finest writings of such American essayists as Emerson and Thoreau.

Robert Greenleaf's own writings are increasingly in demand as both he and the servant-leadership concept have become much better known since his death in September of 1990. Following the publication of his classic book, *Servant Leadership*, in 1977, Greenleaf went on to write a series of separately published essays. Most of these essays, ranging between 12 and 70 pages each, were individually published over a ten-year period by The Greenleaf Center. In the collection of these essays in one book, readers now have an opportunity to delve into some of Robert Greenleaf's very best writings and to understand in greater detail the ideas and practices that make up servant-leadership.

The richness of this volume has been further deepened by Peter Vaill's Foreword and by Jim Shannon's Afterword. Peter Vaill is a noted consultant and professor of human systems and the author of *Managing as a Performing Art* and *Learning as a Way of Being*. Jim Shannon's remarkable career has included time as a former priest, college president, lawyer, and head of the General Mills Foundation. He is currently a senior advisor to the Council on Foundations. Both Vaill and Shannon have read and reread Greenleaf's writings over many years, and through their contributions to this book, each has provided helpful insights into the significance of Greenleaf and servant-leadership.

I view the growing trend toward servant-leadership as a reflection of the ongoing maturation of humankind. It is my sincere hope that this movement toward servant-leadership will find an even greater expression in the decades and centuries to come. Through his writings on the servant-as-leader idea, Robert Greenleaf has increasingly become known as an intellectual trailblazer in leadership and management, and as someone who is helping to lead many of us into a more caring and thoughtful 21st century.

Larry C. Spears
Indianapolis, Indiana
August, 1998

Acknowledgments

I am particularly indebted to my colleagues at The Greenleaf Center for Servant-Leadership—Tamyra Freeman, Nancy Larner, Michele Lawrence, Isabel Lopez, Geneva Loudd, Jim Robinson, Richard Smith, and Kelly Tobe—for their friendship, encouragement, and support. My own journey in servant-leadership has also been enriched through my partnership with the following past and present Greenleaf Center trustees: Bill Bottum; Linda Chezem; Diane Cory; Sister Joyce DeShano; Joe DiStefano; Harley Flack; Newcomb Greenleaf; Bill Guillory; Carole Hamm; Jack Lowe, Jr.; Jeff McCollum; Ann McGee-Cooper; Andy Morikawa; Jim Morris; Paul Olson; Bob Payton; Sister Joel Read; Sister Sharon Richardt; Judith Sturnick; and Jim Tatum.

I am most grateful to two institutions—the W. K. Kellogg Foundation (especially John Burkhardt, Stephanie Clohessey, and Larraine Matusak) and Lilly Endowment, Inc. (particularly Willis Bright and Craig Dykstra)—for their ongoing support of servant-leadership and The Greenleaf Center.

My special thanks go to the wonderful staff at Berrett-Koehler Publishers, especially Valerie Barth and Steve Piersanti.

I wish to thank my family and friends for their love and encouragement, especially my wife, Beth Lafferty; my sons, James and Matthew Spears; and my parents, Bertha and L C Spears. I would also like to thank the following people and institutions for their encouragement and support along the way: James Autry, Walter Brogan, Dick Broholm, Steve Brooks, Max Case, the Central Committee for Conscientious Objectors, the Childbirth Education Association of Greater Philadelphia, Donna Davis, Roberta and Robert DeHaan, Vinton Deming, DePauw University, Max DePree, Karen Farmer, Diann and Allison Feldman, Anne Fraker, *Friends Journal*, Friends Select School, Joe and Laurie Goss, Cathy Gray, the Great Lakes Colleges Association's Philadelphia Center, the Greater Philadelphia Philosophy Consortium, Lisa Greenleaf, Robert K. Greenleaf, John and Mary Gummere, John Haynes, Todd and Ellen Daniels-Howell, Madeline Greenleaf Jaynes, Frank and Marian Killian, Michael Krausz, Eva and Richard Krebs, John and Aline Lafferty, Roger and Verona Lafferty, Jon Landau, Ralph Lewis, Diane Lisco, Isabel Lopez, Robert Lynn, Tjeb Maris, John Nason, National Association for Community Leadership, Hilbrand Nawijn, Marcia Newman, John Noble, Keith Opdahl, Lou Outlaw, M. Scott Peck, Mike and Nancy Revnes, Olcutt Sanders, Gert Schaart, Karen Schultz, Peter Senge, Alice Simpson, Elissa Sklaroff, Debra Spears, Lucian and Chassie Spears, Debra Thomas, Peter Vaill, Wendell Walls, and Signe Wilkinson.

Finally, I wish to express my deep appreciation to the many servant-leaders working within countless organizations around the world. Your efforts at building spirit in the workplace truly inspire others to servant-leadership.

Introduction

LARRY SPEARS

"The servant-leader is servant first. It begins with the natural feeling that one wants to serve. Then conscious choice brings one to aspire to lead. The best test is: do those served grow as persons; do they, while being served, become healthier, wiser, freer, more autonomous, more likely themselves to become servants?"

Robert K. Greenleaf, *The Servant as Leader*, 1970

With that initial definition of servant-leadership in 1970, Robert K. Greenleaf planted a seed of an idea that continues to grow in its influence on society with each passing year. In fact, during the 1990s, we have witnessed an unparalleled explosion of interest and practice of servant-leadership. In many ways, it can be said that the times are only now beginning to catch up with Robert Greenleaf's visionary call to servant-leadership.

Servant-leadership, now in its third decade as a specific leadership and management concept, continues to create a quiet revolution in workplaces around the world. This introduction is intended to provide a broad overview of the growing influence this unique concept of servant-leadership is having on people and their workplaces.

As we prepare to enter the 21st century, we are witnessing a shift in many businesses and nonprofit organizations—away from traditional autocratic and heirarchical modes of leadership and toward a model based on teamwork and community; one that seeks to involve others in decision making; one that is strongly based in ethical and caring behavior; and one that is attempting to enhance the personal growth of workers while at the same time improving the caring and quality of our many institutions. This emerging approach to leadership and service is called "servant-leadership."

The words *servant* and *leader* are usually thought of as being opposites. When two opposites are brought together in a creative and meaningful way, a paradox emerges. And so the words *servant* and *leader* have been brought together to create the paradoxical idea of servant-leadership.

The basic idea of servant-leadership is both intuitive and sensible. In light of the history of the industrial revolution, for a long time there has been a tendency to view people as objects; institutions have viewed people mostly as cogs within a machine. In the past few decades, we have witnessed a shift in that long-held view. Standard practices are rapidly shifting toward the ideas put forward by Robert Greenleaf, Margaret Wheatley, Stephen Covey, Peter Senge, Danah Zohar, Max DePree, and many others who suggest that there is a better way to manage our organizations in the 21st century.

Today there is a much greater recognition of the need for a more team-oriented approach to leadership and management. Robert

Greenleaf's writings on the subject of servant-leadership helped get this movement started, and his views have had a profound and growing effect on many.

> "Despite all the buzz about modern leadership techniques, no one knows better than Greenleaf what really matters."
>
> *Working Woman* magazine (March, 1992)

The term *servant-leadership* was first coined in a 1970 essay by Robert K. Greenleaf (1904–1990) entitled "The Servant as Leader." Greenleaf, who was born in Terre Haute, Indiana, spent most of his organizational life in the field of management research, development, and education at AT&T. Following a 40-year career at AT&T, Greenleaf enjoyed a second career that lasted another 25 years, during which time he served as an influential consultant to a number of major institutions, including: Ohio University, M.I.T., Ford Foundation, R. K. Mellon Foundation, the Mead Corporation, the American Foundation for Management Research, and Lilly Endowment, Inc. In 1964, Greenleaf also founded the Center for Applied Ethics, which was renamed the Robert K. Greenleaf Center in 1985 and is now headquartered in Indianapolis.

As a lifelong student of how things get done in organizations, Greenleaf distilled his observations in a series of essays and books on the theme of "the servant as leader"—the objective of which was to stimulate thought and action for building a better, more caring society.

The idea of the servant-as-leader came partly out of Greenleaf's half-century of experience in working to shape large institutions. However, the event that crystallized Greenleaf's thinking came in the 1960s, when he read Herman Hesse's short novel, *Journey to the East*—an account of a mythical journey by a group of people on a spiritual quest. The central figure of the story is Leo, who accompanies the party as the servant and who sustains them with his caring spirit. All goes well with the journey until one day Leo disappears. The group quickly falls into disarray, and the journey is abandoned. They discover that they cannot make it without the servant, Leo.

After many years of searching, the narrator of the story stumbles upon Leo and is taken into the religious order that had sponsored the original journey. There, he discovers that Leo, whom he had first known as a servant, was in fact the head of the order, its guiding spirit and leader.

After reading this story, Greenleaf concluded that the central meaning of it was that the great leader is first experienced as a servant to others, and that this simple fact is central to his or her greatness. True leadership emerges from those whose primary motivation is a deep desire to help others.

In 1970, at the age of 66, Greenleaf published "The Servant as Leader," the first of a dozen essays and books on servant-leadership. Since that time, over a half-million copies of his books and essays have been sold worldwide. Slowly but surely, Greenleaf's servant-leadership writings have made a deep, lasting impression on leaders, managers, educators, and many others who are concerned with issues of leadership, management, service, and spirit.

In all of these works, Greenleaf discusses the need for a new kind of leadership model: a model that puts serving others—including employees, customers, and community—as the number one priority. Servant-leadership emphasizes increased service to others; a holistic approach to work; the promotion of a sense of community; and a deepening understanding of spirit in the workplace.

Who is a servant-leader? Greenleaf said that the servant-leader is one who is a servant first. In "The Servant as Leader" he wrote: "It begins with the natural feeling that one wants to serve, to serve first. Then conscious choice brings one to aspire to lead. The difference manifests itself in the care taken by the servant—first to make sure that other people's highest priority needs are being served. The best test is: Do those served grow as persons; do they, while being served, become healthier, wiser, freer, more autonomous, more likely themselves to become servants?"

It is important to stress that servant-leadership is not a "quick-fix" approach. Nor is it something that can quickly be instilled within an institution. At its core, servant-leadership is a long-term, transformational approach to life and work—in essence, a way of being—that has the potential for creating positive change throughout our society.

> "Servant leadership deals with the reality of power in everyday life—its legitimacy, the ethical restraints upon it and the beneficial results that can be attained through the appropriate use of power."
>
> *New York Times* (October 2, 1990)

After some years of carefully considering Greenleaf's original writings, I have identified a set of ten characteristics of the servant-leader that I view as being of critical importance, central to the development of servant-leaders.

1. *Listening*: Leaders have traditionally been valued for their communication and decision-making skills. Although these are also important skills for the servant-leader, they need to be reinforced by a deep commitment to listening intently to others. The servant-leader seeks to identify the will of a group and helps clarify that will. He or she seeks to listen receptively to what is being said (and not said!). Listening also encompasses getting in touch with one's own inner voice, and seeking to understand what one's body, spirit, and mind are communicating. Listening, coupled with regular periods of reflection, are essential to the growth of the servant-leader.

2. *Empathy*: The servant-leader strives to understand and empathize with others. People need to be accepted and recognized for their special and unique spirits. One assumes the good intentions of co-workers and does not reject them as people, even when one is forced to refuse to accept their behavior or performance. The most successful servant-leaders are those who have become skilled empathetic listeners.

3. *Healing*: The healing of relationships is a powerful force for transformation and integration. One of the great strengths of servant-leadership is the potential for healing one's self and one's relationship to others. Many people have broken spirits and have

suffered from a variety of emotional hurts. Although this is a part of
being human, servant-leaders recognize that they have an opportunity to "help make whole" those with whom they come in contact. In
"The Servant as Leader," Greenleaf writes, "There is something subtle communicated to one who is being served and led if, implicit in
the compact between servant-leader and led, is the understanding
that the search for wholeness is something they share."

4. *Awareness*: General awareness, and especially self-awareness,
strengthens the servant-leader. Making a commitment to foster
awareness can be scary—you never know what you may discover!
Awareness also aids one in understanding issues involving ethics and
values. It lends itself to being able to view most situations from a
more integrated, holistic position. As Greenleaf observed:
"Awareness is not a giver of solace—it is just the opposite. It is a dis-
turber and an awakener. Able leaders are usually sharply awake and
reasonably disturbed. They are not seekers after solace. They have
their own inner serenity."

5. *Persuasion*: Another characteristic of servant-leaders is a reliance on persuasion, rather than on one's positional authority, in
making decisions within an organization. The servant-leader seeks to
convince others, rather than coerce compliance. This particular element offers one of the clearest distinctions between the traditional
authoritarian model and that of servant-leadership. The servant-
leader is effective at building consensus within groups. This emphasis on persuasion over coercion probably has its roots within the
beliefs of The Religious Society of Friends (Quakers)—the denomination with which Robert Greenleaf himself was most closely allied.

6. *Conceptualization*: Servant-leaders seek to nurture their abilities to "dream great dreams." The ability to look at a problem (or an
organization) from a conceptualizing perspective means that one
must think beyond day-to-day realities. For many managers, this is a
characteristic that requires discipline and practice. The traditional
manager is consumed by the need to achieve short-term operational
goals. The manager who wishes to also be a servant-leader must

stretch his or her thinking to encompass broader-based conceptual thinking. Within organizations, conceptualization is, by its very nature, the proper role of boards of trustees or directors. Unfortunately, boards can sometimes become involved in the day-to-day operations (something that should always be discouraged!) and fail to provide the visionary concept for an institution. Trustees need to be mostly conceptual in their orientation; staffs need to be mostly operational in their perspective; and, the most effective CEOs and managers probably need to develop both perspectives. Servant-leaders are called to seek a delicate balance between conceptual thinking and a day-to-day focused approach.

7. *Foresight*: Closely related to conceptualization, the ability to foresee the likely outcome of a situation is hard to define, but easy to identify. One knows it when one sees it. Foresight is a characteristic that enables the servant-leader to understand the lessons from the past, the realities of the present, and the likely consequence of a decision for the future. It is also deeply rooted within the intuitive mind. There hasn't been a great deal written on foresight. It remains a largely unexplored area in leadership studies, but one most deserving of careful attention.

8. *Stewardship*: Peter Block (author of *Stewardship*, and *The Empowered Manager*) has defined stewardship as "holding something in trust for another." Robert Greenleaf's view of all institutions was one in which CEOs, staffs, and trustees all played significant roles in holding their institutions in trust for the greater good of society. Servant-leadership, like stewardship, assumes first and foremost a commitment to serving the needs of others. It also emphasizes the use of openness and persuasion, rather than control.

9. *Commitment to the growth of people*: Servant-leaders believe that people have an intrinsic value beyond their tangible contributions as workers. As such, the servant-leader is deeply committed to the growth of each and every individual within his or her institution. The servant-leader recognizes the tremendous responsibility to do everything within his or her power to nurture the personal, professional,

and spiritual growth of employees. In practice, this can include (but is not limited to) concrete actions such as: making funds available for personal and professional development; taking a personal interest in the ideas and suggestions from everyone; encouraging worker involvement in decision making; and actively assisting laid-off workers to find other employment.

10. *Building community*: The servant-leader senses that much has been lost in recent human history as a result of the shift from local communities to large institutions as the primary shaper of human lives. This awareness causes the servant-leader to seek to identify some means for building community among those who work within a given institution. Servant-leadership suggests that true community can be created among those who work in businesses and other institutions. Greenleaf said, "All that is needed to rebuild community as a viable life form for large numbers of people is for enough servant-leaders to show the way, not by mass movements, but by each servant-leader demonstrating his [or her] own unlimited liability for a quite specific community-related group."

These ten characteristics of servant-leadership are by no means exhaustive. However, they serve to communicate the power and promise that this concept offers to those who are open to its invitation and challenge.

> "Servant leadership is the essence of quantum thinking and quantum leadership."
>> Danah Zohar, author, *Rewiring the Corporate Brain*

There are a half-dozen major areas in which the principles of servant-leadership are being applied in significant ways. The first area has to do with servant-leadership as an institutional philosophy and model. Servant-leadership crosses all boundaries and is being applied by a wide variety of people working with for-profit businesses, not-for-profit corporations, churches, universities, and foundations.

In recent years, a number of institutions have jettisoned their old heirarchical models and replaced them with a servant-leader approach. Servant-leadership advocates a group-oriented approach to analysis and decision making as a means of strengthening institutions and of improving society. It also emphasizes the power of persuasion and seeking consensus over the old "top-down" form of leadership. Some people have likened this to turning the heirarchical pyramid upside down. Servant-leadership holds that the primary purpose of a business should be to create a positive impact on its employees and community, rather than using profit as the sole motive.

Many individuals within institutions have adopted servant-leadership as a guiding philosophy. An increasing number of companies have adopted servant-leadership as part of their corporate philosophy or as a foundation for their mission statement. Among these are the Sisters of St. Joseph's Health System (Ann Arbor, MI), The Toro Company (MN), Schneider Engineering Company (Indianapolis, IN), and TDIndustries (Dallas, TX).

TDIndustries, one of the earliest practitioners of servant-leadership in the corporate setting, is a Dallas-based heating and plumbing contracting firm that was named "one of the ten best companies to work for," in the January 12, 1998 issue of *Fortune* magazine. TDIndustries was profiled in Robert Levering and Milton Moskowitz's book, *The 100 Best Companies to Work for in America*. In their profile of TDIndustries, the authors discuss the longtime influence that servant-leadership has had on the company. TDI's founder, Jack Lowe, Sr., stumbled upon "The Servant as Leader" essay in the early 1970s and began to distribute copies of it to his employees. They were invited to read through the essay, and then to gather in small groups to discuss its meaning. The belief that managers should serve their employees became an important value for TDIndustries.

Twenty-five years later, Jack Lowe, Jr., continues to use servant-leadership as the guiding philosophy for TDI. Levering and Moskowitz note, "Even today, any TDPartner who supervises at least one person must go through training in servant-leadership." In addition, all new employees continue to receive a copy of "The Servant as Leader" essay.

Servant-leadership has influenced many noted writers, thinkers, and leaders. Max DePree, former chairman of the Herman Miller Company and author of *Leadership Is an Art* and *Leadership Jazz* has said, "The servanthood of leadership needs to be felt, understood, believed, and practiced." And Peter Senge, author of *The Fifth Discipline*, has said that he tells people "not to bother reading any other book about leadership until you first read Robert Greenleaf's book, *Servant Leadership*. I believe it is the most singular and useful statement on leadership I've come across." In recent years, a growing number of leaders and readers have "rediscovered" Robert Greenleaf's own writings through DePree's and Senge's books.

A second major application of servant-leadership is its pivotal role as the theoretical and ethical basis for "trustee education." Greenleaf wrote extensively on servant-leadership as it applies to the roles of boards of directors and trustees within institutions. His essays on these applications are widely distributed among directors of for-profit and nonprofit organizations. In his essay, "Trustees as Servants," Greenleaf urged trustees to ask themselves two central questions: "Whom do you serve?" and "For what purpose?"

Servant-leadership suggests that boards of trustees need to undergo a radical shift in how they approach their roles. Trustees who seek to act as servant-leaders can help create institutions of great depth and quality. Over the past decade, two of America's largest grant-making foundations (Lilly Endowment, Inc. and the W. K. Kellogg Foundation) have sought to encourage the development of programs designed to educate and train not-for-profit boards of trustees to function as servant-leaders. The Greenleaf Center itself does a great deal of work with trustee boards.

The third application of servant-leadership concerns its deepening role in community leadership organizations across the country. A growing number of community leadership groups are using Greenleaf Center resources as part of their own education and training efforts. Some have been doing so for more than 15 years.

The National Association for Community Leadership has

adopted servant-leadership as a special focus. Recently, NACL named Robert Greenleaf as the posthumous recipient of its National Community Leadership Award. This award is given annually to honor an individual whose work has made a significant impact on the development of community leadership worldwide.

M. Scott Peck, who has written about the importance of building true community, says the following in *A World Waiting to Be Born*: "In his work on servant-leadership, Greenleaf posited that the world will be saved if it can develop just three truly well-managed, large institutions—one in the private sector, one in the public sector, and one in the nonprofit sector. He believed—and I know—that such excellence in management will be achieved through an organizational culture of civility routinely utilizing the mode of community."

The fourth application involves servant-leadership and experiential education. During the past 20 years, experiential education programs of all sorts have sprung up in virtually every college and university—and, increasingly, in secondary schools as well. Experiential education, or "learning by doing," is now a part of most students' educational experience.

Around 1980, a number of educators began to write about the linkage between the servant-leader concept and experiential learning under a new term called "service-learning." It is service-learning that has become a major focus for experiential education programs in the past few years.

The National Society for Experiential Education (NSEE) has adopted service-learning as one of its major program areas. NSEE has published a massive three-volume work called *Combining Service and Learning*, which brings together many articles and papers about service-learning—several dozen of which discuss servant-leadership as the philosophical basis for experiential learning programs.

The fifth application of servant-leadership concerns its use in both formal and informal education and training programs. This is taking place through leadership and management courses in colleges and universities, as well as through corporate training programs. A number of undergraduate and graduate courses on management and leadership incorporate servant-leadership within their course curricula. Several colleges and universities now offer specific courses on servant-leadership. Also, a number of noted leadership authors, including Peter Block, Ken Blanchard, Max DePree, and Peter Senge, have all acclaimed the servant-leader concept as an overarching framework that is compatible with, and enhances, other leadership and management models such as Total Quality Management, Learning Organizations, and Community-Building.

In the area of corporate education and training programs, dozens of management and leadership consultants now utilize servant-leadership materials as part of their ongoing work with corporations. Some of these companies have included AT&T, the Mead Corporation, and Gulf Oil of Canada. A number of consultants and educators are now touting the benefits to be gained in building a Total Quality Management approach on a servant-leadership foundation. Through internal training and education, institutions are discovering that servant-leadership can truly improve the way in which business is developed and conducted, while still successfully turning a profit.

The sixth application of servant-leadership involves its use in programs relating to personal growth and transformation. Servant-leadership operates at both the institutional and personal levels. For individuals it offers a means to personal growth—spiritually, professionally, emotionally, and intellectually. It has ties to the ideas of M. Scott Peck (*The Road Less Traveled*), Parker Palmer (*The Active Life*), Ann McGee-Cooper (*You Don't Have to Go Home from Work Exhausted!*), and others who have written on expanding human potential. A particular strength of servant-leadership is that it encourages everyone to actively seek opportunities to both serve and lead others, thereby setting up the potential for raising the quality of life throughout society. A number of individuals are working to integrate the servant-leader concept into various programs involving both men's and women's self-awareness groups and 12-step programs like Alcoholics Anonymous. There is also a fledgling examination under-

way of the servant-leader as a previously unidentified Jungian arche-
type. This particular exploration is discussed in a book by Robert
Moore and Douglas Gillette titled *The King Within*.

For some people, the word *servant* prompts an immediate negative connotation, due to the oppression which many workers—particularly women, and people of color—have historically endured. For
some, it may take a while to accept the positive usage of this word,
servant. However, those who are willing to dig a little deeper come to
understand the inherent spiritual nature of what is intended by the
pairing of servant and leader. The startling paradox of the term *servant-leadership* serves to prompt new insights.

In an article titled "Pluralistic Reflections on Servant-
Leadership," Juana Bordas has written: "Many women, minorities
and people of color have long traditions of servant-leadership in their
cultures. Servant-leadership has very old roots in many of the indigenous cultures. Cultures that were holistic, cooperative, communal,
intuitive and spiritual. These cultures centered on being guardians of
the future and respecting the ancestors who walked before."

Women leaders and authors are now writing and speaking about
servant-leadership as a 21st-century leadership philosophy that is
most appropriate for both women and men to embrace. Patsy
Sampson, who is former president of Stephens College in Columbia,
Missouri, is one such person. In an essay on women and servant-leadership "The Leader as Servant," she writes, "So-called (service-ori-
ented) feminine characteristics are exactly those which are consonant
with the very best qualities of servant-leadership."

> "Servant-leadership works like the consensus building that the
> Japanese are famous for. Yes, it takes a while on the front end;
> everyone's view is solicited, though everyone also understands
> that his [or her] view may not ultimately prevail. But once the
> consensus is forged, watch out: With everybody on board, your
> so-called implementation proceeds wham-bam."
>
> *Fortune* magazine (May 4, 1992)

Interest in the philosophy and practice of servant-leadership is now at an all-time high. Hundreds of articles on servant-leadership have appeared in various magazines, journals, and newspapers over the past few years. Many books on the general subject of leadership have been published that have referenced servant-leadership as an important model for both the present and the future.

The Greenleaf Center for Servant-Leadership is an international, not-for-profit, educational organization that seeks to encourage the understanding and practice of servant-leadership. The Center's mission is to fundamentally improve the caring and quality of all institutions through servant-leadership.

In recent years, the Greenleaf Center has experienced tremendous growth and expansion. Its growing programs include: the worldwide sales of over 120 books, essays, and videotapes on servant-leadership; a membership program; workshops, institutes, and seminars; a Reading-and-Dialogue Program; a Speakers Bureau; and an annual International Conference on Servant-Leadership. A number of notable Greenleaf Center members have spoken at our annual conferences, including: Peter Block (author of *Stewardship* and *The Empowered Manager*), Max DePree (author of *Leadership Is an Art* and *Leadership Jazz*), Stephen Covey (author of *The Seven Habits of Highly Effective People*), Meg Wheatley (author of *Leadership and the New Science*), M. Scott Peck (author of *The Road Less Traveled* and *A World Waiting to Be Born*), and Peter Senge (author of *The Fifth Discipline*). These and other conference speakers have spoken of the tremendous impact the servant-leader concept has had on the development of his or her own understanding of what it means to be a leader.

The last few years have witnessed the expansion of interest in servant-leadership to all parts of the world. Greenleaf Center materials are available in English, Spanish, Dutch, Czech, and Arabic, and other translations are in the works. In addition, The Greenleaf Center now has satellite offices in Europe, Great Britain, and Australia.

The Greenleaf Center's logo is a variation on the geometrical figure called a "mobius strip." A mobius strip, pictured below, is a one-sided surface constructed from a rectangle by holding one end fixed, rotating the opposite end through 180 degrees, and applying it to the first end—thereby giving the appearance of a two-sided figure. It thus appears to have a front side that merges into a back side, and then back again into the front.

The mobius strip symbolizes, in visual terms, the servant-leader concept—a merging of servanthood into leadership and back into servanthood again, in a fluid and continuous pattern. It also reflects the Greenleaf Center's own role as an institution seeking to both serve and lead others who are interested in leadership and service issues.

Life is full of curious and meaningful paradoxes. Servant-leadership is one such paradox that has slowly-but-surely gained tens of thousands of adherents over the past quarter-century. The seeds that have been planted have begun to sprout in many institutions, as well as in the hearts of many who long to improve the human condition. Servant-leadership is providing a framework from which many thousands of known and unknown individuals are helping improve the way in which we treat those who do the work within our many institutions. Servant-leadership offers hope and guidance for a new era in human development and for the creation of better, more caring institutions.

1

Servant:

Retrospect and Prospect

INTRODUCTION

I believe that caring for persons, the more able and the less able serving each other, is what makes a good society. Most caring was once person to person. Now much of it is mediated through institutions—often large, powerful, impersonal; not always competent; sometimes corrupt. If a better society is to be built, one more just and more caring and providing opportunity for people to grow, the most effective and economical way while supportive of the social order, is to raise the performance as servant of as many institutions as possible by new voluntary regenerative forces initiated within them by committed individuals: *servants.*

Such servants may never predominate or even be numerous; but their influence may form a leaven that makes possible a reasonably civilized society.

Out of the perspective that emerges from my long concern for institutions, I have come to believe that a serious lack of vision is a malady of almost epidemic proportions among the whole gamut of institutions that I know quite intimately—churches, schools, businesses, philanthropies. And that needed vision is not likely to be supplied by the administrative leadership of those places. Administrators, important and necessary as they are, tend to be short-range in their thinking and deficient in a sense of history—limitations that preclude their producing visions. If there is to be a constant infusion of vision that all viable institutions need, whatever their missions, the most likely source of those visions is their trustees who are involved enough to know, yet detached enough from managerial concern, that their imaginations are relatively unimpaired. Trustees are most effective when they are led by an able and farseeing chairperson—by a quality of leadership that is rare in our society today. These extraordinary chairpersons are not necessarily "big" people. The most effective trustee chair I have ever seen in action (and I have seen quite a few) was a "little" person in the world of affairs.

The above paragraph offers a view of the crucial role of trustee leadership that is not widely shared today by the populace at large, or accepted as a personal goal by many current chairpersons, and welcomed by even fewer contemporary chief executives as a role independent of theirs. With so little acceptance of the idea, one may ask, why advocate it? The response to that question requires two "ifs." If one accepts that our institution-bound society serves well enough and no basic change in how our institutions are led is called for, then there is no reason to advocate this radical idea. But if one sees too many of our institutions as seriously deficient in their service to society (as I do) and believes (as I do) that that deficiency could be corrected over time, then something rather fundamental has to change. And the most reasonable and manageable change is to begin, gradually, to raise the effectiveness of trustee leadership until trustees are influential enough and farseeing enough to infuse new visions of greatness, one institution at a time, into as many of our institutions as possible. That powerful new trustee influence is not likely to be achieved until strong visionary leaders emerge to chair their efforts.

Beginning in 1970, I started to write on the theme of *servant*. These have been interesting years because responses have brought involvement in some depth with persons and institutions that share my concern. In this process, others have contributed much to my understanding of what may be required for our society to become more serving—to make a substantial move toward a quality of the common life that is reasonable and possible with available resources, human and material.

To such as I who did not write for publication until age 65, this understanding has come rather late in life. In summing it up now, I would like to share some reflections. Then I will speculate on the prospects, as I see them, for the servant motive in the future. But, first, a note about where I have been.

ORGANIZATION—HOW THINGS GET DONE

The major focus of my adult life may best be described as *a student of organization, how things get done*—particularly in large institutions. Fortuitous advice from a wise college professor helped shape this interest and led me, upon graduation, to find my way into the largest business organization in the world, American Telephone and Telegraph Company. Early on, I became a student of the history of what seemed to me to be an extraordinary institution. I managed to carve out a career in which I could be both involved and within watching distance of its top structure, and yet maintain sufficient detachment so that I could be reflective about what was going on. My tenure embraced the expansion of the 1920s, the Depression, World War II, and the growth years of the 1950s and 1960s. I never carried heavy executive responsibility and was spared the debilitating effects of such a role which seem almost inevitable, given conventional organizational structures.

In the latter part of my career, I held the position of Director of Management Research. With the help of a professional staff, and within a broad charter, I could both study and advise regarding the management and leadership of this huge institution—over 1 million employees—immersed as it is in sophisticated technology, elaborate human organization, and regulated public service. I was concerned with its values, with its history and myth, and, intimately, with its top leadership. I learned the hard way about the profound influence that history, and the myths of institutions that have a considerable history, have on values, goals, and leadership. And I was painfully aware of the cost in these terms of any insensitivity to history and myth—especially among the top officers. In any institutional setting, one really cannot understand one's involvement in it *now* without a clear sense of the course of events that form that institution's past, out of which grows the mythology that surrounds the record of those events. History and myth, in my view, need each other in order to illuminate the present.

This experience at AT&T gave me a good perspective and the impetus, in my retirement years that began in 1964, to venture into close working relationships with a wide range of institutions: universities (especially in the turbulent 1960s), foundations (as trustee, consultant, and staff member), churches (local, regional, and national), and related church institutions, professional associations, healthcare, and businesses—in the United States, in Europe, and in the third world.

This post-retirement experience, following 38 years with AT&T, has been enriching and stimulating; but one facet of it, in particular, prompted me to begin to write and to pull together a thread of thinking that has emerged around the *servant* theme.

The servant theme evolved out of close association with several colleges and universities during their disturbed period in the 1960s. This was a searing experience, to be intimately involved with students, faculty, administrators, and trustees at a time when some of these venerable institutions literally crumbled—when the hoops came off the barrel.

My first servant essay, "The Servant as Leader," was prompted by my concern for student attitudes which then—and now, although the manifestations are different—seemed low in hope. One cannot be hopeful, it seems to me, unless one accepts and believes that one can live productively in the world as it is—striving, violent, unjust, as well as beautiful, caring, and supportive. I hold that hope, thus defined, is absolutely essential to both sanity and wholeness of life.

Partly in search for a structural basis for hope, partly out of awareness that our vast complex of institutions—particularly colleges and universities in the late sixties—seemed so fragile and inadequate, two further essays were written: "The Institution as Servant" and "Trustees as Servants." The three essays were then collected in a book with some related writings and published in 1977 under the title *Servant Leadership*. Another projected essay, "The Servant as a Person," turned out to be a book and was published in 1979 with the title *Teacher as Servant: A Parable* [published by The Greenleaf Center].

Out of the struggle to write these things, while contending with the modest ferment they stirred, came the belief that, as a world society, we have not yet come to grips with the *institutional revolution* that came hard on the heels of the industrial revolution, and that we confront a worldwide crisis of institutional leadership. How can we ordinary mortals lead governments, businesses, churches, hospitals, schools, philanthropies, communities—yes, even families—to become more serving in this turbulent world? And what does it mean to serve? I prefer not to define *serve* explicitly at this time. Rather, I would let the meaning it has for me evolve as one reads through this essay.

How can an institution become more serving? I see no other way than that the people who inhabit it serve better and work together toward synergy—the whole becoming greater than the sum of its parts.

I believe that the transforming movement that raises the serving quality of any institution, large or small, begins with the initiative of one individual person—no matter how large the institution or how substantial the movement. If one accepts, as I do, the principle of synergy, one has difficulty with the idea that *only* small is beautiful. The potential for beauty (largely unrealized to be sure) is much greater in large institutions—because of the phenomenon of synergy. Because we are now dominated by large institutions, how to make *big* also *beautiful* is a major challenge for us.

How to achieve *community* under the shelter of bigness may be the essence of this challenge because so much of caring depends upon knowing and interacting with persons in the intimacy of propinquity. The stimulus and support that some individuals need to be open to inspiration and imaginative insight often come from the nurture of groups. There may not be a "group mind" (inspiration and imaginative insight may be gifts only to individuals), but there is clearly a climate favorable to creativity by individuals that the group, as community, can provide. Achieving many small-scale communities, under the shelter that is best given by bigness, may be the secret of synergy in large institutions.

THE IDEA OF SERVANT

The idea of "servant" is deep in our Judeo-Christian heritage. The concordance to the Standard Revised Version of the Bible lists over 1300 references to *servant* (including serve and service). Yet, after all of these millennia, there is ample evidence that ours is a low-caring society when judged by what is reasonable and possible with the resources at hand. There are many notable servants among us, but they sometimes seem to be losing ground to the neutral or nonserving people. It is argued that the outlook for our civilization at this moment is not promising, probably because not enough of us care enough for our fellow humans.

I am personally hopeful for the future because knowledge is

available to do two things that we are not now doing, things that are well within our means to do and that would give caring people great joy to do, things that would infuse more of the servant quality into our society. (1) We know how to mature the servant motive as a durable thing in many who arrive in their teens with servanthood latent in them—and this, I believe, is quite a large number. This is what my book *Teacher as Servant* is about. (2) We know how to transform institutions so that they will be substantially more serving to all who are touched by them. A chapter in *Teacher as Servant* deals with such a transformation. But formidable obstacles stand in the way of using this knowledge, obstacles that I will call "mind-sets."

THE PROBLEM OF MIND-SETS

Mind-sets that seem to restrain otherwise good, able people from using the two bits of knowledge mentioned above are often tough and unyielding. Whether obstacles like these can be sufficiently reduced before the deterioration of this civilization has become irreversible is open to question. For the older ones among us who are "in charge," nothing short of a "peak" experience, like religious conversion or psychoanalysis or an overpowering new vision, seems to have much chance of converting a confirmed nonservant into an affirmative servant. But for some, those few older ones who have a glimmer of the servant disposition *now*, it is worth their making the effort to try to stem the tide of deterioration. Life can be more whole for those who try, regardless of the outcome.

Civilizations have risen and fallen before. If ours does not make it, perhaps when the archeologists of some future civilization dig around among the remains of this one they may find traces of the effort to build a more caring society, bits of experience that may give useful cues to future people. It is a reasonable prospect that, in the civilization that succeeds ours—whether it evolves from ours in a constructive way or whether it is reconstructed from the ruins after long dark ages—those future people will be faced with the same two problems that confront us now: (1) *how to produce as many servants as they can from those who, at maturity, have the potential for it*; and (2) *how to elicit optimal service from such group endeavors (institutions) as emerge.* And, unless some unforeseeable transmutations in human nature occur along the way, those future people may be impeded by the same unwillingness to use what they know that marks our times. Knowledge may be power, but not without the willingness, and the release from inhibiting mind-sets, to use that knowledge.

Over a century ago, when the then-stagnant Danish culture was reconstructed as a result of the work of the Folk High School, the motto of that effort was *The Spirit is Power*. A chapter in the essay "The Servant as Leader" tells the story of a remarkable social transformation that followed when the spirit of the Danish young people was aroused so that they sought to find a way out of their dilemma, a stagnant culture, by building a new social order.

Worth noting about this 19th-century Danish experience is that Bishop Grundtvig, the prophetic visionary who gave leadership to the Folk High School movement, did not offer a model for others to follow, nor did he himself found or direct such a school. He gave the vision, the dream, and he passionately and persuasively advocated that dream for over 50 years of his long life. The indigenous leaders among the peasants of Denmark responded to that vision and built the schools—with no model to guide them. *They knew how to do it!* Grundtvig gave the prophetic vision that inspired them to act on what they knew.

VISION FOR OUR TIMES: WHERE IS IT?

"Where there is no vision, the people perish." This language (Proverbs 29:18) from the King James Version of the Bible stays with me even though modern translators make something else of that passage.

What Grundtvig gave to the indigenous leaders of the common people of Denmark in the 19th century was a compelling vision that they should do something that they knew how to do: *they could raise the spirit of young people so that they would build a new society—and they did*. Without that vision, 19th-century Denmark was on the way to perishing.

Our restless young people in the 1960s wanted to build a new society too. But their elders who could have helped prepare them for that task just "spun their wheels." As a consequence of this neglect, a few of those young people simply settled for tearing up the place. And, in the absence of new visionary leadership to inspire effort to prepare our young people to build constructively, some of them may tear up the place again! Do not be surprised if they do just that. The provocation is ample. We simply are not giving the maturing help to young people that is well within our means to do. Instead, we are acting on the principle that knowledge, not the spirit, is power. Knowledge is but a tool. The spirit is of the essence.

Perhaps the older people who could help them do not do what they know how to do because, as in the 1960s, they are not inspired by a vision that lifts their sights to act on what they know. No such vision is being given in our times. And the paralysis of action that restrains us in preparing young people to live productively in the 21st century is still with us. We may be courting disaster by our neglect.

This is an interesting thesis (as said earlier): (1) We know how to increase the proportion of young people who, at maturity, are disposed to be servants; and (2) we know how to transform contemporary institutions so that they will be substantially more serving to all who are touched by them. What is needed, this thesis holds, is a vision that will lift the sights of those who know and release their will to act constructively. This vision might be prompted by conscience and self-generated out of a conscious search, or it may be without known cause, or it might be forcefully communicated by a strong leader-type person (as Grundtvig did in 19th-century Denmark).

This leader might present a vision that has a benign result, as Grundtvig did; or he or she might be a leader like Adolph Hitler, who brought a major disaster; or the vision might be given by an

Elvis Presley who can release the inhibiting constraints and incite a frenzy of action that has no seeming value-laden consequence, good or bad.

The late Rabbi Abraham Joshua Heschel had given a lecture on the Old Testament Prophets to an undergraduate audience. In the question period a student asked, "Rabbi Heschel, you spoke of false prophets and true prophets. How does one tell the difference?"

The good rabbi drew himself into the stern stance of the prophet of old and answered in measured tones, "There—is—no—way!" and looked intently at his questioner for an embarrassing moment. Then his face broke into a gentle smile, and he said, "My friend, if there were a 'way,' if we had a gauge that we could slip over the head of the prophet and say with certainty that he is or is not a true prophet, there would be no human dilemma and life would have no meaning." Then, returning to his stern Old Testament stance he said emphatically, "But it is terribly important that we know the difference."

Thus, one who is inspired by a vision must know the difference between an action that points toward a benign result, or simply aimless activity. I believe it is possible to prepare most of the emerging adults to know the difference. This is the first step in increasing the proportion of young people who are disposed to be servants. My book, *Teacher as Servant*, describes how a teacher on his own and without the support of either colleagues or university, can prepare young people to know the difference. I will comment later on one other opportunity within colleges and universities. Neither approach costs any money!

WHAT DO WE KNOW—OR DON'T WANT TO KNOW?

I have said that (1) we know how to increase the proportion of young people who, at maturity, are disposed to be servants, and (2) we know how to transform institutions so that they will be substantially more serving to all who are touched by them. But it is not knowledge that is codified and systematized and bearing the appropriate establishment imprimatur. It is knowledge like that which the leaders among the Danish peasants had when they were inspired to build schools which would kindle the spirit of their young people. They had always known how to do that, but until Bishop Grundtvig gave them the vision, they were unable, or lacked the will, to act on what they knew.

There is nothing mystical about the available knowledge to do the two things (as suggested above) that need to be done in our times to raise the servant quality of our society. To my knowledge, clear and complete models do not exist, but there are fragments of experience here and there that can readily be assembled to give a workable basis for moving to solidify that experience—*to know!* Let me give examples from four widely differing contemporary institutions in which, it seems to me, able, honest people lack the vision to act on what they know—or could easily know—*and seem not to want to know!* They seem to have mind-sets that block them.

Business

A certain important industrial field is occupied by half a dozen large companies and many small and medium sized ones. It is a field that is subject to quite wide cyclical economic fluctuations and in which disruptions by labor disputes are common. One of the larger companies (not the largest) stands in conspicuous contrast to the other large ones on three counts: no matter what happens to the economic fortunes of the others, this firm, up to now, has always made money; they have never had a strike or work stoppage; their product is generally recognized as superior. (What makes their product superior will be commented on later.)

Let us call this company X. A close observer of this industry recently asked the head of one of the other large companies in this field this simple question: "What do you folks learn from company X?" The response was a hand gesture of dismissal and the brusque comment, "I don't want to talk about it!"

One can speculate about why, in a highly competitive field, the head of one large company would brush off a suggestion that he might learn something from a more successful competitor. But what distinguishes company X from its competitors is not in the dimensions that usually separate companies, such as superior technology, more astute marketing strategy, better financial base, etc. Company X is not too different from its competitors in dimensions like these. What separates company X from the rest is unconventional thinking about its "dream"—what this business wants to be, how its priorities are set, and how it organizes to serve. It has a radically different philosophy and self-image. According to the conventional business wisdom, company X ought not to succeed at all. Conspicuously less successful competitors seem to say, "The ideas that company X holds *ought* not to work, therefore we will learn nothing from them." They "don't want to talk about it."

University

In the field of higher education, there is another consequence of a lack of vision that cannot be as clearly identified as in the above business example. For many years, I have tried to stir an interest in universities in making a more determined effort to develop the servant-leadership potential that exists among their students. When new money is produced to support such an effort, a pass will be made at doing it. But when the money stops, the effort stops. It does not take root. Here and there the occasional professor, on his own, without the support of his university, and sometimes with the opposition of his colleagues, has taken an interest in this aspect of student growth—with conspicuous success.

In contrast, a student with athletic potential will find elaborate coaching resources available to develop this talent—even in the poorest and feeblest of institutions. But the young potential servant-leader will find that the position of the best and strongest university is that the development of leadership potential is something that just happens, and nothing explicit is to be done about it in the crucial undergraduate years. I wrote an article about this in an educational journal stating that the only way I see for work in the undergraduate years to help alleviate the leadership crisis we seem now to be in is to find and encourage the rare professor who will take it on—unrecognized and uncompensated, and perhaps denigrated by his colleagues. A university president responded to my article with this concurring comment:

> I am coming more and more to agree with your opinion that it is almost impossible to mount anything like an organized program in developing leadership in our university students. Reluctantly, I am reaching your conclusion that the best and only hope of success will be an effort on the part of a few dedicated individuals who will take that cross upon themselves. If this is truly the case, then we need to try to discover who and where they are and give them all the assistance we can.

When John W. Gardner wrote his sharp criticism of universities for administering what he called the *antileadership vaccine* (his parting message when he left the presidency of Carnegie Corporation for a career in politics in 1964), the response from academe seemed to be, "We don't want to talk about it!"

Health Profession

In the medical profession, there is a widely held position against accepting nutrition as an important factor in health. The average doctor knows that the human body is a chemical-psychic organism. But in treating illness or in advice regarding health building, there is not much concern for nutrition.

The Hill Foundation in St. Paul, Minnesota, which has a long record of generous giving to medical education, recently made a grant to establish a program in nutrition in a *new* medical school. The foundation's annual report for 1973 commented on this grant as follows:

It is a true paradox: Americans are often overweight and under-nourished. We are wasteful of our food assets and unwise in our dietary patterns; meanwhile, much of the rest of the world struggles to assure its people an adequate food supply. There is an immediate need for more basic research in nutrition; more communication on ways to plan and control food production, processing, presentation and preparation; and for more public education on sound nutritional practices. But the fact is that there are too few well-trained people to perform this task. . . .

An important aspect of the nutrition problem is related to the medical school curriculum. Few medical schools have major departments devoted to the field of nutrition research and education. Generally the young doctor gets a briefing on aspects of nutrition as they relate to specific diseases such as diabetes, allergies or coronary problems. Most of the emphasis, however, is on the remedial care of patients, with little attention devoted to the maintenance of health or the prevention of illness. . . . The same weaknesses exist in the training of such paramedical personnel as nurses and dietitians. . . . The Foundation believes Mayo Medical School ideally suited to develop and implement a broad nutrition education program *because it is a new institution* (italics ours), and hence is still flexible in its approach to medical training.

What this says to me is that the mind-set among doctors on nutrition is such that only a new medical school will offer a chance to use fully the available nutritional knowledge as an important factor in health building. The medical establishment would seem to say, as the head of the business said when asked what he learned from his more successful but unconventional competitor, "We don't want to talk about it!"

Church Leader

My interpretation of a bit of 19th-century history is that when Karl Marx sat in the British Museum composing the doctrines that would shape so much of the 20th-century world, he was filling a void that was left by the failure of the churches of his day to deal adequately with the consequences of the industrial revolution. If the 19th-century churches (or church leaders) had taken the trouble to suggest a design for the new society that the industrial revolution made imperative, and if they had advocated it persuasively as a new vision, Marx might still have written his tracts; but they would not have found the field relatively unoccupied.

Recently, I met with a group of church leaders, professionals, who were convened for three days on the subject of "The Churchman as Leader." I listened for a day as they discussed their leadership opportunities and problems as they saw them. Then, in commenting on what I had heard, I noted three words that are sometimes used interchangeably but have quite different connotations: *manage* (from *manus*—hand) suggesting control; *administer* (from *administrare*—to serve) suggesting to care for; and *lead*, of uncertain origin, but commonly used to mean "going out ahead to show the way." Manage and administer, along with the ceremonial aspects of office, are the *maintenance* functions—they help keep the institution running smoothly—*as it is*. Important as maintenance is in the current performance of any institution, it does not assure adaptation to serve a changing society. That assurance can come only from *leading*—venturing creatively. Having made this distinction in the meaning of terms as they are commonly used, I commented that, as I observed their discussion, these churchmen were talking mostly about *maintenance*, not *leading*.

In most institutions, churches included, managing and administering, the maintenance functions, are delegated and resources are allocated in order that those to whom these functions are assigned can carry on. Those who manage and administer (maintain) may also *lead* —*go out ahead to show the way*. But leadership is not delegated; it is assumed. If there are sanctions to compel or induce compliance, the process would not qualify as leadership. The only test of leadership is that somebody follows—*voluntarily*.

At this point, I was asked by the church leaders, "If you do not see us as *leading*, in your terms, what could persons in positions like ours do in order to lead?"

I repeated my credo, as stated in the beginning of this essay, which concludes with ". . . If a better society is to be built, one more just and caring and providing opportunity for people to grow, the most open course, the most effective and economical way, while supportive of the social order, is to raise the performance as servant of as many institutions as possible by new voluntary regenerative forces initiated within them by committed individuals—*servants.*" Then I said:

"What church leaders can do to really *lead* in our times is to use their influence to bring into being a contemporary *theology of institutions* that will underwrite the commitment of church members within our many institutions and support them as they become new regenerative forces: to the end that their particular institution, in which they have some power of influence, will become more serving—and continue to grow in its capacity to serve.

"The leadership of the 19th-century churches did not accept the challenge to suggest a new design for postindustrial revolution society, and they left a void to be filled by a concerned and articulate atheist. The leaders of late-20th-century churches are not accepting the challenge of an institution-bound society (which Marx did not provide for in his doctrines, and, as a consequence, Marxist societies today have the same problem in getting their institutions to serve as we have). The opportunity that church leaders have today is to take the initiative to see that an adequate theology of institutions evolves so the churches have a firm basis for preparing their members to become regenerative servants in the institutions with which they are involved. *Leadership is initiating—going out ahead to show the way.*"

There was not much response to this suggestion in the meeting of church leaders. When we concluded, I noted this paucity of response and said that I would write to them about it when I got home. I later sent to those present a memorandum entitled "The Need for a

Theology of Institutions," in which I suggested a detailed procedure that a church leader might follow in producing this new theology. Only 2 of the 16 present at the conference acknowledged the receipt of the memo, and they were noncommittal. A supplementary memorandum six months later got the same response.

I would conclude that these church leaders—all responsible, able, good people—took the same position as the head of the business did when asked what he learned from his much more successful (if unconventional) competitor: "We don't want to talk about it!"

When 19th-century church leaders were confronted with the radical impact of the industrial revolution, if some audacious consultant had suggested that a new theology was needed to deal with this problem, the response of church leaders of that day might have been the same—"we don't want to talk about it."

My reflection on these last ten years leads me to conclude that *vision*, without which we perish, is required to open us to willingness to use what we know and to work to extract hard reality from a dream. In the absence of a powerful liberating vision, church leaders, like others in responsible roles, "don't want to talk about it." Why, over such a long span of history, has the production of vision been so difficult to do? Why are these liberating visions so rare?

WHY ARE LIBERATING VISIONS SO RARE?

It seems to me important to accept that the mind-sets that are so frustrating to all reformers, those who are urging others to use what they know, actually serve a useful purpose. What if every person and every institution was "open" in the sense of being free of all inhibiting mind-sets that block action on what we know? Every question and every situation would be faced as if nothing like it had happened before. This would be a reformer's dream; but the world would be in chaos. Few of us can survive without a good deal of dogma that prompts reflexive actions. We would not be able to act quickly in emergencies, and moral choices that require prompt action would paralyze us. Most of us get along as well as we do by a good deal of "what if?" anticipatory thinking that pre-sets responses to common situations. If we were all completely "open," much of our traditional wisdom might be lost, as might "manners" that enable us to interact spontaneously in appropriate ways with fellow humans.

Liberating visions are rare because ours is partly a traditional society—but only partly. It is also an evolving society about which Cardinal Newman is quoted as saying, "To live is to change; to live well is to have changed often." The mixture of *traditional* and *changing* is an important aspect of the human dilemma.

Therefore, in answer to the question, "Why are liberating visions so rare?" one must say that they are rare because a stable society requires that *a powerful liberating vision must be difficult to deliver*, and that the test for the benign character of such a vision shall be rigorous. Yet to have none, or not enough such visions, is to seal our fate. We cannot run back to be a wholly traditional society, comforting as it may be to contemplate it. There must be change—sometimes great change.

Moods and spirit of people vary. There are moments when people are more open to charismatic vision than others. Some times seem "plastic"; others seem "hard." We but dimly understand the forces that open and close people to liberating visions.

The word *prudence* comes to mind. We should try to change with a minimum of threat of damage to stability—as embodied in the four kinds of mind-sets I have described. If stability is significantly lowered or lost, no matter how noble the end sought, the cost in human suffering may be inordinate. When an imprudent effort toward change, one in which the liberating vision is not sufficiently compelling and benign in intent, may make it more difficult for a later prudent effort to succeed, reformers take note: in the end, most people choose *order*—even if it is delivered to them by brutal nonservants. The ultimate choice of order is one of the most predictable mind-sets because it is a first condition of a civilized society.

If the writer in Proverbs 29:18 is correctly quoted in saying

"Where there is no vision, the people perish," there is remarkable consistency between the common dilemmas in ancient times and in ours. The four examples of firm mind-sets in the fields of business, education, health, and church suggest that there has been failure to give sufficiently powerful liberating visions. This kind of deprivation has been the common lot of humankind from the earliest times. And because of that, the threat of perishing is always with us.

SUMMONING AND ARTICULATING A VISION

So far I have given only half an answer to the question, Why are liberating visions so rare?—because it is so difficult to give them. The other half is: because so few of those who have the gift for summoning a vision, and the power to articulate it persuasively, have either the urge or the courage or the will to try! And it takes all three. We in America may be in a transition period between an era of "growth" and one of "restraint" and liberating visions may have a hollow sound. This is discouraging to visionaries!

One of the requirements of a caring, serving society, in both favorable and discouraging times, is that it provides in its structures a place for visionaries and surrounds those in that place with the expectation that they will produce those liberating visions of which they are capable. A new view of a structure of the institutions that serve us may be in order—a view that embraces both internal structure as well as the relationship between institutions and how they influence one another.

When "The Servant as Leader" was published in 1970, I had this to say about prophetic vision:

> I now embrace the theory of prophecy which holds that
> prophetic voices of great clarity, and with a quality of insight equal
> to that of any age, are speaking cogently all of the time. Men and
> women of a stature equal to the greatest of the past are with us now
> addressing the problems of the day and pointing to a better way and
> to a personeity better able to live fully and serenely in these times.

The variable that marks some periods as barren and some as rich in prophetic vision may be in the interest, the level of seeking, and the responsiveness of the *hearers*. The variable may not be in the presence or absence or the relative quality and force of prophetic voices. The prophet grows in stature as people respond to his message. If his or her early attempts are ignored or spurned, the talent may wither away.

It is *seekers*, then, who make the prophet; and the initiative of any of us in searching for and responding to the voice of a contemporary prophet may mark the turning point in her or his growth and service.

I came by this point of view from reading the history of the Religious Society of Friends (Quakers), and I concluded that George Fox, the powerful 17th-century voice in England that gave this Society its remarkable vision, probably would not have been heard had there not been in existence in England for 100 years prior a group known as *seekers*. This was a small band of people whose common bond was that they were *listening* for prophetic vision. They were held together by a religious concern, but they knew that it lacked articulation in a contemporary formulation that would make of them a vital social and religious force in their day. And as they heard and responded to George Fox, they became for a short time a great movement that had a remarkable impact on English institutions, notably a new business ethic and a pervasive social concern that influenced the western world and carried forward to 18th-century America, where it made of the Quakers the first religious group to formally condemn slavery and forbid slaveholding among its members—100 years before the Civil War.

But this movement very quickly crystallized into a church, as too many of its members ceased to be seekers. Instead of *seeing*, being open to new prophecy, they "*had it*," tested and tried—what churches have always done. What they had was, and remains, good. But the Quakers were no longer on the growing edge.

The servant-leader may be not so much the prophetic visionary (that is a rare gift) as the convener, sustainer, discerning guide for seekers who wish to remain open to prophetic visions. The *maintenance* functions within all sorts of institutions may not require leaders of any sort, but, *seekers*, of which every institution should have some, *must* have servant-leaders. But from where, in our vast complex of institutions, will liberating visions come? I have a suggestion.

A STRUCTURE OF INSTITUTIONS
THAT ENCOURAGES LIBERATING VISIONS

In search for a structure that encourages liberating visions, the institutions that make up our society might be arranged in a three-level hierarchy.

In the base level are what may be called "operating" institutions: governments, businesses, hospitals, schools, labor unions, professional associations, social agencies, philanthropies, families, communities.

In the second level are churches and universities, because of their concern for values and for continuity of the culture, and because of their capacity for nurturing the serving quality in both individuals and institutions.

At the third level are seminaries (theological and nontheological) that are sustaining resources for churches, and foundations that could perform a similar service for colleges and universities. Both foundations and seminaries are suggested because they have sufficient detachment and freedom from daily pressures to maintain a reflective overview of the whole society, and because they have greater latitude than most institutions to be what they want to be and to do what they think they should. They have the unusual opportunity to harbor and encourage prophetic voices that give vision and hope. *Unfortunately, in our times, little prophetic vision seems to come from either seminaries or foundations.*

Further, foundations and seminaries have the opportunity to become the source of nurturing that is mediated through churches and universities to individuals and operating institutions. Thus a major preoccupation of seminaries and foundations might become *the nurture of institutions*—institutions that in turn serve people. And it is hoped that, in time, *all* institutions will come to acknowledge their insufficiency and their need for constant nurture from a source that has the necessary detachment and freedom from daily pressures. I suggest that this source could be foundations and seminaries.

The utility in such an idea of a hierarchy of institutions is that when there is faltering in any institutions, as there is likely to be in the best of them from time to time, a fair question to ask is, wherein has there been a lack of caring concern for this institution for the level next above?

This assumption leaves the question, To whom do seminaries and foundations turn when they need caring concern? Since these two stand at the top of the hierarchy, there are no resource institutions that serve them. Therefore, seminaries and foundations need a quality and depth of trustee care that would not be possible for all institutions. These two kinds of institutions need the most dedicated and discerning trustees of all. And these trustees have the greatest of all opportunities for constructive service to the society of the future. The opportunities are great, but the challenge to astuteness of trustee leadership is also great—because most seminaries and foundations, as they now stand, have well-set patterns that do not favor their occupying the role I have described as possible, and natural, for them as level-three institutions—at the top of the hierarchy.

SEMINARIES

As seminaries have evolved, they have tended to take on the values and mind-sets of universities. A few of them are schools within university structures. But most are independent institutions with their own trustees, even where they are affiliated with religious denominations.

If seminaries take on the full scope I will suggest, they will not be at all like universities. To be sure, they have a curriculum of courses and they grant degrees. But this is incidental to their major function: to harbor and nurture prophetic voices that give vision and hope, and to serve as a sustaining support for churches. These are not primary functions of a university, and the university tradition may not be useful as a model for seminaries.

I have a gnawing suspicion that the strongest role, a viable structural model for a seminary, has not yet evolved. It is the opportunity for seminary trustees, under the leadership of their chairperson, to help the seminary get into its strongest role. It is not the trustee mission to design the seminary, authoritatively. Rather, trustees have the opportunity to *lead* a process out of which the design for the seminary of the 21st century may evolve. All of the several constituencies of each seminary should be full participants in the evolution of that design. And it should be *evolution*—over time, and never ending. The seminary should rest firm, at all times, in its contemporary mission, while the process of transcending that mission is carried forward simultaneously.

As trustees undertake to lead their seminary toward its full stature as a serving (level-three) institution, one of their concerns should be for the seminary to make, out of its own experience, a contribution to an evolving theology of institutions—a theology that gives a critical, contemporary view of the purpose and program of both seminary and church. This concern, consistently manifest, will help clarify the goals of the seminary. It will also help prepare the seminary to support the churches in their ministry, both to individuals and to the full range of "operating" institutions that churches have the opportunity to influence, to the end that these institutions will be more serving of all persons whose lives they touch.

Seminaries differ widely in their doctrinal positions; but most share the desire to bring about conditions of life that will favor all persons reaching their full stature as religious beings (in the root meaning of the word *religion*). It is regarding this common goal that new vision is needed.

FOUNDATIONS

Foundations, as institutions with funds to dispense for legally approved purposes, are a relatively recent addition to our extensive gallery of institutions. There is considerable disagreement as to what the function of foundations should be, and there are persistent public pressures to restrict their autonomy. There is some sentiment that foundations should not exist at all, or only for a limited term of years.

Foundations are unique in that they are free of "market" pressures. All other institutions have constituencies that must be satisfied if they are to continue to exist. Foundations have only to obey the law—which is stricter than it once was, and may get more so.

While foundations still have some latitude to choose what they will do, it is suggested that some of them elect to become, in part at least, support institutions for universities and colleges—not just to give them money, although they may continue to do some of that. Could not some foundations become for universities and colleges what seminaries now are (or could be) for churches? This will not come about quickly or easily, but foundation trustees might assume the kind of leadership suggested above for seminary trustees: leadership to a process out of which the design for a foundation role for the 21st century will evolve.

Large, sophisticated businesses sometimes set aside staffs whose role is to think about the firm as an institution and give intellectual guidance to its development. Universities tend to rely on committees of faculty to render this kind of service to the university itself; and it is not enough. American railroads are the classic example of large businesses that did not set people aside to think about the business they were in. Everybody was busy running the railroad day to day. And few railroads survived this neglect as viable businesses. There is some question that universities will survive, unharmed, from their own self-neglect; and they have been badly scarred in recent years.

It probably will be more difficult for a foundation to become effective in this support role for universities than for seminaries to do it for churches. This is partly because of the great size and complexity of some universities as well as the scarcity of persons who could (or would) staff a foundation that undertakes this difficult task. As with seminaries, the prime concern is *trustees*. Trustees of a foundation that uses its resources for this important purpose will need to be unusually caring and dedicated and persevere over a long period. They will accept the fact that their foundation must *earn* the kind of role suggested here.

Some universities and colleges face a drop in enrollment and are experiencing financial stringencies. They have difficulty thinking of any problem they now have as other than something that more money would solve. As a somewhat detached observer, I suspect that universities and colleges are suffering—even today—more for want of ideas, and for vision to liberate them to use ideas, than for want of money. If their governing ideas were better suited to their needs and opportunities in these times, the want of money might not be such a problem. But, the university tradition being what it is, it is unlikely that they have the power to be sufficiently self-regenerating. They, like the churches, need the sustained caring support that only a most able foundation staff is likely to give.

It is humbling for any institution to accept that it is not self-regenerating and that it should welcome conceptual leadership from another institution like a foundation—one that has the resources, human and material, to give that help, and that has managed to assemble a few unusually able trustees whose exceptionality give the foundation self-regenerating power. Most universities, like most people and institutions, could use a good measure of humility. Humility is one of the distinguishing traits of the true servant—as willing humbly to accept service as to give it.

SELF-REGENERATING INSTITUTIONS

Continuous regeneration is essential for viability of persons and institutions and society as a whole. A prudent use of human resources is to concentrate the ablest trustees, who will always be few in number, in those institutions that are best positioned to be self-regenerating and thereby to gain the strength to give clear and compelling regenerating vision to others.

If seminaries and foundations can be accepted as being appropriately placed in the hierarchy of institutions to assume this guiding role (as I believe they are), then a concerted effort should be made to provide these two kinds of institutions with trustees who will persevere with determination to assure sustained self-regeneration in themselves in order to give strong support to churches (by seminaries) and colleges and universities (by foundations) with the hope that, between the influence of churches and universities, "operating" institutions will be helped to a sustained high level of caring and serving.

INSTITUTES OF CHAIRING

One of the practical steps that foundations and seminaries might take, collectively or separately, is the conduct of institutes for those who chair trustees. They could do this, first, for themselves to prepare their own chairpersons to give the leadership that will help assure the quality of trustee oversight that self-regenerating institutions require. The institutes could then extend the availability of this chairing preparation to universities and colleges and to churches and church-related institutions so that, between them, they could provide this service for those who chair the trustees of all operating institutions that have trustees or directors. Such Institutes of Chairing would be a permanent thing: to give initial and continuing preparation for the chair leadership; to serve as a medium of exchange between those who undertake this role; and to provide a consulting resource for chairpersons who want help on specific problems.

This is a large order. But if the voluntary character of our complex society is to be preserved and enhanced, a major investment in strengthening and maintaining the trustee role of all institutions that have governing boards seems imperative. This is one of those invaluable social supports that we know how to provide and that we can afford to supply. What is needed, first, is a liberating vision that will make it a feasible thing to do. Where better might we look for that liberating vision than among seminaries and foundations? If just *one* in each category will take it on and advocate that vision persuasively and with spirit, they may infect the rest. Visions, both good and bad, can be contagious. An *Institute of Chairing* could be one of the good ones.

I suggest that a prime concern of all seminaries and foundations could be to become self-regenerating institutions—with their own able and caring trustees. They could stand as models for the others.

SERVANT LEADERSHIP—BY PERSUASION

In my personal credo stated earlier I said, "If a better society is to be built, one more just and more caring and providing opportunity for people to grow, the most effective and economical way, while supportive of the social order, is to raise the performance as servant of as many institutions as possible by new voluntary regenerative forces initiated within them by committed individuals—*servants*."

So far I have not found it helpful to define *servant* and *serving* in other terms than the consequences of the serving on the one being served or on others who may be affected by the action. In *Teacher as Servant*, I describe a semifictional servant in some detail.

In "The Servant as Leader," the definition was: "Do those being served grow as persons: do they, while being served, become healthier, wiser, freer, more autonomous, more likely themselves to become servants? *And* what is the effect on the least privileged in society; will she or he benefit, or, at least, not be further deprived?" I would now add one further stipulation: "No one will knowingly be hurt by the action, *directly or indirectly*."

Thus the servant would reject the "utilitarian" position, which would accept a very large gain in, say, justice at the cost of a small but real hurt to some. The servant would reject the nonviolent tactic for societal change, however noble the intent, if, as a consequence, some who are disposed to violence are likely to resort to it, or some may be threatened or coerced. (I would fault Mohandas Gandhi on these grounds. Great leader and tremendous person that he was, I do not find his tactic an appropriate model for the servant. John Woolman, as described in "The Servant as Leader" is, for me, such a model.)

The servant would reject the rapid accomplishment of any desirable social goal by coercion in favor of the slower process of persuasion—even if no identifiable person was hurt by the coercion.

To some determined reformers, such a set of beliefs would lead to paralysis of action. The servant (in my view) is generally a "gradualist." And, while granting that, in an imperfect world, because we have not yet learned how to do better, coercion by governments and some other institutions will be needed to restrain some destructive actions and to provide some services best rendered authoritatively, the servant will stand as the advocate of persuasion in human affairs to the largest extent possible.

This view is supported by a belief about the nature of humankind, a belief that leads to a view of persuasion as the critical skill of servant leadership. Such a leader is one who ventures and takes the risks of going out ahead to show the way and whom others follow, *voluntarily, because they are persuaded that the leader's path is the right one—for them*, probably better than they could devise for themselves.

One is persuaded, I believe, on arrival at a feeling of rightness about a belief or action through one's own intuitive sense—checked, perhaps, by others' intuitive judgment, but, in the end, one relies on one's own intuitive sense. One takes that intuitive step, from the closest approximation to certainty one can reach by conscious logic (sometimes not very close), to that state in which one may say with conviction, "This is where I stand!" The act of persuasion will help order the logic and favor the intuitive step. And this takes time! The one being persuaded must take that intuitive step alone, untrammeled by coercion or manipulative stratagems. Both leader and follower respect the integrity and allow the autonomy of the other; and each encourages the other to find her or his own intuitive confirmation of the rightness of the belief or action.

To the servant (as I view that person), *persuasion*, thus defined, stands in sharp contrast to *coercion* (the use, or threat of use, of covert or overt sanctions or penalties, the exploitation of weaknesses or sentiments, or any application of pressure). Persuasion also stands in sharp contrast to *manipulation* (guiding people into beliefs or actions that they do not fully understand).

If one accepts such definitions, has the servant become limited to a passive role and yielded the carrying of the tougher burdens to those with fewer scruples? No, I do not believe so; not if the preparation of servants can begin when they are young. There are some old and valuable burden carriers around who are much too coercive and manipulative; and they might lose their usefulness if they attempted too radical change. It may be better to tolerate their ways as long as they are useful so long as they do not hurt others.

I realize that in adding to the definition of servant the admonition, "no one will knowingly be hurt," some people who might otherwise think of themselves as servants (as I have defined it) will reject that identification. The problem is that some do not believe they can carry the leadership roles they now have without causing some hurt, or that necessary social changes can be made without some being hurt.

In an imperfect world, some will continue to be hurt, as they always have been. I know that, in the course of my life, I have caused some hurt. But, as my concern for servanthood has evolved, the scars from these incidents are more prominent in my memory and self-questioning is sharper: Could I have been more aware, more patient. more gentle, more forgiving, more skillful? The intent of the servant, as I see that person now, is that, as a result of any action she or he initiates, *no one will knowingly be hurt*. And if someone *is* hurt, there is a scar that henceforth will endure to be reckoned with. Hurting people, only a few, is not accepted as a legitimate cost of doing business.

I find eleemosynary institutions most at fault on this issue—particularly with their employed staffs. There seems to be the assumption that since the cause being served is noble, what happens to the people who render the service is not a particular concern.

I once sat with the governing board of a large church as they discussed the many ramifications of their affairs. In listening to their discussions I was appalled at some of the attitudes they held and the cavalier actions they took regarding their employed staff. When it was appropriate for me to comment, I noted my observation on their attitudes and actions and I said: "I have spent my life in a business and had responsibility, directly or indirectly, for the careers of many people. If I had held attitudes like those you have revealed and had your record of hiring and firing people, at some point I would have been taken aside and told, 'Greenleaf, you may be good for something, but we will not let you manage people. We can't afford this!' With the predominantly economic motive, most businesses I know about take greater care with their people than you do. This may have been part of what Emerson had in mind when he said (in *Works and Days*), 'The greatest meliorative force in the world is selfish huckstering trade!' "

It all reminds me of that powerful line with which Shakespeare opens his 94th sonnet:

> They that have power to hurt and will do none.

(Not very little, but none.) This is the sonnet that concludes with those caustic lines:

> For sweetest things turn sourest by their deeds;
> Lilies that fester smell far worse than weeds.

The intervening eleven lines will bear close scrutiny.
The firm aim of the servant is that *no one* will be hurt.
Preparation of a servant, particularly for the exacting role of servant-leader, should start not later than secondary school (before if possible) because, I believe, the servant needs to learn to stand against the culture on two critical issues: *power* and *competition*.

POWER

I have no definite view of power to offer: only some fragmentary thoughts. I grant that, in an imperfect world, some raw use of power will always be with us. But as ours has become a huge, complex, institution-bound society, power seems more of an issue than it was in simpler times when it was easier to identify where coercive pressures came from. Also, within the past 200 years, the damage to power wielders has been clearly signaled—beginning with William Pitt's statement in the House of Commons in 1770, "Unlimited power is apt to corrupt the minds of those who possess it"; and then, in the late 19th century, Lord Acton's more quoted line, "Power tends to corrupt and absolute power corrupts absolutely." It is interesting to note that Lord Acton, a Catholic layman, made this statement in heated opposition to the assumption of Papal infallibility in 1870. And what is the corruption that both Pitt and Acton might have had in mind? I believe it is *arrogance*, and all of the disabilities that follow in the wake of arrogance.

In "The Servant as Leader," I tell of John Woolman, the 18th-century American Quaker who persuaded slaveholding Quakers, one by one, to free their slaves. Half his persuasive argument was concern for the slave, the other half was concern for the damage done to the slaveholder and his family. John Woolman also used the word *corruption* in referring to the legacy of the slaveholder to his heirs.

Along the way, in a conversation I had with the chief executive of a large business concerning the incentives that make his job attractive, he listed as first "The opportunity to wield power!" This came before monetary reward, prestige, service, and creative accomplishment—all of which, together, he said, would not compensate for carrying such a heavy burden.

A few years ago, a friend called to tell me that he had just been made head of a philanthropic foundation—his first work of this kind. My immediate response, drawing on my own considerable experience with foundations, was, "The first thing that will happen to you is that you will no longer know who your friends are." This is a serious disability.

I will never forget my first venture as a foundation representative when I made a tour of a dozen universities on a new grant program. My wife met me at the airport when I returned and asked how it went.

"I have no idea," was my reply.

"I have never experienced anything like this before. In most of my work life, I have had to do battle for my ideas every inch of the way, and nothing I have tried to do has been a pushover. But here, in these conversations with high-ranking officers of prestigious universities, every word I uttered was received as a pearl of wisdom." *This was a corrupting experience.*

I am aware that some foundation representatives seem to rise above this corrupting influence; but I hold that the power of the almoner is near the absolute; and it is corrupting, as I am sure all power is. If it were not so clear in my own experience, I would not be so sure of it.

Somehow, the young potential servant should be helped to an awareness of power and its consequences on both the wielder and the object. In my essay *Trustees as Servants*, I contend that "No one, *absolutely no one*, is to be entrusted with the operational use of power without the close oversight of fully functioning trustees." I would now generalize further and say that young potential servant-leaders should be advised to shun any power-wielding role which is not shared with able colleagues who are equals. (See *The Institution as Servant* for an elaboration of this thesis.) If a young potential servant-leader can accept that the first protection against the corruption of power is never to undertake a power-wielding role alone; if this can be established when one is young, a lifestyle may be built on this principle that will be easy and natural. It is not easy and natural for one who is deeply entrenched as a lone wielder of power to contemplate carrying a major responsible role without a firm grip on power—in one's own hands, *alone*. One who is firmly established as a chief executive officer (a lone power wielder) will almost universally say, "It won't work, one person *must* hold the ultimate power." But if enough of today's able youngsters catch the vision of servant-leadership and incorporate it into their lifestyles early, the day may come, when these people are in their prime years, that they will label, categorically, the current commonly accepted power striving of some successful people as *pathological*—because it makes for a sick society. Those who embrace the spirit of servant-leadership early in their lives are likely to take a similar view of competition—and come to see it as an aberration, not a normal human trait. And when enough able people take that view, it will make a different world. But that will take some time.

COMPETITION

It is difficult to know whether humankind's seemingly "normal" competitive urges are innate—the nature of the human animal—or whether they are acquired. It is difficult to know because the culture is so thoroughly competitive, and imposes its shaping imprint from infancy onward, that one cannot sort out what *homo sapiens* would be like if raised in a noncompetitive culture.

Recently I was on a panel in a conference in a medical school that was discussing the subject of "the ethics of the drug industry." In preparation for the conference, someone had made a video recording of drug ads on TV over a period of weeks; and we sat for 20 minutes watching these, one after another.

It is bad enough to have to look at these zany ads when they appear once in a while as the price of watching commercial TV. But to sit through 20 minutes of nothing else—well, it was nauseating, an affront to taste, intellect, and integrity; and the conference erupted in indignation—"Something ought to be done about this!" After listening for a minute or two of this heated reaction I interjected with, "You shouldn't be so upset by these ads. As a nation, we have made a clear social policy, backed by tough laws with criminal sanctions, that an

industry like this will be *forced* to serve by requiring dog-eat-dog competition as a rule of doing business. When you decide to *force* service
this way (and you really don't influence much but price), then you
should not be surprised if you get a result like we have just witnessed."

The conference erupted again, "What would *you* do, repeal the
antitrust laws?" And I answered, "I don't know what I would do. I
have only one point: if you decree (and you have so decreed) that
dog-eat-dog competition is to be the regulator, then do not be surprised if you get this kind of result. Anyway, what is so sacred about
the antitrust laws? They were not brought down off the mountain
chiseled in stone. They are crude man-made devices to deal with a
clear social problem: how to elicit the best service we can get from a
business. But there are several unhealthy by-products, one of which
you have just seen." This promoted considerable discussion, without
conclusion. And there is not likely to be a better answer to the question: How can we elicit optimal service from people and institutions,
as long as competition is uncritically accepted as *good* and is deeply
imbedded in the culture? In the preparation of young potential servants to be servant-leaders, the issue of competition must be critically
examined and alternatives sought.

This is a curious bit of history of usage of the word *compete*.
Modern usage puts it as "To strive or contend with another," while
the Latin origin of the word is *competere*—to seek or strive together.
The clear implications of the origin of this word is that competition
is a cooperative rather than a contending relationship.

This reference may not help us to resolve our own personal
dilemmas as we find ourselves in a struggle to beat out somebody
else, in a society that supports that struggle with both moral and legal
sanctions. (Recently I attended a conference on the subject of "The
Judeo-Christian Ethic and the Modern Business Corporation."
There were about 25 theologians of the major faiths present. In the
papers and the discussions there was frequent reference to "unfair"
competition, but I do not recall a single question by a theologian
about competition per se.)

My position is: if we are to move toward a more caring, serving society than we now have, competition must be muted, if not eliminated. If theologians will not lead in this move (and I sense no initiative from that quarter), practicing servants will, and theologians will rationalize the result after the fact. The servant will be noncompetitive; but what can be the servant's affirmative position?

I believe that serving and competing are antithetical; the stronger the urge to serve, the less the interest in competing. (Read Petr Kropotkin's classic *Mutual Aid* for perspective on this issue.) The servant is importantly concerned with the consequences of his or her actions: those being served, *while being served* become healthier, wiser, freer, more autonomous, more likely themselves to become servants. *And*, what is the effect on the least privileged in society; will they benefit, or, at least, not be further deprived? *And*, no one will knowingly be hurt by the action?—the servant is strong *without* competing. But, unfortunately, we have decreed that ours shall be a competitive society. How does a servant function in such a society?

Servant-Leader: Strong or Weak?

The power-hungry person, who relishes competition and is good at it (meaning: usually wins) will probably judge the servant-leader, as I have described that person, to be weak or naive or both. But let us look past the individual to the institution in which he or she serves: what (or who) makes that institution strong?

The strongest, most productive institution over a long period of time is one in which, other things being equal, there is the largest amount of voluntary action in support of the goals of the institution. The people who staff the institution do the "right" things at the right time—things that optimize total effectiveness—because the goals are clear and comprehensive and they understand what ought to be done. They believe they are the right things to do, and they take the necessary actions without being instructed. No institution ever achieves this perfectly. But I submit that, other things being equal, the institution that achieves the most of this kind of voluntary action will be judged *strong*, stronger than comparable institutions that have fewer of these voluntary actions.

Earlier, in the discussion of mind-sets, I gave the example of the more successful business in a highly competitive field that stands above its competitors in profitability, in the quality of the product it delivers, and in the absence of labor conflict that plagues all of the others. The principal difference is that this unusual company has more voluntary effort; its people do more, voluntarily, than other companies' people do for them. And it is not accidental. The man who built this business, dead for some years, put the people who worked for him *first*. As a consequence, his employees delivered all that people can deliver—and the business came to lead its field. It is a "people" business. There are other companies in other fields that have taken this view and, when other things are equal, they are all strong when compared with competitors who do not take this view of people.

From my own experience with businesses, I would say that even when "people first" is not the policy of the top executives, "*strong*" subordinate executives may take the "people first" position and add strength to the business. In AT&T, when we occasionally conducted attitude surveys, we noted what we called the "umbrella" effect. A strong subordinate manager would produce positive attitudes among his or her subordinates when the stance of higher level managers caused the prevailing attitudes in other parts of the company to be more negative. I believe that able subordinate managers who are servants can build strength in the people they lead even when the policy that is projected on them from above works to destroy it. But such subordinate managers must be really strong in terms of toughness, conviction, and tenacity.

Further, when there is a sticky organizational problem in a business, an astute power-wielding executive sometimes tries to find a person who is accepted as servant who will get into the situation and correct it—with persuasion. *And for purely practical reasons*: it comes out better than if somebody swings on it in a coercive or manipulative way!

Both the words *servant* and *persuasion* are "soft" words to some people. They do not connote the tough attitudes that are thought to be needed to hold this world together and get its work done.

In 1970, when I chose to advocate, in writing, the servant-leader concept, both words *serve* and *lead* were in a shadow. *Lead* seems to have recovered some stature, but *serve* is still questioned by many thoughtful people. I chose to stay with *serve*, *lead* and *persuade* because I see, through the meaning they have for me, a path to restoring much of the dignity that has been lost through the depersonalization that industrialization has brought to us. And dignity adds strength both to individuals and to the institutions of which they are a part—strength to serve.

PROSPECTS FOR THE SERVANT IDEA—SOME SPECULATIONS

In much of what I have written on the servant theme, including most of this essay, I have dealt with issues of leadership and institution building. After ten years of circulation of these writings and considerable interaction about them with people who have their hands on the levers of power and influence, I am not persuaded that much movement toward our society becoming more caring is likely to be initiated by those who are now established as leaders. Mind-sets like the four discussed earlier are much too prevalent and entrenched, and we seem not to have the resources to generate, or the openness to receive, liberating visions. Whatever older people can do to make ours a more serving, caring society should be encouraged; but I do not expect much from my contemporaries.

We (some of us) do know how to prepare and inspire young people to press the limits of the reasonable and possible, with some of them becoming skilled builders of more serving institutions. The over-arching vision that will inspire and energize mentors of the young is my prime concern. These mentors are strong, able people who believe that well-prepared young people, in whom servant-leadership is an integral part of their lifestyles, are likely to bring to reality some of what we oldsters can only dream about.

My hope for the future, and I do have hope, is that some (perhaps many) young people whose lifestyles may yet be shaped by conscious choices may be helped to more serving roles than most of their elders occupy today. What I have written is not likely to give this help directly to young people. But it may be useful to those who have the gifts and the will and the courage to be mentors of the young. And I believe that the psychic rewards to these mentors can be very great. What could bring more satisfaction to oldsters than helping some of the young to become servant-leaders?

In *Teacher as Servant*, I described in detail how a university teacher could, without the support of university or colleagues, encourage, in a decisive way, the growth as servant of a large number of students. I hazarded a guess that, if there were a way to alert them to the opportunity, perhaps as many as one in a thousand of the 500,000 or so university and college faculty in the United States might take the initiative to give this precious help to students. And I reasoned that the 500, if they worked at it over a career, could favor the time of the next generation becoming a golden age of leadership in our country. It can be done without adding to college and university budgets. It would require no changes in the curriculum, no administrative or faculty actions, no trustee initiatives. All that is needed is a handful, really, of determined and perceptive faculty members who, deep down inside, are true servants and who, without extra compensation and recognition—perhaps in the face of some opposition— will *lead* in this most fundamental way. They will go out ahead to show, by their example, how one may be a servant in what appears to be a cold, low-caring, highly competitive, violence-prone society. These servant teachers may be a saving remnant, in the biblical sense. And saving remnants are usually not empowered, approved, or well-financed.

I would now amend the language of this assertion in just one particular way. In place of "alert them (the one in a thousand teachers) to the opportunity" I would substitute "inspire them with a vision of the opportunity."

One who might respond to this suggestion is the president, especially in a small college; but it also might be a large university. The president might personally offer to lead a noncredit seminar for elected student leaders. The agenda of the seminar might be discussions with invited resource people and sharing between the president and these student leaders on matters of mutual concern in their current leadership roles. In my conversations with student leaders, I have found them concerned with some of the same issues that are on the minds of presidents—matters of the spirit. Presidents might find in these seminars a helpful close contact with students, and students would have the opportunity to learn about leadership from each other and from the president—experientially. The president may learn something about leadership, too—a new perspective on that job.

The prospect for the servant idea rests almost entirely, I believe, on some among *us investing the energy and taking the risks to inspire with a vision.* In our large and complex society, a single compelling prophetic voice may not, as Grundtvig did in 19th-century Denmark, move those few who will educate and inspire enough young people to rebuild the entire culture. In our times, the orchestration of many prophetic visionaries may be required. But I believe that the ultimate effect will be the same: *teachers* (individuals, not institutions) will be inspired to raise the society-building consciousness of the young. And *teachers* may be anybody who can reach young people who have the potential to be servants and prepare them to be servant leaders. These teachers may be members of school faculties, presidents of colleges and universities, those working with young people in churches. Some may be parents, others may be either professionals or volunteers working with youth groups. But whoever and wherever they are, these teachers will catch the vision and *do what they know how to do.* First, they will reinforce or build hope. Young people will be helped to accept the world, and to believe that they can learn to live productively in it *as it is*—striving, violent, unjust, as well as beautiful, caring, and supportive. They will be helped to believe that they can cope, and that, if they work at it over a lifetime, they may leave a little corner of the world a bit better than they found it. Then these teachers will nourish the embryo spark of servant in as many as possible and help prepare those who are able—*to lead!*

Thus I do not see the prospect for the servant idea being carried by a great mass movement—not soon.

I have premised this discussion on building hope in the young and preparing some of them to serve and lead. As an oldster, I have hope that is supported by the belief that some seminaries and foundations will have (or find) trustees of the stature who will help them (seminaries and foundations) to be self-regenerating institutions. These then will become sources of prophetic visions for, and supports of organizational strength in, schools and churches which will minister to individuals and to the vast structure of operating institutions that make up our complex society. Central to this ministry will be the encouragement of teachers of servants—some of whom will become leaders who make their careers as regenerating influences within institutions of all sorts, including seminaries and foundations—thus closing the loop. But the prime movers in this process are trustees of foundations and seminaries. It is for these exceptionally able and dedicated trustees to initiate and to sustain the process. I believe that a few will. This is the basis of my hope.

Beyond my hope, I have a speculative prospect to share: that some of these servant-leaders will bring together communities of seekers who find—and *continue to seek*, thus adding a new building force that works toward an evolving caring society.

I envision that these communities (of seeking servants who find—and continue to seek) will bring a new kind of institution that is radically different from anything we now have. It may be a business, a church, a school, a unit of government. Or it may be an institution that embraces aspects of several of these. But it will be *new*, and its emergence will be a hopeful augury for everybody, especially for young people.

In this way a prophetic vision for the 21st century may be delivered to us—not in words, but by a few humble servants saying simply, "Here it is; come and see."

The reader is invited to speculate on what this new institution might be like and what its presence might mean to the quality of our common life. These speculations might help this new institution to come, by creating receptivity for a new vision.

NOTE ON LIBERATING VISIONS

A final note on receiving, communicating, and responding to *liberating visions*. This is an illusive term. What could it mean? Let me give an example out of my experience.

When I was working closely with several colleges and universities in the late 1960s I became aware that one of the student preoccupations of that period was reading the novels of Herman Hesse. College book stores had stacks and stacks of them—and some still do. Because I was deeply concerned with what was going on in students' minds at that time, I made a project of reading all that Hesse wrote, in the order that he wrote these stories. Along with them I read a biography that told me what was going on in Hesse's life as he wrote each book.

Hesse, in the early part of his life, was a tormented man, in and out of mental illness that is reflected in what he was writing at the time. His book *Journey to the East* marks the turning point toward the serenity that he achieved in his later years when he wrote his greatest novel, *Magister Ludi*, which earned a Nobel Prize for literature. I found *Journey to the East* a hopeful book because it is the story of Leo, the central figure who accompanies a band of men on their mythical journey (probably Hesse's own journey) as the *servant* who does their menial chores, but who also sustains them with his spirit and song. He is a person of extraordinary presence. All goes well with the journey until Leo disappears. Then the group falls into disarray and the journey is abandoned. They cannot make it without the servant Leo. The narrator, one of the party, after some years of wandering, finds Leo and is taken into the Order that has sponsored the journey. There he discovers that Leo, whom he had first known as *servant*, was in fact the titular head of the Order, its guiding spirit, a great and noble leader. The story of Leo gave me the idea of "The Servant as Leader."

Later a Catholic Sister came to talk about what I had written in "The Servant as Leader." In the course of the discussion she asked me where I found the earliest reference to the idea of servant. I replied, in the Bible, of course, beginning early in the Old Testament. Her rather sharp question was, "Then why do you attribute it to reading Hesse?" I responded, "Because that was where I got the idea to write on the Servant as Leader theme. If I had not read the story of Leo, I might have never written anything on this subject. There was something in Hesse's story that moved me in a way that I had not been moved before."

In the terms that I have been discussing the subject of liberating visions, I was prepared to receive one by my deep immersion in the student turmoil of the sixties and by reading Hesse as part of my search for understanding of what was going on in student minds. The liberating vision that took me into one of the most interesting and productive chapters of my life was delivered by Hermann Hesse.

This essay, "Servant: Retrospect and Prospect," has had much to do with receiving, communicating, and responding to *liberating visions*. What I learned from the experience noted above is that liberating visions can come from anywhere at any time and that they may or may not bear any particular theological label. Important to me are:

- Immerse oneself in the experiences this world offers.

- Be accepting of the people involved in these experiences, and seek to understand what moves them.

- Acknowledge—and stand in awe before—the ineffable mystery

that shrouds the source of all understanding of human motives that leads to visions.

• *Be open to receive, and act upon, what inspiration offers.*

Along the way, I had a dream that may have had something to do with the course of my experience these last ten years.

It is a beautiful summer day, and I am in a lovely, extensive woods in which there is a labyrinth of paths. I am riding a bicycle through these paths, holding in my hand a map of them to guide my journey. It is a buoyant, joyful experience and there is a delightful certainty about it. Suddenly a gust of wind blows the map out of my hand. I stop and look back to see it flutter to the ground, to be picked up by an old man who stands there holding it for me. I walk back to retrieve my map; but when I arrive at the old man, he hands me—not my map—but a small round tray of earth in which fresh grass seedlings are growing.

> Where there is no vision, the people perish.
> *Proverbs 29:18 (King James Version)*

> What is now proved was once only imagin'd.
> *William Blake (The Marriage of Heaven and Hell)*

POSTSCRIPT

As I was writing this an invitation came to visit a small church-related college where they wanted to talk about a new goal for the college: to make preparation for servant-leadership a central concern, in the work of the college. I visited with faculty, as a whole and in groups, and with student leaders. It was an encouraging experience, to find that a college wanted to consider such a move. My parting advice was not to try to "legislate" such a change but to give leadership and encourage wide discussion, and let new directions come as individuals find ways to work toward such a goal with the hope that, ultimately, a consensus will emerge. This is what servant-leadership is about: helping consensus, voluntary and durable consensus, to evolve.

2

Education and Maturity

A talk before the faculty and students of Barnard College, at their fifth biennial vocational conference, November 30, 1960

Maturity has many meanings, especially when applied to people. But in my own association, there is a strong link between the word *maturity* and the word *becoming*. Education, in particular a liberal education, can be a powerful maturing force. Depth of meaning about process emerges only out of experience. This, briefly, is the framework within which I shall try to deal with the subject of education and maturity.

A friend of mine in Madison, Wisconsin, tells a story about Frank Lloyd Wright many years ago when his studio, Taliesen, was at nearby Spring Green. Mr. Wright had been invited by a women's club in Madison to come and talk on the subject "What is Art?" He accepted and appeared at the appointed hour and was introduced to speak on this subject.

In his prime, he was a large impressive man, with good stage presence and a fine voice. He acknowledged the introduction and produced from his pocket a little book. He then proceeded to read one of Hans Christian Andersen's fairy tales, the one about the little mermaid. He read it beautifully, and it took about 15 minutes. When he finished he closed the book, looked intently at his audience and said, "That, my friends, is art," and sat down.

As I thought about this talk today, I wished that I knew how to do this with the subject of maturity. Maturity is like art and virtue; it is best demonstrated, and I feel presumptuous to be talking about it at all.

I do not have a how-to-do-it formula for achieving maturity to hand you. My sole aim is to encourage you to be thoughtful about your problem of finding the meaning of maturity in your own lives and the times you live in. Because we are all different, the problem will be different for each of us. The common ground I shall try to find is a way of thinking about the meaning of maturity.

The most important lesson I have learned about maturity is that the emergence, the full development, of what is uniquely *me* should be an important concern throughout my entire life. There are many other important concerns, but this particular one must never be submerged, never be out of sight.

This I learned the hard way. There was a long "wilderness" period in which I sought resources outside of myself. I looked for an "answer" to the normal frustrations of life (*frustration* used in the sense of the blocking of motives to which one cannot make a constructive response). Good years went by. No answers came. It took a long time for me to discover that the only *real* answer to frustration is to concern myself with the drawing forth of what is uniquely me. Only as what is uniquely me emerges do I experience moments of true creativity; moments which, when deeply felt, temper the pain of long periods of frustration that are the common lot of most of us and give me the impulse and the courage to act constructively in the outside world.

Every life, including the most normal of the normal, is a blend of experiences that build ego strength and those that tear it down. As one's responsibilities widen, these forces become more powerful. As good a definition as I know is that maturity is the capacity to withstand the ego-destroying experiences and not lose one's perspective in the ego-building experiences: "If you can meet with triumph or disaster—," to borrow a phrase from Mr. Kipling.

One of my special interests is the field of management development. I have made a point of looking into a few organizations in which, in a certain period, there was an unusual flowering of managerial talent. Usually there was one person, an able manager who had the gift of guiding his understudy so as to help bring latent talent to fruition, to the mature ability to carry heavy responsibility successfully. The most outstanding developer I know about had at the center of his philosophy the idea that the really important lessons in the managerial art are learned only as the result of error, suffering the consequences of error and learning from the total experience. This is an important test of maturity: to seek to avoid error, to accept the consequences of error when it comes (as it surely will), and learn from it and to wipe the slate clean and start afresh, free from feelings of guilt.

But this takes a special view of the self. The sustaining feeling of personal significance is important. It comes from the inside. I am *not* a piece of dust on the way to becoming another piece of dust. I am an instrument of creation, unlike any that has ever been or ever will be. So is each of you. No matter how badly you may be shaken, no matter how serious the failure or how ignominious the fall from grace, by accepting and learning you can be restored with greater strength. Don't lose this basic view of who you are.

A friend of mine once said of his 4-year-old son, "His world is a six-foot sphere. He's in the center of it and moves it around with him wherever he goes."

The conventional view is that this is youthful egocentricity and that one grows out of it as he matures, as he becomes social and accepts responsibility. I would rather say that there is a transmutation as one matures. One is *still* at the center of his world. (How could one be unique and be otherwise?) But with maturity one's world becomes the limitless sphere of people, ideas, and events which each of us influences by each thought, word, and deed; and each of us, in turn, is open to receive influence. The individual capacity of each of us to influence and be influenced and to absorb the shocks—this capacity is in proportion to the emergence of the sentient person, the drawing forth of what is uniquely *us*. This is an important idea to keep as your own private lamp when somebody undertakes to grind you down—as they surely will sometime, if you have not been aware of it already.

This is the central idea of maturity: to keep your private lamp lighted as you venture forth on your own to meet with triumph or disaster or *just plain routine*. And this is what a liberal education is about; because this is what life is about. If, in your college years, you learn nothing other than who you are, that you have a private lamp, your stay here will have been amply justified.

The notion of uniqueness will bear some exploration. I will leave to the theologians the speculation as to whether part of what is uniquely a person is inherently evil. I prefer to say: whatever it is, draw it forth and face it; then make something creative and good out of it. Oscar Wilde has left for us the observation, "Every saint has a past, every sinner has a future."

We are all conditioned by the culture in which we have lived, more than we can ever know. So many of the conflicts of the world today may have had their origins in the sudden impact of modern travel and communication, which bring these cultural differences face to face in sharp encounter. This makes it imperative that each of us understands the biases of his own culture which he brings to the confrontation.

Yet, acknowledging all of this, I believe that something of unconditioned uniqueness is prepared to show through in every person. It is the process of drawing it forth with which each of us needs to be concerned. It is a process which, at best, will be only dimly perceived; yet we must conjure with it. The remainder of this talk will deal with some ideas about the process which seem particularly important to me at this time.

I see four major issues that need to be faced and dealt with if this drawing forth is to proceed as an important life involvement. The relevance to your concern in this vocational conference is this: in choosing a vocation, you should have as your primary aim (there are other necessary aims, but this one should be primary) that of *finding in the work in which you are engaged that which is uniquely you.* If you miss on this, you will likely wind up as one of T. S. Eliot's hollow men—

> Between the potency
> And the existence
> Between the essence
> And the descent
> Falls the Shadow

No other achievement, no other end sought, will be worth the effort if through the work that occupies your best days and years you do not find a way to fan your own creative spark to a white heat—at least once in a while. So I want to talk about four of many issues, four that have emerged rather sharply out of my own experience, in the hope that something will resonate in your own experience, while you still have many choices before you.

First, *the consequences of stress and responsibility!* All work—whether in business, profession, government, home—both develops and limits. It stretches one out in some ways and narrows one in others; it both fans the flame and seeks to quench it. This has no doubt happened to some extent in the educational and other choices you have already made. It will happen more in work.

I see no exceptions: no completely whole persons, nor any chance of it. You must not look forward to any idealized achievement, no perfect or enduring adjustment to your life work. Whenever I think I have really achieved something, up come those powerful lines from Walt Whitman's "Song of the Open Road":

> Now, understand me well—It is provided in the essence of things, that from any fruition of success, no matter what, shall come forth something to make a greater struggle necessary.

The greater struggle that will be necessary as you learn to bear more stress and carry responsibility comes because long exposure to these conditions tends to narrow the intellect unless a valiant effort is made to achieve an ever-expanding outlook. It is not enough just to try to keep up, to maintain the level of intellectual curiosity you have achieved in college. The intellectual life must expand. The great risk which the bearers of responsibility assume is that intellectual curiosity, the search for understanding, will atrophy and that only a calculating rationality will remain.

The test is in the heat of action. If one has a problem on which it is appropriate to act, and if one doesn't know what to do (which is the constant dilemma of all bearers of responsibility), one *should* turn to the search for greater depth of understanding about the problem.

If you are only going to remember one thing from this talk, I hope you will remember this: the main reason you will ever be aware of a problem is that your understanding of yourself, of the other people involved, and of the area in which the problem lies is limited. Therefore, the search for understanding—an intellectual pursuit—is the most practical of ideas, even though the "practical" people often spurn it. But it is a difficult idea to hold onto when one bears the weight of responsibility for action, especially if the need is urgent. It is difficult to seek to understand when the heat is on. If one is to be well served by a liberal education, one needs to use this period of relative isolation from real life pressures to develop the firm habit of seeking to understand when the heat is *not* on. This is the best rationale I know of for concentrating such an important educational influence in your present age range. Learn how to seek to understand now, when the heat is not on; make it a firm habit, and try to be aware that this will only serve you well if the habit is firmly enough fixed so that you can manage it when the going is rough, when the stakes are real, and when the consequences of failing to understand may be overwhelming.

One of the important testing grounds in decision making is the meeting of personal conflicts, when ideas or interests differ. Please give some thought to Dr. Carl Rogers' wonderful formula for meeting conflict. It is this: try to state to the *other person's* satisfaction your *understanding* of *his* position; then identify and state as much of *his* proposition as you can agree with; *then*, and not until then, state your own point of view.

The risk in this procedure is that *you* might change. Opening one's self to understanding always entails this risk. This is bad advice for the brittle, the fearful, the dogmatic, the "allness" people. But then, our subject *is* maturity.

If change is too painful to contemplate, then one had best adjust his blinders to shut out all peripheral understanding. But if one does this and winds up hating the world, then one shouldn't blame the world for it.

There is a poignant line from *The King and I* when Anna is getting to the King with some new ideas and, in desperation, he pounds the table and shouts, "If you're going to be King, you've got to be King!" He seemed to me to be saying, "Don't mix me up with ideas when, at this point, the only thing I know how to do is to act!" This portrays dramatically the awful consequences of a life of action in which the intellectual lamp was not kept bright, in which the search for understanding was not a constant quest. And in this play, the end, for the King, is tragic.

The second issue is *the tension between the requirement to conform and the essential person.*

Conformity has become a nasty word. It has almost become the battle cry of those of our generation who see their role as the modern version of the muckrakers of 50 years ago.

The attacks on conformity confuse the issue because in any organized society there must be a lot of conformity. Whenever two people undertake to work and live together, there must be some conformity.

All organized effort, any concerted influence, requires to some extent that those who participate must think and act alike. Nothing important can be accomplished without a good deal of conformity. Only a hermit in his cave can completely eschew conformity and carry out his role. As our society becomes more complex, more highly integrated, it demands more conformity than was called for in simpler times.

The problem is to know conformity for what it is: a completely external adjustment to the group norm of behavior in the interest of group cohesiveness and effectiveness. Then, knowing conformity for what it is, always keep it in rational focus as a conscious adjustment in the interest of an effective society. Keep it external, never let it become a part of *you*. Hold it firmly on the outside. The great danger is that one will lose one's identity in the act of conformity, not knowing which is the essential person and which is the conforming act, and thereby forfeit his right to be respected as an individual (by himself or by anybody else).

When I was a boy, one of the weapons of discipline held over little boys who used profane language was that their mothers would wash their mouths with soap. My mother never did it to me, although there was ample provocation; but it was one of the things I heard about. I recall a story about a determined little character who did receive this punishment, and he is alleged to have sputtered out through the soap suds, "You can soap my talk, but you can't soap my think!" Don't ever let anybody soap your think.

The third issue that needs to be dealt with, if the drawing forth of what is uniquely each one of us is to proceed, is *the struggle for significance—the complications of status, property, achievement.*

One of the hazards of prolonged schooling is that one becomes accustomed to living in a system in which the ends of the system are to nurture significance for the individual. This is what a school is for.

Once in the world of work, the institution one is in—whether it is home, school, business, social service—uses people for other ends. All such institutions have other obligations, and they commit people who do the work to these obligations. Most modern institutions are also concerned that the people who do the work find personal significance in their work. But this is a qualified obligation and one must not expect that any work will automatically provide the feeling of significance. A requirement of maturity is that one *learns to find his own significance*, even under circumstances in which powerful forces may seem to operate to deny it.

But what is it that one is expected to find? I see it as something latent in the individual to be fulfilled. It is the seed of what is uniquely each person. Providing the conditions for its germination, emergence, and growth is the *search*.

A healthy adulthood requires that one find it, and find it among the available choices. History and literature are surfeited with examples of barren lives in which the search was thwarted because the searcher could not accept the choices available to him. If only some out-of-reach circumstances were present, the search might go on.

One fictional account that has meant a great deal to me is Nathaniel Hawthorne's *Great Stone Face*. This is a simple story that can be read in 15 minutes, and I commend it to you.

In this story, we are in a small New England town nestled in the mountains with a view of a nearby mountain whose profile resembles a majestic face. The people in this town are living out a myth. Someday a noble man will come to them whose own profile resembles the great stone face. His presence will bring into their lives the qualities of majesty which the great stone face symbolizes.

In the course of the story, there comes a procession of people from the outside world, people of wealth and external status. The coming of each is heralded with great expectation; but always there is disappointment. The resemblance is not true.

Years go by. We see a generation live from youth to old age carrying this hope that the image of the great stone face will come and that their lives will be enriched by the presence of the man who bears this likeness. Finally they recognize the resemblance to this image among them—one of their own people. He has been there all the time, a living demonstration of those qualities which in his old age gave him the resemblance to the profile on the mountain.

Viewed symbolically, this community is a person seeking from external sources the qualities which are latent to emerge—if only they will be permitted to emerge. They did not realize that the external marks of character are the product of the way a life is lived. If they were truly seekers, they would not have been so preoccupied with the external marks. Rather they would have attended more to the process, to what was going on in the lives they were examining. Had they been examining lives in process, lives around them to be seen, they would have seen right before their eyes the demonstration of how to live nobly. And they would have seen it when they were young enough for it to make a difference in the way their lives were lived.

We see in this story the collective life of the community denied fulfillment because it is looking for a stereotype. Significance is more likely to come from holding an attitude of unqualified expectancy, of openness and wonder.

So often, too, significance is blocked by compulsive drives for goals that do not provide fulfillment, something we pursue that we really don't want. When we achieve what we pursue, whether it is a tangible external thing or an internal state of mind, there is an emptiness. If we can name it and describe it precisely, the chances are we are seeking the wrong thing. I have seen so much of this among my contemporaries. If only they could lay aside the pursuit of over-specific and (therefore) meaningless goals and let their own uniqueness flower. The warning here is that our society holds up values which confuse the search—status, property, power, tangible achievement, even peace of mind—which subvert the emergence of true uniqueness, the only real significance. These are necessary elements of the society we live in at its current stage of development. We must make our peace with them and accept them as important, but we should not view them as basic or primary. Personal significance *is* primary.

Neither institutions nor aggregates of people have significance, except as it is given to them by living individuals who comprise them. Even traditions, powerful as they sometimes appear to be, are not viable unless contemporary people understand and believe in them and, by their thoughts, words, and deeds, give them current significance.

One of my favorite stories is about a now-prominent New York minister who was starting his career in the depression of the 1930s in a very poor church. He had no car and he needed one for his parish work. But since neither he nor the church had any money, this was a problem. Finally he bought an old battered jalopy for $25. It wasn't much of a car, but it ran and served his needs. However, he was soon confronted by an objection from his parishioners. Poor as they all were, they didn't like the idea of their minister riding around in that kind of car, especially parking it in front of the church. Finally it came out at a meeting of the governing board when one of the members said that their minister should have a car that "added to his dignity." At this point the young minister rose and spoke one short sentence that disposed of the question about his car. "Gentlemen," he said, "no automobile adds dignity to a man; man adds dignity to the automobile."

This is a point ever to keep sharply in mind. Dignity, significance, character are wholly the attributes of individual people. They have nothing to do with anything external to the person.

The fourth major issue I see is *facing the requirements for growth; accepting some process for drawing forth one's uniqueness.*

I would like to see a word that has fallen into disuse restored to common usage. That word is *entheos,* from the same roots as *enthusiasm,* which means "possessed of the spirit." These two words, *entheos* and *enthusiasm,* have had an interesting history in the English language, coming down side by side through separate channels of meaning from the 16th century. *Entheos* has always been the basic spiritual essence; enthusiasm, until recently, its perverter and imitator. *Entheos* is now defined as *the power actuating one who is inspired*, while *enthusiasm* is seen as its less profound, more surface aspect.

I want to use *entheos* as it is now defined, the power actuating one who is inspired; and, at the risk of laboring it, I want to build a concept of growth around this one word. For those who are concerned with maturity *seen as becoming*, it is important to see *entheos* as the lamp and to keep one's own private lamp lighted as one ventures forth into a confused, pressure-ridden world, but nevertheless a hopeful world for those who can maintain their contact with the power that actuates inspiration. From the little I know of history, I cannot imagine a more interesting time to be alive *provided one can make it with entheos.*

I see *entheos* as the essence that makes a constructive life possible; it is the sustaining force that holds one together under stress; it is the support for venturesome risk-taking action; it is the means whereby whatever religious beliefs one has are kept in contact with one's attitudes and actions in the world of practical affairs; it lifts people above the prosaic and gives them a sense of timelessness; it is the prod of conscience that keeps one open to knowledge, so that one can be both aware and sensitive, when the urge to be comfortable would keep the door closed. I like that line from William Blake:

> If the doors to perception were cleansed, everything will
> appear to man as it is, infinite.

Entheos does not come in response to external incentives. In fact, it may persist when incentives operate to destroy it. The individual cannot will it, it comes when it will and sometimes it goes when most needed. *But it does grow.*

All that can be willed is the search. There is no one pattern I know of. Each must find his own pattern. One of the great challenges of maturity: find your own growth pattern in the search for *entheos*.

I can suggest some tests. If one has a few tests in mind, these might help to plot the individual search. We are reaching for *entheos*, the power actuating one who is inspired. First some misleading indicators—some achievements that might throw one off.

Status of material success. One's external achievement may be impressive and praiseworthy and yet, in the process of achieving, one may be destroying much that is really important to him.

Social success. The nongrowth people are sometimes more comfortable to be with.

Doing all that is expected of one. Who is doing the expecting, and what do they know about what I should be expecting of myself?

Family success can be a misleading indicator. Fine and desirable as it is, it can be an egocentric, narrowing development. Internally, the family may appear in good balance; but it may be taking more out of the wider community than it is contributing.

Relative peace and quiet. This may simply mean that the doors of perception are closed.

Finally, *busyness—compulsive busyness.* Beneath the surface of much action, there is the drive to avoid the implications of growth. "This is for monks in a monastery; I'm too busy," they seem to say (Read the Mary-Martha story and ask, What does it have to say on this point?)

These are six indicators of achievement that can be misleading as evidences of growth. These can all be positive and worthwhile; but they don't necessarily add up to growth of *entheos.*

Now, what I believe to be some valid tests, some indicators that there may be real growth of *entheos.*

First, two paradoxes, *a concurrent satisfaction and dissatisfaction with the status quo.* One is not so unhappy with his current level of achievement that he can't live with himself. Neither is he so pleased with it that he has no incentive to break out of it. Then there is a concurrent feeling of broadening responsibilities and centering down. One is constantly reaching out for wider horizons, new levels of experience and at the same time the idea of "This one thing will I do" is in the ascendancy.

There is a growing *sense of purpose* in whatever one does. The idea of purpose becomes important. Without being obsessive about it, the most penetrating and disturbing of all questions, "What am I trying to do?" becomes a constant query. One never loses sight of this question.

There are *changing patterns and depths of one's interests.* Old interests to which one was once attached drop away and newer and deeper ones take their place. Choices must be made.

> Somewhere ages and ages hence:
> Two roads diverged in a wood, and I—
> I took the one less traveled by
> And that has made all the difference.
>
> *Robert Frost*

As *entheos* becomes a more constant companion, one moves toward the minimum of difference between the outside and inside images of the self; *one becomes more willing to be seen as he is.* Living as we do in an unreal world, to some extent we all wear masks. Convenient as it is to let the mask do what only serenity can *really* do, I submit that *all* masks chafe; I never saw a well-fitting mask. It is a great relief to take them off. The power of *entheos* makes this possible; and the urge to remove the mask is one of the surest signs of its potency.

Then *one becomes conscious of the good use of time and unhappy with the waste of time.* As awareness opens, one of the measures it takes of our contemporary society is the number of elaborate and seductive devices lurking about that serve no other purpose than to waste time.

A further test is the growing *sense of achieving one's basic personal goals through one's work,* whatever it is—however menial, however poorly recognized. One of the popular illusions in our kind of culture is that one must reach a high status position in order to achieve one's goals. In my observation, there is really nothing in status but status, and the proportion of frustrated people is just as great in high places as in low places. I know it is an old truism, but the only place to achieve one's personal goals is where one is. Looking for a greener pasture for this purpose is almost certain to seal off the opportunity for achievement.

Going with some of these tests is the *emergence of a sense of unity*, a pulling together of all aspects of life. Job, family, recreation, church, community all merge into one total pattern. While there remain obvious allocations of time to specific pursuits, the sense of leaving one and going to another diminishes. Peripheral time-consuming activities that cannot be brought within this view are laid aside. None of us needs to accept all of the obligations that others would impose upon us, and one way of making the separation is to test their compatibility with the core of *unified* activities. As *entheos* grows, one becomes more decisive and emphatic in saying *no!*

Finally, there is a developing *view of people. All* people are seen more as beings to be trusted, believed in, and loved and less as objects to be used, competed with, or judged. It is a shifting of the balance from use to esteem in *all* personal relationships. In an imperfect world, one never achieves it fully; but there can be measurable progress. This is a critically important test. Unless this view of people becomes dominant, it is difficult for the inward view of one's own significant uniqueness to emerge. Love of oneself in the context of a pervasive love for one's fellow man is a healthy attribute and necessary for the fulfillment of a life. Out of this context, love of oneself is narrowing, introverting, and destructive.

The ultimate test of *entheos*, however, is an *intuitive feeling of oneness, of wholeness, of rightness;* but not necessarily comfort or ease.

These seem to me to be some valid tests that give assurance that *entheos* is growing. If this kind of thinking doesn't strike a responsive chord with you today, please make a note of it, tuck it away in the back of your diary, and look at it 10 years, 20 years from now.

In closing, I want to return for a moment to work, vocation, and its relevance to growth, to the drawing out of the unique significance of the person.

Don't just look for a job; even for an interesting and remunerative job.

Think of yourself as a person with unique potentialities, and see the purpose of life as bringing these into mature bloom.

Don't think of your career in terms of finding a nice fit for your skills and abilities. You will find some work more rewarding than other work; but the perfect job doesn't exist. Anyhow, neither the person nor the job stays put.

Since there are no perfect jobs, no ideal fields, take one that challenges you as a piece of work to be done. Make other requirements subsidiary to this one, because nothing else really matters if the job is not rewarding in this sense.

Whatever your work is, make something out of it that enriches *you*. Work itself cannot be truly significant except as it is seen as the means whereby the people who do the work find themselves in it. Do your work well; keep your sense of obligation high; cultivate excellence in everything you do; but above all *use* your work, use it as a means for your own fulfillment as a person—your own becoming.

If you have goals, be sure to state them in terms of external achievement, not in terms of what you will become. You don't know what you *can* become, and no one can tell you.

This can be one of the great excitements of life—the surprise when you discover what you *have* become and realize that more is yet to come.

3

The Leadership Crisis

A Message for College and University Faculty

INTRODUCTION

In the eight years since I wrote the following essay on "The Leadership Crisis," I have moved into a more meditative life with greater concern for the forces and influences that either nurture or depress the human spirit. And I have come to see the conditions that raise or lower the quality of life in colleges and universities as not materially different from those that operate in other institutions: governments, hospitals, churches, schools, businesses, philanthropies. Therefore, what I first addressed to colleges and universities and published in an academic journal, now seems to me to be much more widely relevant. And what is being said today in the flood of literature about how to lead in business seems equally applicable in the academic world.

ortant, as I noted in the earlier essay, "an indispensable
the persuasive power (of leaders) to be effective is that
on is living out a great dream. . . . Institutions function
the idea, the dream, is to the fore, and the person, the
leader is seen as servant of the idea. It is not 'I,' the ultimate leader,
that is moving this institution to greatness; it is the dream, the great
idea. 'I' am subordinate to the idea. 'I' am servant of the idea along
with everyone else who is involved in the effort. . . . It is the idea that
unites people in the common effort, not the charisma of the leader. .
. . Far too many of our contemporary institutions do not have an adequate dream, an imaginative concept that will raise people's sights
close to where they have the potential to be. . . . that has the energy
to lift people out of their moribund ways to a level of being and relating from which the future can be faced with more hope than most of
us can summon today." That was the way I saw the crisis of leadership eight years ago: the need to produce in more of our institutions
the overarching dream that will have this energy.

I am indebted to Peter Senge for the idea of a "shared vision," for
the importance of the individual, regardless of status, to claim the
dream as one's own. A condition for such a shared dream to prevail
may be wide participation in the evolution of the vision, especially if
it is an old institution that has lost a great dream it once had and
wants to get a new one.

What goes on in the participative process? Let me speculate:
those who are the best dreamers and most adept at articulating
dreams will periodically "test the waters." Those who have the gift of
leading will periodically say, "Let's get together and talk about this."
Those who have the gift of statesmanship will listen carefully to all of
this and search for the ideas and the language that will be the basis for
consensus.

What evolves from this process, in which the key leader may take
a hand, may not emerge as a written statement one can hang on the
wall. It may best exist as an oral tradition that is continually reexamined, modified, or given new emphasis. In a well-led institution,

there will always be a consensual tradition that most will summon in answer to the question, "What are we about?"

What I identified as a crisis of leadership in colleges and universities eight years ago, after considerable involvement with academic institutions, I now see as a symptom of the failure of faculties to accept that the price of freedom everywhere—in their case academic freedom—is responsibility, the obligation to be constantly alert to opportunities to make one's share in forming the dream one lives by a real and meaningful thing, an obligation that persists as long as one has the wits to participate.

Top leaders in all institutions have the opportunity to reduce the sense of crisis in our times by helping everyone involved to understand the responsibility that freedom entails, and to create an atmosphere in which consensual dreams can emerge that have the power to guide purpose and decision in way that makes for greatness.

A critical aspect of leadership, whether in a university in which a substantial piece of the power to govern has been ceded to faculties, or in business in which, structurally at least, all the ultimate power usually resides with the chief executive, or something in between, is this: *Can the key leader accept that optimal performance rests, among other things, on the existence of a powerful shared vision that evolves through wide participation to which the key leader contributes, but which the use of authority cannot shape? And can that key leader be persuasive enough that responsibility for generating and maintaining that vision is widely accepted as a serious obligation?*

The ambiguity in this process may be that the effective key leader may never talk explicitly about vision or its generation. The process may be much too subtle for that. The generation of a shared vision may be one of those wonderful things that just happens when genuine respect for persons, for all persons, is consistently manifested. Within the climate of that pervasive attitude, and in the normal course of decision making, the first response of both the key leader and all subordinate leaders may be the simple question, "What are we trying to do?"—*Robert K. Greenleaf, 1986*

The leadership crisis of our times is without precedent.

People have been poorly served by their leaders before; but in the past 100 years, we have moved from a society comprised largely of artisans and farmers with a few merchants and professionals, and with small government, to widespread involvement with a vast array of institutions—often large, complex, powerful, impersonal, not always competent, sometimes corrupt. Nothing like it before has happened in our history. This recent experience with institutions may have brought a new awareness of serious deficiencies in the quality of our common life that are clearly traceable to leadership failures. Some of these lacks have become so painful to bear that *leadership crisis* is an apt term to describe an important aspect of our present condition. Why are we in this dilemma, and what can we do about it? From the perspective of my experience, in these few pages I will suggest some tentative answers to these questions. And I will continue to search.

NEGLECT OF PREPARATION FOR LEADERSHIP

Colleges and universities assumed a unique place in American culture early in this century when, with the growing percentage of college-age young people enrolled, public service was added to the traditional roles of teaching, learning, and scholarship. Now that nearly 50 percent of college-age young people are on campus, the presence of a pervasive crisis of leadership raises the question about the impact of higher education. The traditional civilization-building role of the universities is as important as it ever was. But is it being sustained adequately in these times? The tradition seems not to have been adapted to carry all of the obligations that contemporary universities, with their massive influence, may be expected to assume—including explicit preparation for leadership. (Please note that I have not said "training" for leadership. "Preparation" is a much more subtle process.)

In the turbulent 1960s, the charge was made that universities were effectively administering an "anti-leadership" vaccine to their students. Now, with declining enrollment and new financial urgencies, I sense that, from within universities, the fragility that they demonstrated in themselves in the 1960s is seen as an attribute of society at large. Appreciated, but perhaps not clearly understood, is weakness of leadership as an underlying cause. And there is concern about this condition. There are evidences of hunger for leadership that is denied by a seeming unwillingness of faculties to respond to such leadership as they have. If these are correct surmises, why then is there not a vigorous stirring in the universities to bring their great civilizing tradition to bear on this problem? It may be that the crisis of leadership in society at large is also the universities' own crisis. It is a baffling enigma to those who make the effort to interest universities in preparation for leadership. Yet I believe there is a reasonable basis for it. Let me speculate on what I think it is.

THE NEW AWARENESS OF POWER

Since World War II, there has evolved a new sensitivity to the issue of power, particularly coercive power—its abuses and legitimate uses. Along with this new concern about power, perhaps because of it, has come a fresh critical judgment of our many institutions, all of which wield power, whether they are governmental or voluntary, for profit or not for profit.

I am a nonacademic who has made a few soundings within universities. My estimate of the perception of the typical faculty member, as she or he looks out from academe on the world of institutions, is as follows: Valuable and necessary as these institutions are—businesses, churches, schools, governments, hospitals, social agencies (they are all we have)—the whole gamut of them is seen as not serving well. Slavish adherence in these institutions to rigid hierarchical structures is viewed as an anachronism and a destroyer of values in the leaders that emerge. Some of these institutions are seen as mechanisms for manipulation and exploitation. Many who work for them are regarded as diminished and used up. And there is the suspicion that the root cause is low-grade top leadership: inept, not knowing, not caring, and, above all, the abuse and misuse of power. What makes it a crisis is that the fault is seen in an abstraction called the "system." Leader and follower are both victims of the use of power in the "system." There is no evident handle on the problem.

If, from within the university, one looks out on a scene as just described, including the university itself in that scene; if, accurate or not, that is the perception, would not a sensitive academic person be likely to hesitate to venture into leadership preparation for such a society? There is little in the background of a scholar that would give the average teacher a reasoned basis for reacting to that perception; nor is it likely that, in the prevailing structure of university leadership, there would be respected advice that would be persuasive in changing either that perception or the reaction to it.

If, as I believe, a concern about power, including the ramifications of power within the university itself, is the barrier that blocks universities from accepting an explicit obligation for preparing leaders, is it possible to reach an understanding of power that will help universities see their way around the barriers that now restrain them? Let me suggest an approach to that question.

THREE KINDS OF POWER

As a basis for sorting out what people do when they undertake to lead, let us consider three dimensions of power. These are not sharply delineated from one another by external markings. The distinctions exist more in the attitudes and values of wielders of power.

Coercive Power

Coercive power exists because certain people are granted (or assume) sanctions to impose their wills on others. These sanctions may be overt, as when one may be penalized or punished if one does not

comply; or the sanctions may be covert and subtle, if one's weaknesses and sentiments are exploited and thus pressure is applied. The
power to coerce has a long history of use. But now, with constantly
expanding government, the domination of the social structure by institutions—especially large ones—the expansion of techniques of
surveillance, the proliferation of weapons of destruction, the growth
in sophistication of methods of crime and oppression, and the bewil-
dering complexity of life in which it is more and more difficult for
people to gauge where their interests lie; with all of these we seem
more vulnerable to coercion than we once were.

Another complication is that some coercion is masked behind
ideal aims and is employed by people who are highly civilized and are
motivated for noble ends.

Universities are involved in the use of coercive power in their
role of "credentialing" (Thomas Jefferson, founder of the University
of Virginia, would not allow degrees to be granted as long as he was
Rector—on the ground that degrees are pretentious.) When universities were small and were concerned largely with esoteric scholarship, degrees were a relatively harmless honorific. But now that
universities are huge and degrees are so often, by law or custom, the
ticket of admission to a "good" job—the means for upgrading oneself
in society—the university holds, and uses, great coercive power. Even
when it is sensitively and benignly used, it is still coercive power; and
having that power has the same liabilities to corrupting influences as
would any other kind of coercive power.

One of the problems of the use of coercive power by the more
civilized people, even though for noble ends, is that, when conditions
are right, the use of that power may cause destructive violence to be
unleashed in the less civilized, sometimes on a disastrous scale. It may
be plausibly argued that, although the Vietnam war and the civil
rights crisis were seen as the proximate causes of the student disor-
ders in the late 1960s, one of the ultimate causes may have been the
universities' own long-standing use of coercive power.

Is there a moral principle here: when coercive power is used in any form and for any purpose, does not the user of that power bear some responsibility for what may be inevitable harmful effects, including the unleashing of violence? If coercive power is used (and I do not foresee a utopian society in which it will not be used), do not the users of that power have the obligation to be aware of the potential danger and prepare a meliorative strategy that minimizes the damage to the social fabric?

Coercive power is more pervasive than most are aware of, and its consequences are traceable to evils that we ordinarily do not connect with it.

Manipulative Power

I see manipulation as distinct from coercion because it rests more on plausible rationalizations than on the threat of sanctions or on pressure. People are manipulated, I believe, when they are guided by plausible rationalizations into beliefs or actions that they do not fully understand. By this definition, some manipulation by leaders is unavoidable because some who follow are not capable of understanding or will not make the effort to understand. But not all manipulation by leaders can be justified on these grounds. The heart of the problem, I believe, is that effective leaders, those who are better than most in charting the path ahead, who willingly take the risks and expend the energy that leadership requires—those people are apt to be *highly intuitive*. Thus leaders themselves, in their conscious rationalizations, may not fully understand why they chose a given path. Yet our culture requires that leaders produce plausible explanations for the directions they choose to take. These rationalizations are useful because they permit—after the fact—the test of conscious logic that "makes sense" to leader and follower. But the understanding required by the follower, if she or he is not to be manipulated, is not necessarily contained in this rationalization that makes sense. Because we live in a world that pretends a higher validity to conscious rational thinking in human affairs than is warranted by the facts of our existence, and because many sensitive people "know" this, *manipulation* hangs as a cloud over the relationship between leader and led almost everywhere, and is the subject of much pejorative comment.

Can this cloud be dispelled? Not easily. But something can be done about it if both leaders and followers are constantly aware of the presence of this murkiness, and if they accept that dispelling it requires a determined effort by both of them. Within this framework of awareness, what would the effort be, what would they try to do? The essence of leadership, I believe, is that the leader makes the effort first. The leader takes the first step in the belief that, if it provides a clear demonstration of the intent to build a more honest relationship, followers will respond.

I suggest that the leader try persuasion!

Persuasion as Power

Unfortunately there is ambiguity in the word *persuasion*. One of the dictionaries I consulted, in a series of definitions, gives three that do not imply coercion. A fourth implies coercion. And the fifth states flatly, "to bring a desired action or condition by force." I prefer to use the word *persuasion* for a process that does not allow either coercion or manipulation in any form. One is persuaded, I believe, upon arrival at a feeling of rightness about a belief or action *through one's own intuitive sense*. One takes an intuitive step, from the closest approximation to the certainty to be reached by conscious logic (sometimes not very close), to that state in which one may say with conviction, "This is where I stand." The act of persuasion, as I limit the definition, would help order the logic and favor the intuitive step. *And this takes time!* The one being persuaded must take that intuitive step alone, untrammeled by coercion or stratagems. Both leader and follower respect the autonomy and integrity of the other and each allows and encourages the other to find his or her own intuitive confirmation of the rightness of the belief or action. If this relationship prevails whenever it is possible, then, when a quick action is required, one supported by the skimpiest of rationalizations, it will be accepted with the assurance that at some future time there will be the opportunity for intuitive mutuality to be reestablished. A leader who practices persuasion whenever possible sets a model that, in time, will encourage followers to deal with the leader by persuasion. Power is generated in this relationship because it admits of mutual criticism, spirited arguments can occur, and it does not depend on artful stratagems.

This poses a problem for conventional organization structures in which those "at the top" hold coercive power and, because of their superior informational sources, are in a good position to manipulate. Such persons should take note that those who are seen as holding coercive power, even though they use it sparingly, are somewhat disqualified to persuade. "Where is the hidden agenda?" is often the unasked question. Since in our imperfect society it is difficult to conceive of a functioning organization in which there is not an ultimate locus of coercive power, two suggestions are made so that unqualified persuasive power can make its contribution.

The first is that every institution should harbor able persuaders who know their way around, who are dedicated servants of the institution, whose judgment and integrity are respected, who do not manipulate, who hold no coercive power, and who, without the formal assurances that faculty members usually have, feel free and secure. Those who hold the ultimate power will accept that these nonpowerful persuaders can accomplish things for the good of the institution that the powerful cannot command. Therefore, the powerful will permit radical criticism to be made. Every institution that wants the benefits that only persuasion can accomplish needs to support such persons on its staff, because the value of coercive power is inverse to its use.

My second suggestion is that an indispensable condition for persuasive power to be effective is that *the institution is living out a great dream*. I speak with some conviction on this because, near the end of my career, I was party to an unsuccessful effort to persuade the top command where I worked that a new goal was needed. The great dream on which the institution was built had lost its force and, as seems the plight of so many contemporary institutions, ours was in the mood of struggling to survive.

Those in command where I worked were honest, able, dedicated, and caring—like so many who head other institutions with which I am familiar. But they were not guided by a great dream, not a dream that was shared by those who followed them. The idea that inspires and unifies was muted. Leaders were seen, too much, as self-symbols; they did not come through as servants of the dream. Consequently, there was not enough trust in the institution by any of its constituencies.

Great institutions are a fusion of great ideas and great people. Neither will suffice without the other.

NEW DREAMS ARE NEEDED

Where would the leader of an institution get the idea that a dream is needed? How would he or she learn what it would serve? Where, in all of our vast communication, educational, and religious resources is the suggestion being made?

Regardless of the stress of circumstance, institutions function better when the idea, the dream, is to the fore, and the person, the leader, is seen as servant of the idea. It is not "I," the ultimate leader, that is moving this institution to greatness; it is the dream, the great idea. "I" am subordinate to the idea; "I" am servant of the idea along with everyone else who is involved in the effort. As the ancient Taoist proclaimed, "When the leader leads well, the people will say, 'We did it ourselves.'" The leader leads well when leadership is, and is seen as, serving the dream and searching for a better one. Dreams should be articulated by whomever is the ablest dreamer, and leaders should always be open to persuasion by dreamers. It is the idea that unites people in the common effort, not the charisma of the leader. It is the communicated faith of the leader in the dream that enlists dedicated support needed to move people toward accomplishment of the dream. Far too many of our contemporary institutions do not have an adequate dream, an imaginative concept that will raise people's sights close to what they have the potential to be.

If the dream has the quality of greatness, it not only provides the overarching vision for the undertaking; it also penetrates deeply into the psyches of all who are drawn to it and savor its beauty, its rightness, and its wisdom. The test of greatness in a dream is that it has the energy to lift people out of their moribund ways to a level of being and relating from which the future can be faced with more hope than most of us can summon today. Persuasion, as an art of leadership, is tenable because of the persuasive power in the dream itself.

A GREAT DREAM FOR A UNIVERSITY

Just from reading the newspapers, one would question whether universities have an adequate dream for these times, one in which the roles of teaching and learning, scholarship, and public service are inseparable. And the great dream that might be theirs seems remote indeed. In the context of the subject "the crisis of leadership," what evidence supports this assertion?

It is specious, I believe, to argue as some do, that general education nurtures leadership and prepares people for discriminating followership. Quite the reverse may be true. How else, in view of the massive level of higher education, would one explain either the leadership crisis in which we are now enmeshed or the gross misjudgments in selecting whose leadership to follow that has characterized recent years?

Then, if, as I have suggested, the university degree has become the ticket of admission to better jobs, these tickets are being issued to at least twice as many as there are jobs that warrant preparation.

Perhaps more serious, academic higher education is not suited to everybody. Informed guesses on how many will profit by such education run as low as 15 percent. If this, or anything close to it, is a fair judgment, with nearly 50 percent of the college age population enrolled, what is the effect on the leadership potential of the other 35 percent—those who should receive some other kind of education?

A determined effort to educate minority peoples has been made. One effect on the black community has been to give favored job treatment to those who make it through a university—to the disadvantage of the large numbers of less educated whose dependence on welfare has increased and who may have been deprived of their indigenous leadership.

These evidences of an inadequate dream in universities are cited not to censure them—they are doing as well in their obligations as are other institutions that serve us. But, as I see it, they hold the key to recovering us from the leadership crisis. Therefore, universities merit priority in concern about this problem.

I submit that universities are in urgent need of a great new dream. No small dream will suffice. How will they find that dream and unite to bring it to reality? Who will lead them to it?

A BASIS FOR HOPE

One would hope that university administrators would give that leadership; the signals are clear enough that they should. But faculties have held too much power too long, and administrators are too much caught up in the common mores of our institutional life. They need an infusion of leadership vision as much as others do. Then, pressed as most of them are by financial urgencies and by the intractable nature (as they see it) of faculties, it is not likely that the initiative to redirect universities to a new role of nurturing leadership will come from administrators, even though they might thereby establish their own leadership in a healthy way and make financing easier.

Neither private nor public funding sources for university programs appear eager to initiate new concerns for the preparation of leaders. Like the universities, they, too, seem caught up in the crisis of leadership. Ours may be said to be *the age of the anti-leader*.

Where, then, will the initiative come from? Is there no hope that a resource equal to the need will emerge? Yes, there is hope. Hope lies in the great strength of the academic tradition (which some see as its most troublesome aspect): academic freedom and tenure.

The transforming movement will arise, I believe, from the source it usually comes from in a crisis: from a *saving remnant*. At first, from a few faculty members who act alone, within the scope of autonomy they now have, finding their own way to be effective, using some of their own free time, and, in some cases, putting in a little money. A few such far-seeing faculty members may start the transforming movement without the support of their culture, possibly incurring some opposition from it. This is characteristic of saving remnants. They are not usually empowered, approved, or well financed.

The teachers who make up this saving remnant will come to one understanding in common: they will have a clear sense of how institutions change, prudently. They will accept that change takes place slowly as a result of diligent work to acquire competence to lead. Revolutionary ideas do not change institutions. *People* change them by taking the risks to serve and lead, and by the sustained painstaking care that institution building requires.

I know of a few teachers who have taken such initiative to prepare their students to lead and to deal with the realities of institutional life. I had the good fortune to have had one of those teachers in college over 50 years ago. Advice from him set the direction of my career to find my own way as a building and meliorating influence within institutional structures. The most open course I can see for meeting the leadership crisis in the next generation (too late for this one; we will have to muddle along as best we can) is to encourage a few faculty members to move on their own, without the support of their institutions, and to start now on the preparation of the next generation of leaders.

If one in one thousand among the half-million or so faculty members in our country will move on this now (not an unrealistic expectation if there were a way to alert them to the opportunity) *the 500, on their own and without anybody's help*, could produce a flowering of talent in the next generation that would make a golden age of leadership. I am absolutely certain of it. I am so certain that I have written a guide to encourage their venturing as lone unsupported individuals, and, perhaps, to point a way. It is called *Teacher as Servant, a Parable*. [Available through the Greenleaf Center.]

> *If* the one in one thousand will respond to this encouragement,
> *If* they will articulate persuasively what they are doing,
> *If*, having established that students will respond, they take further
> steps to educate university trustees and persuade them to accept
> a more affirmative institution-building role for themselves,
> *If* trustees will then install and guide administrators who are prepared to be, and disposed to be, effective leaders-by-persuasion, and
> *If* those administrators will gather the help of all constituencies of
> the university to establish means for explicit preparation for
> both leading and following, by persuasion,

then, someday, someplace, a design for a new contemporary university may emerge, *wholly as a result of persuasion*. In the course of this evolution, that university's goals, program, leadership, and governance may be reexamined, not so much in the light of tradition of what universities have been, but, rather, in recognition of the obligation that has been assumed because of access to several formative years of half the population.

The leadership crisis in society at large will begin to be meliorated when *one* university, in its new awareness of its obligations and opportunities, moves into, and then resolves, its own crisis of leadership, and emerges with a great new dream.

When, in the persuasive atmosphere of that dream, the trustees and administrators lead by persuasion, and faculties, students, and staff respond with persuasion, that university will regenerate, in the late 20th century, the civilizing influence that universities once had and move to the center of our institutional life as a bastion of strength in what may prove to be a gathering storm.

4

Have You a Dream
Deferred?

What happens to a dream deferred?
Does it dry up
like a raisin in the Sun?
Or—?

Langston Hughes

Do you have a dream deferred, now that you are nearing the end of your freshman year? And what about the charge of idealism and the high expectations you brought here last September; what shape are they in? How does your university adventure look to you at this point?

We are here today because you have applied to be appointed Ohio

Fellows. The objective of the Ohio Fellows program, as I understand it, is to help you realize your potential for service in the public interest. It is not concerned with what vocation you choose for your life work. But it assumes that, in your work or outside it, you want to make a social contribution through becoming a self-actualizing person.

Because you want to be admitted to this group, I assume that you are still searching, within the resources of the university, for something you have not yet found—perhaps to renew your faith in your dream. If my assumption is correct, what is the nature of your search? What is your personal strategy for the optimal use of the opportunity which the next three years offers?

As I recall it, no one raised these questions near the end of my freshman year in college. No one suggested that it was my responsibility to manage my own life at that point. I am not sure that much is made of it today. Yet, at age 18 or 19, are you not mature enough to manage your own growth? All that my generation can do is to help clarify the problem; and, out of our greater experience, point to alternatives that you may not yet have discovered. You cannot compress or extract experience by listening to us. Every person has to live every minute of his own existence and make his own meaning out of it. *But you can widen your awareness so as to make your experience more intense and more meaningful.* Thus I urge you to open up to influences and seek opportunities that will expand your awareness. These may come in unexpected ways.

In my own case, a remark by a professor in the course of a rambling lecture shaped my career. He was neither a great scholar nor an exciting teacher; but he was wise in the ways of men and institutions. What he said and what I did as a result of receiving this signal are not important here; but I have often wondered whether, on that fateful day, something exceptional was said or whether I just had my doors of perception open a wee bit so that a significant signal could come through.

After much reflection on my own education and a sustained interest in what colleges do, I have concluded that there is no one right way to provide education. One of the disadvantages of the level of academic effort required today may be that the signal that shapes your life is even harder to hear than mine was when educational endeavor was considerably more relaxed.

I once heard Robert Frost asked the meaning of one of his poems. "Read it and read it and read it," he said, "and it means what it says to you." What he was saying, I think, was that meaning, that subtle signal that may shape one's future, is an elusive thing; it does not emerge, necessarily, as the logical end-product of a conscious analytical process. In fact, it may defy such an approach. It is more likely to come as a gift, as an insight, peripheral to the analytical process rather than the target of it. It requires an attitude, and openness, belief in the vastness of knowledge just beyond our conscious rational searching. "If the doors of perception were cleansed," wrote William Blake, "everything will appear to man as it is, infinite." I think of this as the attitude of wonder.

Reading and reading and reading the poem would, in effect, be an act of submission to the poem, a willingness to let one's guard down and be taught, to let a significant signal come through. This is why I want to talk to you about the next three years; to encourage you to seek and respond to your own signal, received or generated out of your own experience. And it will not be quite like anyone else's signal because you are uniquely you and your signal will be what *you hear*.

Be aware! Be open to insight from your own experience and from what you see and hear around you. This is the best advice I can give you for the next three years: keep those dreams alive; persist in the attitude of wonder. What follows are a few ideas that bear on these concerns.

A LIFE STYLE OF GREATNESS

I hope you will manage your lives these next three years so that you leave the university with a well-set lifestyle of greatness, with attitudes and values and ways of initiating and responding that will assure service in the public interest with distinction. Distinction is not synonymous with fame. Whether your life is long or short or your opportunities large or small, *distinction* or *greatness* is a combination of the moral and the excellent. It is doing the very best you can with the talents you have and the opportunities you can find.

Your vocation can be any legitimate calling your talents justify, be you poet, scientist, or businessman. A lifestyle of greatness will augur for a total impact that will leave some segment of society a little better than if you had not tried. It is important that some of you make this choice now because plenty of people, by design or by accident, will leave it worse. It takes a lot of hard work by responsible individuals for a society just to stay even. (I use the word *responsible* advisedly. I am not using it in the sense that so many of my generation use it when what they mean is that they want you to behave so that their comfort, their sense of propriety, are not disturbed. Responsible people build; they do not destroy. They are moved by the heart. The prime test of rightness of an act is: How will it affect people, are lives moved toward nobility?)

It is so easy to assume that simply by meeting the requirements of the university the preparation one needs for life will follow as a matter of course. You will do well to conform to the requirements for a degree and make the most of the courses you elect to take. But do not assume that automatically out of this will emerge a well set lifestyle that favors a distinguished public service role. If you want that, you have the opportunity to take charge of your own growth now, with your own strategies. You cannot leave this to the university or to anyone else.

How do you do this? You can wait until you graduate and use this opportunity to prepare and prepare and prepare; or you can begin living now, accept this university as "real," and find your own best way to influence this community so that it becomes a better institution to serve those who come after you. Make as your goal that three years from now you will leave here with a well-set, clearly demonstrated lifestyle of greatness, a way of dealing with your environment that is both moral and excellent. And let it not be a tentative abstract idea. Rather, let it be a concrete achievement, tested and refined in the arena of real experience, a firmly set and durable lifestyle.

A word of caution, however. Do not set out to remake your personality. Few people I know are wholly satisfied with the way they are, and much that is *you*, you will best learn to live with. Read E. B. White's perceptive essay, "The Second Tree from the Corner,"[1] particularly the closing paragraphs. It is about a troubled man who decided not to make himself over. Much that is you is pretty firmly established at this point; and you cannot choose another set of parents or relive the past 18 years. Accept what you are; make note that no one is perfect and resolve that you will build on what you now are, within a consciously chosen self-image of a responsible person. Make the very best you can out of it these next three years. You will never have a better chance.

A few years ago Edwin H. Land spent some days visiting with undergraduates at Massachusetts Institute of Technology. Then he talked to them on "Generation of Greatness, the Idea of a University in an Age of Science." In this talk, he said, "Everywhere I could sense a deep feeling in the undergraduates I met—that if a way could be found of nurturing the timid dream of his own potential greatness which he brought from his family and school, if somehow he could tie on to the greatness in the faculty and the administration, then his dream might be coming out differently."

"What do I mean by greatness?" he asked. "I mean—an opportunity for greatness for the many—as distinguished from genius.— Within his own field he will make things grow and flourish; he will grow happy helping other people in his field, and to that field he will add things that would not have been added, had he not come along."

CULTIVATE YOUR CREATIVENESS

When I came of age 40 years ago, it seemed not so important to be creative because ours was a pretty settled world (or so we saw it), and

I could begin to be constructive by learning to do well those things that were in the established patterns of society. For you it is different; you must start out creative or you will never really be in the ball game. Otherwise, you may be useful and prestigious, and you may even make a lot of money. But, you are not likely to be a constructive influence, an important contributor to the public interest, if you are not creative, because the important initiatives and responses will require new inventions—*prudent, feasible inventions that unlock the social impasses and raise people's sights and aspirations above the ordinary.* If you are to do this, at any stage of your life, your creative power must flower while you are young, and it must be sustained as long as you expect to function productively.

Your major contribution may come at any age. Theodore N. Vail, who built the business in which I spent 38 good years, made his impressive contribution to institution building between the ages of 62 and 75. Pope John XXIII achieved his prime influence between 80 and 84. In both, creativity flowered early and was nurtured carefully throughout their long lives. One never knows when his big creative opportunity will come. And it makes a more interesting life to keep one's creativity alive even though a "big" opportunity never comes.

Some large social contributions have been made by persons with small but well-nurtured creative endowments. If one is to make his way as a mathematician, scientist, artist, or composer, his creative powers had best mature early and be exceptional. However, in the area of social contribution, a more modest creative resource, coupled with values, skills, knowledge, attitudes, and experience, may be the greater asset.

I counsel you then to be aware of your priceless gift of creativity. No matter how small and flickering a light it may seem to be at the time, cultivate it as a pearl beyond price. Whatever your competence in your chosen field turns out to be, and regardless of the size of the opportunities that may come your way in the foreseeable world, your imaginative capacity will measure the productive use of your strengths and opportunities.

The skill of *foresight* is crucial. The "lead" that a leader has is his ability to foresee an event that must be dealt with before others see it so that he can act on it his way, the right way, while the initiative is his. If he waits until everybody sees it, he has waited too long; he cannot be a leader—at best, he is a mediator. Therefore, cultivate the greatest of the creative skills, foresight. Practice on every significant event you observe; ask yourself, where did it come from, where is it going? Note your projections and check them in the future. Practice living partly in the future—all of the time.

Creativity, however, is only part of the picture. Adolph Hitler was creative, diabolically so. One must have a dependable value system and a reasonably sane outlook to make a constructive social contribution. Then some creative people miss because they are ignorant or unskillful. Others are hampered by a restrictive set of attitudes, like perfectionism or an over-inflated ego. Still others are unaware and miss the necessary cues. And then there is the overarching matter of balancing one's trust between intuition and reason. If you have a dream deferred, bring it to life by beginning to live it—no matter how discouraging the circumstances may be. Learn to relax, so that the elements of your life fall, of themselves, into context and proportion. You may have more going for you than you are aware of. If you end up in middle age an uncreative, crusty reactionary—the kind of person your generation complains about so vociferously, it will probably be because you *chose* not to allow the idealism that is so characteristic of your present age to operate and elected, instead, a less courageous path, not "the path less traveled by" which, Robert Frost said, "makes all the difference."

BUILD A NEW MORALITY

Yours may be the first generation since the time of Moses to face, as an explicit task, the problem of building your own morality. Most of the time, from the Mosaic law down to now, there has always been a law, a code. To be sure, it was honored in the breach by many people, but it was always there. Those who violated it, for the most part acknowledged the law and thought of themselves as deviants. Now, since you have been alive, the law has all but disappeared. Many will assert that there still is a moral law, a code of ethics, and that they know what it is. I think of myself somewhat in this category. But the *level of consensus necessary for traditional morals to be accepted as law no longer holds.* Therefore, your generation may well be the first to face the condition of producing your own. Many will advise you, such as Professor Joseph Fletcher and his principle of "what love requires in the situation."[2] But you cannot be rescued from the confusion you may find in a lawless world as handily as Moses did it for his followers, by bringing it down from that mysterious encounter on the mountain chiseled in stone and bearing God's imprimatur. For better or for worse, you will have to achieve it on your own, with your own resources, and without much help from my generation, which has not faced the problem. I am not saying that the present state of affairs is good or bad; that is simply the way it is.

If this is a valid assumption, then building your own morality map may well be one of your major concerns these next three years. And a good deal of what you seek may come to you intuitively if you will be open to understand what goes on around you that most people condemn.

While I have stressed that the level of consensus on what constitutes morality has dropped, within your lifetime, to a point where it is difficult to affirm, "this is the moral law," the shift is only one of degree. Every person has always been, and must always be, his own theologian, his own moralist, his own value finder. It is just more confusing for your generation to try to find your way amid the babble of conflicting opinion from mine. Every strong moral person has always had to choose the ground upon which he or she would stand.

One of the qualities of a lifestyle of greatness is the ability to know with some certainty the solid ground one stands on at any one time. It gives one a toughness of mind with which one looks out upon a seething, troubled world with a quiet eye and asks the meaning of it all—not so much to judge it as to enlarge the perspective from which to build even more solid ground for one's own two feet to stand on. In the end, each man builds his own solid ground to stand on—and stands alone. In Robert Frost's one poem clearly addressed to the "inner circle," the one called "Directive," he says: "And if you're lost enough to find yourself/By now, pull in your ladder road behind you/And put a sign up *closed* to all but me./Then make yourself at home."

I must confess ambivalent feelings about the college-age group today: its outlook and its behavior. I am enough the creature of my generation to be shaken at times and wishing to be insulated from yours. But then, I really envy you who may face the greatest creative opportunity, as individuals and as a society, which any young people may ever have faced: as a matter of conscious choice, the chance to resolve the prevailing confusion with a new level of ethical insight.

As you think of your opportunity to build a new ethic, do not set out to reinvent the wheel. There are thousands of years of moral history to build upon, even though the behavior of us older people may look pretty wobbly to you. None of us, no existing institution, owns the tradition. Our moral tradition is there for you to use as a fresh resource. I wish for you the strength and the insight to use it well and to pass it on to your children as a nobler ethic *because of your efforts*.

GROW IN WISDOM

I see the next three years as open space for you to rise to this opportunity to build a new ethic. Use your participation in the university program to this end, but beware of accepting that it will chart the course for you to follow to this end. It will provide a clear path to intellectual growth, but the path to wisdom, indispensable for ethical choices, is not so clear. Walt Whitman had something to say about wisdom in his "Song of the Open Road." "Here is the test of wisdom,/Wisdom is not finally tested in schools,/Wisdom cannot be passed from one having it to another not having it,/—is not susceptible of proof, is its own proof,—" Clearly it is a different sort of thing from intellectual growth, which is the major concern of a university.

You can easily be deceived that you are wise because you are academically proficient, articulate, can reason well, and understand another's wisdom. Wisdom is not the antithesis of intellect. But intellectual growth can interfere with wisdom if not kept in perspective. Since in three years you are likely to emerge well started on your education, do not assume that you will therefore be wise. If you want to see a spectacular dramatization of this, read the novel *Herzog*.[3]

In the laudable pursuit of intellectual development, it is well to remember that the great hazards of personal choice, such as alcoholism, drug addiction, broken marriage, reactionism, the "educated" are just as vulnerable as the "uneducated." Only wise people have some protection against these hazards. And even with wisdom, it takes a bit of luck.

Wisdom, common sense (a better term would be *uncommon sense*), *judgment* are all terms that refer to something that is of the essence; it is not codifiable or teachable, except perhaps by a mentor who goes with his understudy into the real-life situation, asks him what he sees and hears (thereby training his awareness), asks for his tentative judgment, lets him commit an error and discusses the consequences (some of our best wisdom comes from error and suffering the consequences of error), and thereby helps him in acquiring a disciplined, thoughtful approach to real-life problems. Thomas Jefferson had such a mentor in George Wythe, the Williamsburg lawyer under whom Jefferson apprenticed. Without the influence of a George Wythe, there might not have been a Jefferson to write The Declaration of Independence or to draft the statutes in Virginia that shaped the Constitution. He might have settled for the role of the eccentric Virginia scholar.

Find such a mentor if you can. There may be one for you here on this campus. At the very least, be aware that intellectual prowess is not wisdom, and approach real life situations humbly. Only through testing your judgment, risk of decision in real-life situations—with an openness to learn what only experience teaches—will you grow in wisdom. Read Abraham J. Heschel's wonderful essay, " To Grow in Wisdom."[4]

One of the ways you may grow in wisdom, here on this campus, is to learn to challenge—by challenging, experimentally. In so doing, you may be wrong part of the time. Thus you must learn to accept challenge: from faculty administration, the community, fellow students. In doing this you will become, in part, a politician. Because politics is the art of the possible, you must learn to compromise.

The university is a total learning situation—for everybody: students, faculty, administrators, trustees—even for old consultants like me. And if you are to be well served by it, it needs to be a society in which the art of the possible is practiced by enough people so that those who aspire to grow in their ability to serve society will, in fact, learn.

In theory, at least, the university exists solely to nurture your growth and development. Later your involvement will be largely with institutions that exist to *use* you. But the university is a *real* place. It will use you too; and the people and their dilemmas are real. And you will never have a better chance to grow in wisdom than by entering into the life of the university with openness and humility, the necessary conditions for your experience here to favor the growth of wisdom.

Words cannot describe what it will mean to the ultimate fullness of your life if you can learn a measure of wisdom while you're here these next three years.

TRUST—AN ASPECT OF GREATNESS

One of the resources offered here at the university is the chance to study the problem of trusteeship, both the specific role with a capital "T," and the more general one of how people acquit themselves of the obligations assumed in the various constituencies—student, faculty governing bodies—which make up the university. I once asked the president of a great university this question: "Who in the university is responsible to the student for the obligation which the university assumes when it accepts him as a student?" His answer was, "Not I." That was 20 years ago, and I have never really recovered from it.

When the institution of American democracy ultimately declines, as it may one day, a major cause will be a failure of trusteeship—both the capital "T" and the small "t" varieties. And it will not decline so much because of the ineptness of the less favored as by the failure of those endowed with intelligence, values, training, judgment and experience which bring men to positions of trust—their failure to accept with sufficient commitment the obligations of trusteeship which they assume, and to perform with distinction in the public interest. Far too many good, competent, honest people settle for mediocre performance in these trustee positions. They meet the prevailing standards of adequate performance. But since it does not rise to the level of distinction, it must be judged mediocre. Only distinguished performance in positions of trust can support a long life for the institution of American democracy. In any endeavor, one must strive for distinction just to come out reasonably good.

Ours is an institution-bound society. While there remain large opportunities for individuals to act on their own, most influences that make a difference have the effect of changing what goes on in institutions. And institutions are necessarily instruments of trust. For many of you, your individual contributions will largely be measured by how you perform in institutional roles of trust, whether it be the management of a home or the presiding office in world government.

So much will be determined by the quality of the interpersonal relations among your colleagues. Do they work, figuratively, with knives out and backs to the wall (an expression I hear all too often in off-the-record descriptions of the inner workings of institutions—the whole range from businesses to churches), or is there an esprit that buoys the institution and makes possible a performance at the level of distinction?

As I have found it, the institutional elements that have most to do with *esprit* are *goals*—what are you trying to do in material or behavioral terms. And *strategy*, how do you intend to get there? What are you trying to do? is the easiest of questions to ask and the hardest to answer. There is nothing that builds organizational strength quite like a high order of consensus about goals and strategy. Unfortunately, there is a tendency, in institutions where the aims are more idealistic, like universities and churches, for this consensus on goals and strategy not to be firm.

I give you these views of institutions in general and educational institutions in particular because of my belief that one of the best preparations you can make for a high level of trusteeship, in roles you may assume later, is to be concerned about the institution you will be a part of these next three years. You will never have a better opportunity to learn the ways of institutions, what makes for mediocrity and what makes for greatness, than you have right here at your university.

The university provides a good laboratory for the study of responsibility. Remember the response that President Kennedy made when a reporter asked him why he had not taken an action which, during the campaign, he had criticized President Eisenhower for not taking? President Kennedy's reply was, "When you are responsible, things look different." When you observe an action here in the university, practice being responsible by putting yourselves in the shoes of those who are responsible.

As you study the university look for models of men and women who account for trust at the level of personal greatness. Think of yourselves as being like them, someday.

REALISM—TRY TO SEE IT STRAIGHT AND PLAY IT STRAIGHT

One of the gifts of those whose mature lives measure up to their estimated potential as young people is that their early assumptions about the nature of the society they will live and work in are realistic. One can make too optimistic assumptions and suffer endless frustration or too pessimistic ones and curb one's aspirations. Yet one must err on the side of optimism and accept the frustration.

"The real trouble with this world of ours is not that it is an unreasonable world, nor even that it is a reasonable one. The commonest kind of trouble is that it is nearly reasonable, but not quite. Life is not an illogicality; yet it is a trap for logicians. It looks just a little more mathematical and regular than it is; its exactitude is obvious, but its inexactitude is hidden; its wildness lies in wait."[5] This was written by G. K. Chesterton in 1924, when the world looked much more settled and predictable than it does today.

My concern for the many crises in the world today suggests a view of the human dilemma: problems, but no solutions; nevertheless challenges that must be worked on creatively—a more realistic view. Who would want to live in a world in which the "problems" were one-by-one laid eternally to rest to mark steady progress back to the Garden of Eden? I don't want to live there; do you? I would rather accept that every seeming solution brings a new problem, like progress in lengthening life expectancy breeds overpopulation. It is not the accomplishment, but the search, the struggle, that should excite our interest. And we should, without becoming depressed, be able to face Wordsworth's judgment: "And much it grieved my heart to think/What man has made of man."

What we call civilization has made a little progress toward Emerson's goal of amelioration. But when Emerson asked himself what was the greatest meliorative force operating in the world (he was an optimist and believed there was one), he did not name the usual virtuous activities such as religion, science, education, art. "Selfish huckstering trade!" was his answer. It is something to think about. Why do you suppose a perceptive idealist like Emerson would make a judgment like that?

ANXIETY—LEARN TO LIVE WITH IT

One of the anomalies of the age we live in is that we are acutely conscious of the destructive effects of anxiety (as it is generally defined, not as a medical term); and we work to alleviate it. Yet my worm's-eye view of things tells me that anxiety is deeply rooted in every facet of the design of our society and that it is exploited at every turn by the best people with the best of intentions.

Anxiety is a part of the human condition. If I were handed a magic wand and given the power to banish anxiety, I would not choose to do it because this is one of the things that gives life its challenge. I see no point in rejecting our society because of its disposition to produce anxiety (or for any other reason). This is the way it is. Just make note of it the way it is and devise your strategy for dealing with it. And it can be dealt with by most people with their own resources; one can learn to live productively with anxiety.

Such a strategy, as I have tried to live it, sees two somewhat separate *me's*: the outward me with a deep involvement in the world of affairs, and the inward me—the essential person as viewed from the inside, who is at one with all creation. In that quiet communion when my ladder road is pulled up (and I really pull it up sometimes) and my sign is posted *closed* to all but me, I am truly at home with a level of serenity that transcends the outer world of stress and conflict and tension which beset all institutions at their best, as well as most human relationships, at least part of the time.

I do not believe there ever has been in this world, certainly there is not now, a promise of outward peace. There is more external stress and confusion and pain in some places than others; but the only true serenity is inward. Serenity is the window through which one looks out on the world of affairs. It is how one feels inside as he engages, with spirit, in the turmoil and strife of the world of affairs.

I prefer to view the inward world as real, and the external world as contrived and transient. When Emerson said that "a foolish consistency is the hobgoblin of little minds," he was probably saying that our mastery of the external world is not such that we can ever really make it fit together. We work with intelligence, courage, and honesty to make the world as tolerable as we can; but we also maintain a detachment from it that puts external achievement, however laudable, in a lower priority than attention to growth in our capacity for wonder.

What has wonder to do with anxiety? "Wonder is the seed of knowledge." Wonder is an attitude, it is the filter through which one perceives the world, a filter that tends to substitute moral concern for criticism. It prompts one to ask, "What is going on here?" before one acts; and, though the provocation may be extreme, it leads to a response of thoughtfulness—even amusement, rather than of fear, anger, or dismay. It lifts one above the tumult and gives one perspective. And to wonder is humbling, it opens one to learn:

"I am waiting," writes Lawrence Ferlinghetti, "I am waiting/for a rebirth of wonder."

A LARGE BUT NOT IMPOSSIBLE TASK

I have urged you to attend to the use of these next three years. You have much to do. It is a large but not impossible task.

It will never be easy to live your life optimally. There will be obstacles, always. And they will be just as real here on this campus these next three years as they will be later on. What will some of these obstacles be?

First, the pressure of time—you will have too much to do. If you are who I have assumed you are, you will always have too much to do. And the kind of concerns I have laid before you will not make it any easier. You will have to choose—life's most difficult task.

Then there will be distractions, plenty of distractions. You will want a normal social life; nobody wants to be a grind. But time wasting and unproductive distractions are as abundant here on this campus as anywhere.

Finally, the environment here these next three years will not be encouraging. The university has many purposes and it cannot attend to anything as individual and personal as your own growth strategy. You will have to make it on your own.

At this point you may be asking, "This is a pretty big load you have piled on me, a college freshman. How do I do all of this?"

I do not have a how-to-do-it formula to give you. I have tried to illuminate the problem from the perspective of my own reflection and experience in the hope that it would help you to design your own strategy for the optimal use of these next three years, a strategy that is congruent with your own unique potentiality. Beyond this, my best suggestion to you is to clarify, for yourself, what you believe about yourself; because, if you seek to go very far in realizing your potential for service, you will be venturing into the dangerous and the unknown and the ever-present anxiety may defeat you if you do not have some kind of faith. Leo Tolstoy, writing his answer to the question, What is faith?—after emerging into relative peace from a rampant early life, posited it for me in one simple sentence. "I believe," he said, "that the sole meaning of my life lies in living by that light which is within me."

If you can learn, in the stress of circumstance, to pull in your ladder road behind you and put a sign up *closed* to all but me; and, then, if you can believe that the light within you will guide your path, you are on your way!

THIS UNIVERSITY—YOUR LABORATORY

You are attending a good university. Someday it may become a great one. But the paths to institutional greatness are many. Any person in the close constituencies of the university, any one person with his own efforts can help move it toward greatness—if he is persuasive and can lead. And the initiative can come from wherever the strong, able people are—among faculty, administration, trustees, *or* students. Greatness is best assured when the initiative comes from all four.

The great university of the future may earn this status by different standards than at present. Whereas, up to now, the great university has been the center of esoteric scholarship and the seat of prestigious graduate schools, a generation from now these resources may be more widely spread. Then, the distinguished university, the one that stands out above the others, may be the one which, in addition to scholarly competence, influences explicitly, directly, and substantially the shape of contemporary society through the preparation of its students for exceptional performance in building and serving and leading the whole range of institutions upon which our complex society depends.

Your university might, in these terms, become one of the great universities of the future. If it becomes so, it will be the result of conscious calculated influence from among its present constituencies. It will not just happen.

Why don't you freshmen take it on? Take on, for these next three years, the task of being a responsible, effective influence within this university. The test of whether you are responsibly effective is that you leave the institution, three years from now, in better shape to educate, with distinction, the student generations following you—educate them in a manner congruent with the standards of a distinguished institution as it will be judged then, standards which neither you nor I comprehend now.

I leave it with you, as an opportunity for the next three years. You will have the time of your lives if you take it on. And you will emerge from the experience with well-set individual lifestyles of greatness that will carry you for the rest of your days; and you may realize your dream.

Notes

1. "The Second Tree From the Corner," by E. B. White, Harper & Row, 1954.

2. *Situation Ethics,* by Joseph Fletcher, Westminster Press, 1966.

3. *Herzog,* by Saul Bellow, Crest Books, 1964.

4. *The Insecurity of Freedom,* by Abraham J. Heschel, Jewish Publication Society, 1966.

5. *Orthodoxy,* by G. K. Chesterton, Image Books, 1924.

5

The Servant as
Religious Leader

Much of the literature on leadership deals with those who head great institutions or who leave a mark on history. Such persons can carry their large roles only because many lead effectively in smaller ways that support them. This essay is as much concerned with those who lead small molecular forces—whether as part of a large movement or as lone individuals—as with those whose names go down in history.

This is written, not as the ultimate treatise on religious leading (I doubt that that will ever be written), but rather to stimulate and contribute to dialogue about the critical issue of religious leading in our times. My perspective is that of a student of organization, not of a scholar or theologian. What I have to share about religious leading is

largely what I have gleaned from experience, both my own and
others', from reading literature and history, and from thinking.
Not much of it has come from formal study of either leadership or
religion.

I am a creature of the Judeo-Christian tradition in which I grew
up, as modified by the Quaker portion of that tradition that I acquired after maturity. I cannot judge how I would have addressed the
subject of religious leading if I had been raised in another culture, or
if my life experience had been other than what it was; but I am quite
sure that I would have a different view of it. What is written here is
offered in the hope that no persons will exclude themselves from
consideration of the issues raised because of their religious beliefs or
their biases about leadership.

I am deeply grateful to John C. Fletcher and Robert W. Lynn
without whose help and encouragement this piece would not have
been written.

Part of my excitement in living comes from the belief that leadership
is so dependent on spirit that the essence of it will never be capsuled
or codified. I was less than a year out of college when I was tapped for
what proved to be the most formative experience of my adult life. I
had just joined American Telephone and Telegraph Company, and
that company's first venture into formal management training in the
1920s was a two-week program called a "Foremen's Conference."
This was in the construction and maintenance department of the
company, at that time all men. I attended a short intensive program
to prepare me to lead foremen's conferences. Then, for the next year,
every other Monday morning I received a group of twelve foremen.
With no reading and no published agenda (I had one), for two weeks
we sat around a big table and just talked about the multifaceted job of
being a foreman, the lowest level of management. The pedagogical
theory was that these men would learn from each other—not from
me. But I was the chief learner. There was not then, and there seems

not to be now, much hard knowledge about what proved to be the major focus of my work: how things get done in organized efforts. This is a fact of life with which I have learned to be comfortable.

My conferees ranged in age from 30 to nearly 70. I was 23. These fellows were where the buck stopped. The elaborate management hierarchy above them could think their great thoughts about what they wanted done; but what *was* done was what those foremen who sat around my conference table were willing and able to do. I learned much from these wise and seasoned men.

This was my graduate education; it set the course of my life. During the 55 years since this intense formative experience, I have been deeply involved with people who were trying to lead or manage something. In the last few years before retirement from AT&T, I held the position of Director of Management Research, a post that brought me in close contact with top management and gave me wide latitude, with the help of a professional staff, to examine how this giant company did its work, including the values that guided it. There was ample opportunity to communicate our findings when we learned something that might be useful. The tradition of the company disposed it to listen carefully to research findings in all relevant fields.

In the nearly 20 years since "retirement," my work has expanded to include a range of businesses, large and small, foundations, universities, and churches and church-related institutions including seminaries—in the United States, in Europe, and in the Third World. Some of my best years have been in retirement.

I cannot give a precise logical explanation for how I have come, near the end of my active career, to center my attention on *religious leading*, but I believe the reader may discover enough of it from what I have chosen to discuss here. I have said that leading is so dependent on *spirit* that the essence of it will never be capsuled or codified. Part of that essence lies beyond the barrier that separates mystery from what we call reality.

Spirit, as the animating force in living beings, is value-free. Hitler had it; he was a great, if demonic, leader. Putting value into it, in my judgment, makes it religious. And what is value? Again, I will leave it to the reader to judge what I value. In my intense formative experience with these rough-hewn, sometimes crude, foremen, I realized that what enabled them on occasion to lead (not just to use their authority, but *lead)* under difficult and sometimes dangerous conditions was that they were able to communicate to other rough-hewn men what they, the foremen, valued. Some of what I learned about leadership in that experience was how to create the conditions in which they would talk freely to each other about what they valued.

The premise here is that *to lead is to go out ahead and show the way when the way may be unclear, difficult, or dangerous*—it is not just walking at the head of the parade—and that one who leads effectively is likely to be stronger, more self-assured, and more resourceful than most because leading so often involves venturing and risking. Occasionally something important happens when there is no discernible leader who prompted it, but usually there are persons who take the initiative to say, "Let's go here, or do this," or some may lead with a subtle inconspicuous gesture. Either way, what makes them leaders is that a significant force of people responds.

Few, if any, who have these qualities of strength, assurance, and resourcefulness are equally effective as leaders in all situations. Therefore, even the ablest leaders will do well to be aware that there are times and places in which they should follow. And one who seems deficient in one or more of these qualities may, on some occasion, rise to save the day. But, in general, those who lead well in affairs both large and small, and who sustain their leadership in good times and bad, are exceptional people, an elite. They may not be "high status" people by the usual criteria. The best trustee I have seen in action (and I have seen quite a few) was not a high status person, but he was truly exceptional as a trustee, and remarkable in the chair.

It is further premised that what distinguishes a leader as *religious* (in its root meaning of *religio*—to bind or rebind) is the quality of the consequences of her or his leadership. Does it have a healing or civilizing influence? Does it nurture the servant motive in people, favor their growth as persons, and help them distinguish those who serve from those who destroy?

Countless persons who lead by these criteria, in large ways and small, are judged religious. At times in the past the combined influence of all such persons was not sufficient to check destructive tendencies that are always at work. It was not sufficient in Germany in the 1930s. A religious leader simply makes his or her best effort to build and sustain a good society. The result will be whatever it is. It is not within the power of any of us mortals to determine the outcome (fortunately). A "good" society is seen as one in which there is widespread *faith as trust* (to be discussed later) that encourages and sustains ordinary, good people as constructive influences in the world as it is—violent, striving, unjust as well as beautiful, caring, and supportive.

Among many facets of a "good" society that might be achieved with finite resources are: the opportunity for as many as possible to engage in useful and remunerative work—with the feeling of belonging and being a part of a constructive effort where they are; children get good preparation for a life of service; strong young people are encouraged and prepared for religious leadership; health is encouraged and the environment is protected; the needy, the aged, and the disabled are cared for. There are enough able people to give this care and prepare the young for service and leadership, and their lives would be more rewarding for doing it—*if* these able people could be brought together as an effective force. This is the essence of religious leading as that term is used here: to bring people together and sustain them as an effective force for the building of faith as trust under conditions in which powerful forces may be operating to destroy that faith.

Religious leading is a vast subject. I have ventured here to deal only with that portion that nurtures and supports the religious motive in those who, as they do the work of the world, will labor to build a good society in terms like those given above.

The central idea of this essay is: *work to increase the number of religious leaders who are capable of holding their own against the forces of destruction, chaos, and indifference that are always with us!* Those who are in the vanguard of this effort will find ways to *strengthen the hands of the strong* by helping them, while they are young, to acquire a vision of themselves as effective servants of society, plus an awareness of both the opportunities and the pitfalls for those who would be such servants, and a clear perception of what it takes to lead—in religious terms . This is written as a sharing with those who aspire to be in the vanguard of that work.

ORIGINS

Much of the thinking that culminates in this essay emerged during the stressful years of student unrest in the 1960s when I was deeply immersed in the traumatic experiences of several universities in which the fragility of those prestigious institutions was exposed. Against the background of my knowledge of universities of that period, all of the student attitudes, destructive as they sometimes were, did not seem irrational. I wondered whether, in view of the flaws revealed in universities, ours is a sufficiently caring, serving society to endure. My conclusion was that if it is to endure, something has to change! And the most significant change of all might take place in churches because, unless churches become more effective, it is unlikely that people and institutions will do much better than at present. And that is not good enough. As I see it now, churches are not likely to become more effective unless seminaries develop a capacity to lead them that they do not seem to have. The big change of the future, if it comes, may be initiated by seminaries.

Reflections on these issues led me, in 1970, to begin to write on the *servant* theme. Three essays that suggested some things that might change issued from that effort: "The Servant as Leader," "The Institution as Servant," and "Trustees as Servants." These essays, and some related writings, were later gathered in a book, *Servant*

Leadership (Paulist Press), followed by *Teacher as Servant, a Parable* (The Greenleaf Center). In 1980 another essay, "Servant, Retrospect and Prospect," summarized my experience in working with these ideas over a ten-year period. In 1981 *Seminary as Servant, Essays on Trusteeship* was published. This reflected where my thinking had come regarding the strategic role available to seminaries. I understand the misgivings that many informed people (including some in seminaries) have about seminaries. But I am convinced that seminaries occupy a spot from which a profound influence for the good of society could be wielded—and it is not forthcoming. Too many who are in a position to help seminaries have written them off. I contend that the service needed from seminaries must be forthcoming from existing seminaries because we do not have the time or the resources to replace them with adequately serving institutions. It is imperative that a way be found to raise existing seminaries to the full stature that their position requires. This is a prime challenge for religious leaders of our time. I will return to this issue later.

These writings had some circulation among religious institutions, and I have had several close relationships with pastors, church administrators, lay leaders, governing boards, and congregations. In these experiences, I found considerable concern for the present state of leading in churches and for a consequent diminished influence of churches on their members and on society at large. Paralleling these reported findings from within churches, I made my own observations during this period from involvements with businesses, foundations, and universities. All of these soundings, plus what is available in the news, suggest a deteriorating society with little evidence of effective restorative forces at work.

One could simply view this with alarm and join the chorus of lament that one hears from some who have made similar observations. I prefer to turn my energies to the support of efforts that might set restorative forces in motion. All that any individual can do is to make one's best effort, alone or in concert with others—now!

I begin with the assumption that the enormous resources of

religious institutions in the United States could, within a generation, help turn this faltering society around and start us on a long-term constructive course *if* a substantial number of them, each from its own unique set of beliefs, could work toward a common goal of a "good" society.

Is it not possible that many religious institutions, as they now stand, have within them the human resources from which effective leaders might evolve who would move institutions in which they have some influence to become more constructive elements of a good society? Could a new, persuasively articulated, prophetic vision generate the faith required for those who have the potential to lead to take the risks, develop the strength, and make a new determined effort to lead? If seminaries design programs that will attract the strongest and ablest young people, could they not become the chief source of wisdom about religious leaders, not only for churches but for all segments of society? This essay is written with the hope of contributing to a dialogue out of which a solid conceptual base for such an effort may emerge.

The phrase, "Generate the faith required" seems to me to be the key. A suggested view of the nature and role of *faith* in religious leaders will be discussed later.

"But is this not the age of the anti-leader!" some protest. "People simply do not respond to leadership in these times."

So it seems to be, in the conventional terms in which much leadership is now offered. Could it be that what is called for now is new language, new concepts, new skills—all of which may be needed if we are to have a quality of leading that will be effective in our times? Can those who are moved to make common cause pool their resources in a creative effort to produce new forms of religious leadership which will be accepted by contemporary people as realistic and useful? In the hope that others will respond and contribute, I offer what my experience suggests—all from my perspective of a student of organization.

Who is the religious leader?

THE RELIGIOUS LEADER AS A PERSON

Ours is a stressful world, and both people and institutions are fragile. Anyone who was involved as I was with universities in the 1960s is sharply aware that both people and institutions are fragile. They break easily.

All but the crude and insensitive live under the constant threat of coming unbound, alienated. *Alienated*, in these pages, designates those who have little caring for their fellow humans, who are not motivated to serve people as individuals or as institutions, and who, though able, do not carry some constructive, society-supportive role, or who miss realizing their potential by much too wide a margin. Any influence or action that rebinds—that recovers and sustains such alienated persons as caring, serving, constructive people, and guides them as they build and maintain serving institutions, or that protects normal people from the hazards of alienation and gives purpose and meaning to their lives, is religious. And any group or institution that nurtures these qualities effectively is a church, synagogue, mosque, or temple. Both of the words *religion* and *church* may have additional or differing meanings for individuals and groups. What is suggested here is offered as a common basis for viewing religious leadership among people of many differing beliefs in separate churches.

Together, as *religious leadership*, these two words are used here to describe actions taken to heal, or build immunity from, two serious contemporary maladies: (1) widespread alienation in all sectors of the population, and (2) the inability or unwillingness to serve on the part of far too many of the institutions, large and small, that make up our complex society. Each of these maladies is seen, in part, as a cause of the other, and neither is likely to be healed without coming to terms with the other. The test of the efficacy of religious leadership is: does it cause things to happen among people, directly or indirectly, that heal and immunize from maladies like these two?

One test of any kind of leadership is: Do leaders enjoy a mutual relationship with followers? Are these followers numerous enough and constant enough to make an effective force of their effort? The leader, if in fact a leader, is always attached to an effective force of people. Among those who are normally followers are those who, from time to time, sometimes in major ways, will also lead. The titular leader gives continuity and coherence to an endeavor in which many may lead.

An additional test for religious leaders may be: are they seekers?

We seem today to have few prophetic voices among us. It is possible (I think quite likely) that they are here and speaking as eloquently to the problems of today as the greatest in any age. The lack in our times may be a paucity of seekers who have the critical judgment required to test the authenticity of a prophet. *Is anybody listening?* Are able and discriminating persons listening, people who are willing to work hard to get the skills, to put forth the effort, and take the risks to lead? If a prophet speaks and is not heard, the prophet's vision may wither away.

An important aspect of religious leadership is the nurture of seekers. The religious leader may not have the persuasive ability to put power behind a particular prophet's vision, but she or he may be able to sustain the spirit of seekers and encourage them to listen so that they will respond to prophets who are speaking in contemporary, realistic, and perhaps hard-to-take terms.

Prophet, seeker, and leader are inextricably linked. The *prophet* brings vision and penetrating insight. The *seeker* brings openness, aggressive searching, and good critical judgment—all within the context of the deeply felt attitude, "I have not yet found it." The *leader* adds the art of persuasion backed by persistence, determination, and the courage to venture and risk. The occasional person embodies all three. Both prophet and leader are seekers first. But in religious leadership, as the term is used here, persuasion is only as effective as the quality of the prophetic vision that inspires it and infuses it with spirit. In the end, the quality of prophetic vision shapes the quality of society. The religious leader who is not a prophet is but the instrument of whatever vision is available. The effective religious leader, like other leaders, is apt to be highly intuitive in making judgments about what to do and what not to do. Such a leader also draws heavily on inspiration to sustain spirit. But intuitive insight and inspiration are not apt to be dependable guides in an ignorant, uncritical, or unreflective person. Careful analytical thought, along with knowledge and reflection, provides a check and a guide to intuition and inspiration, gives a solid basis for communicating with informed and prudent people, and offers a framework of assurance to those who would follow.

This discussion of religious leadership presumes that the effective leader will have firm beliefs, whether explicit or implicit, but no particular beliefs are postulated as a condition of being accepted as a religious leader. *Any* set of beliefs that undergirds a leader who causes things to happen among people, directly or indirectly, that heal or immunize from the two pervasive maladies named above, is accepted as having validity that warrants respect. Such acceptance permits people of good will, but with widely differing beliefs, to work in concert as religious leaders on matters that make for a good society.

LEADERSHIP TOWARD FAITH AS TRUST

It may not be possible to find a basis for all people of widely varying beliefs to work together toward a "good" society, but it is hoped that enough of them can find common ground to give the culture more solidity and resiliency than it now seems to have. What is required is that enough people who hold differing beliefs can accept a common definition for religion as is suggested here: any influence or action that rebinds or recovers alienated persons as they build and maintain serving institutions, or that protects normal people from the hazards of alienation and gives purpose and meaning to their lives, is religious.

In this context, theology is seen as the rational inquiry into religious questions supported by critical reflection on communal concerns. Such an inquiry into the influences and actions that do rebind, with results like those named in the paragraph above, may yield the basis for beliefs that make religious leadership possible. And what would we like to see them rebound into? An integrated, loving, caring community? For this to happen on a large scale (and the needs of contemporary society in this regard are large scale), what theologians think about will need to evolve in a way that provides seminaries with both the ideas and language with which to lead.

To the extent that traditional beliefs now attract and hold followers when persuasively advocated, they provide this unity of faith as trust. The disturbing lack of solidity and resiliency in contemporary society may be due to the failure of traditional beliefs to provide the basis for faith as trust in enough people, even in some who "belong" to churches and profess their creeds. Some of the latter, deep down inside, may be just as alienated.

The challenge to contemporary religious leaders, both those professionally or otherwise engaged in churches and those who lead in other settings, is to establish, in contemporary terms, through rational inquiry and prophetic vision, beliefs that sustain those actions and influences that do in fact rebind, heal alienation in persons, and render institutions more serving. Prudence suggests that the central thrust of this effort may be to evolve these beliefs within existing institutions, since an urgent need of our times is for beliefs that unify rather than further fragment society. The first concern of religious leaders may be to learn to rebuild existing institutions as serving rather than to abandon old ones and create new ones. Such leaders may prefer evolution to revolution, persuasion to coercion and manipulation, and gradual to precipitous change. But some change is imperative. Far too many institutions (including some churches) are failing to serve adequately.

Faith is a many faceted concept, a subtle and complex notion. It is discussed here only in relation to leadership. What can it mean in a leader who is successful in bringing and holding together an effective force of people? It may be that it is communicated confidence that a mutually agreed-upon goal can be reached and is worth achieving. This confidence sustains the will to persevere and contend with the inevitable vicissitudes. Such a definition would, of course, fit the successful leader of a gang of thieves. One large step away from this broad definition would insert some clear dimension of justice or mercy as the goal. But would such a qualification, by itself, merit the label religious? I think not. How can we define religious leading without specifying a particular theology or set of beliefs? It may require an operational definition such as I suggested earlier for *religious*.

This definition involves the word *serve*. In my first essay, "The Servant as Leader," I suggested that the servant-leader is servant first. It begins with the natural feeling that one wants to serve, to serve *first*. Then conscious choice brings one to aspire to lead. Such a person is sharply different from one who is a *leader* first, perhaps because of a need to assuage an unusual power drive or to acquire material possessions. The difference manifests itself in the care taken by the servant, first to make sure that other people's highest priority needs are being served. The test I like best, though difficult to administer, is: Do those served grow as persons; do they, *while being served*, become healthier, wiser, freer, more autonomous, more likely themselves to become servants? And, what is the effect on the least privileged person in society; will she or he benefit, or at least, not be further deprived? No one will knowingly be hurt, directly or indirectly.

Faith, to one who aspires to be in the vanguard of the effort to increase the number of effective religious leaders in our time, requires willingness to deal with the issue of *strengthening the hands of the strong*.

STRENGTHEN THE HANDS OF THE STRONG

Earlier I suggested that those who are in the vanguard of the effort to increase the number of religious leaders will find ways to *strengthen the hand of the strong* by helping them, while they are young, to acquire a vision of themselves as effective servants of society.

Strengthen the hands of the strong! Who is strong and how does one strengthen that person's hands? I can only speculate.

In addition to the more ponderable qualities of competence, stability, resiliency, and values, there are the elusive ones of a sense of
the unknowable, contingency thinking, and foresight. All of these are
best strengthened by experience. A mentor leads a potential leader
into a high risk situation and asks, What do you sense or see? What
might happen that would threaten you, but rarely does? What is
likely to happen next, or down the road? The person who, in the heat
of action, can accurately and promptly sense what is going on, is prepared for what might happen but rarely does, and foresees what is
likely to happen next, is *strong*.

A Sense of the Unknowable—Beyond Conscious Rationality

The requirements of leadership impose some intellectual demands
that are not usually measured by academic intelligence ratings. They
are not mutually exclusive, but they are different things. The leader
needs three intellectual abilities that may not be assessed in an academic way: one needs to have a sense for the unknowable, to be prepared for the unexpected, and to be able to foresee the unforeseeable.
The leader knows some things and foresees some things which those
one is presuming to lead do not know or foresee as clearly. This is
partly what gives the leader his "lead," that puts him out ahead and
qualifies him or her to show the way.

As a practical matter, on most important decisions there is an information gap. There usually is an information gap between the solid
information in hand and what is needed. The art of leadership rests,
in part, on the ability to bridge that gap by intuition, that is by a judgment from the unconscious process. The person who is better at this
than most is likely to emerge the leader because he contributes something of great value. Others will depend on him to go out ahead and
show the way because his judgment will be better than most.
Leaders, therefore, must be more creative than most; and creativity is
largely discovery, a push into the uncharted and the unknown. Every
once in a while a leader finds himself needing to think like a scientist,

an artist, or a poet. And his thought processes may be just as fanciful as theirs—and as fallible.

Intuition is a feel for patterns, the ability to generalize based on what has happened previously. The wise leader knows when to bet on these intuitive leads, but he always knows that he is betting on percentages—his hunches are not seen as eternal truths.

Two separate "anxiety" processes may be involved in a leader's intuitive decision, an important aspect of which is timing, the decision to decide. One is the anxiety of holding the decision until as much information as possible is in. The other is the anxiety of making the decision when there really isn't enough information—which, on critical decisions, is usually the case. All of this is complicated by the pressures building up from those who "want an answer." Again, trust is at the root of it. Has the leader a really good information base (both hard data and sensitivity to feelings and needs of people) and a reputation for consistently good decisions that people respect? Can he defuse the anxiety of other people who want more certainty than exists in the situation?

Intuition in a leader is more valued, and therefore more trusted, at the conceptual level. An intuitive answer to an immediate situation, in the absence of a sound governing policy, can be conceptually defective. Overarching conceptual insight that gives a dependable framework for decisions (so important, for instance, in foreign policy) is the greater gift.

CONTINGENCY THINKING

"It is the unexpected that most breaks a man's spirit."

Pericles

Foresight is anticipating what is likely to happen and taking precautionary steps. *Contingency thinking* relates to things that might happen but rarely do. Sometimes the latter appear as emergencies to which there is a preset response. Part of the confidence of followers in a leader rests on the belief that the leader will not be surprised by the unusual and will act promptly in response to it. Let me give two examples out of my experience that are vivid in my memory, although they happened long ago.

About 50 years ago, my wife and I were attending a concert in Carnegie Hall in New York in which the Boston Symphony Orchestra was playing under the direction of Serge Koussevitsky, the Russian-born conductor. The orchestra was well into their program when a great billow of smoke rolled out under the proscenium, someone shouted FIRE, and a full blown panic was almost instantly under way with shouting, running, and pushing—in the orchestra floor and boxes. We were sitting in the front row on the side of the top balcony, high up with a good view of the whole auditorium. Nobody got excited up where we were.

In a matter of seconds Koussevitsky stopped the orchestra, spun around and in a loud voice that could be heard above the tumult he ordered sternly, "sit down, everything will be all right." He stood there motionless with his arms upraised as he looked reprovingly at the unruly audience. The shouting stopped but some people continued to go out in an orderly way. The orchestra members sat motionless, the violinists with their instruments poised on their knees as if a soloist were playing a cadenza. If one of them had broken and run, there might have been a serious panic.

Soon a man appeared from the wings and announced that there had been a small fire in a paper bailer under the stage which was quickly extinguished. The smoke had stopped. But the wail of the sirens on the arriving fire fighting equipment suggested that the fire had been taken seriously.

The point in relating this incident is that the speed, forcefulness, and rightness of Koussevitsky's response suggest that he had anticipated this emergency and that his response was firmly preset. A few seconds delay to think it over and the panic might have been out of hand.

Such occasions are so rare that an orchestra conductor may go through a whole career and not once confront a situation of the gravity that I witnessed. Yet if it suddenly comes, and if one is to deal with it prudently as Koussevitsky did, one must have firmly preset one's response.

The concert resumed for those who remained, which was everybody up in the second balcony where we were—we were all too fascinated by the spectacle of the uproar down below among those rich people in their fancy evening clothes, about half of whom left and did not return. It concluded with a great ovation for the conductor and the orchestra. They were interrupted in that melodious and much-played second movement of Tchaikovsky's Fifth symphony. Every time I hear that music, the memory of that dramatic incident is refreshed.

The news report next day gave Koussevitsky's answer to a reporter's question of how he managed to keep his tempo after a shakeup like that. "Tempi are tempi," he said, "and tranquility is tranquility." He was not thrown by the unexpected.

The second incident, about 35 years ago, was when I had occasion to pull the emergency cord on a New York subway train to save a man's life. It was the only time in 40 years of riding those subways that I saw the cord pulled.

I was seated in the center of a well-filled car in which quite a few were standing, at about the middle of a ten-car train. As the train took off from a station, accelerating as they do at a good clip, a commotion broke out at the door in the forward end of the car where a man had tried to enter as the doors closed and, from the outside, one arm was firmly hooked in the door because of a cuff on a heavy overcoat. The guards who are supposed to look over the train when it takes off had missed it and he was being dragged along to his almost certain death if the train was not stopped before he reached the end of the platform.

The crowd inside was tugging at the door and shouting, "pull the emergency cord!" A cord hung right over their heads, but nobody pulled it. I could not see because of people standing, and it was several seconds before I realized that it was up to me to pull the cord in the other end of the car. I ran as fast as I could, bowling over a couple of people as I went, and got to the cord just in the nick of time. When the train stopped the man was about 25 feet from the end of the platform.

This incident was the cause of considerable reflection. There were about 60 people in that car who were closer to one of those two cords than I was, and some of them were closer to the incident and were alerted sooner than I was. I was not aware that any of them made a move to pull the cord. Why was it up to me to do it? I concluded that I was probably the only one in that car who knew beforehand where those cords were and had preset the response that someday it might be up to me to pull one. Those cords are deliberately not made too conspicuous. If one does not know beforehand where they are, in the heat of the emergency it is not likely that one would discover them by looking around—not in time. So I performed an experiment.

As I met New Yorkers over the next few months, persons who used the subways frequently, I would describe the incident. Then I would say, "There are three different subway systems in New York, and the cords are in a different location in each. This is the Independent System. You have six seconds, Where is the cord? One-two-three-four-five-six; you're too late; the man is gone." Usually there was a protest, "Your counting put me under pressure and I couldn't think." To which I would respond, "In the actual event, I was under pressure too. But take your time, where is the cord?" I tried this on about 25 people without finding one who could say where the cord was, given indefinite time. I concluded that contingency thinkers are a bit rare, but they need not be if the formative years of young people included some preparation for it.

I learned to be a contingency thinker from my father, who was good at it and to whom I was very close. He was a contemporary of G. K. Chesterton, but I doubt that he read him. He would, however, have agreed with what Chesterton had to say in the following paragraph.

The real trouble with this world is not that it is an unreasonable world, nor even that it is a reasonable one. The commonest kind of trouble is that it is nearly reasonable, but not quite. Life is not an illogicality; yet it is a trap for logicians. It looks just a little more mathematical and regular than it is; its exactitude is obvious, but its inexactitude is hidden; its wildness lies in wait. (*Orthodoxy*, 1908)

FORESIGHT—THE CENTRAL ETHIC OF LEADERSHIP

Machiavelli, writing 300 years ago about how to be a prince, put it this way: "Thus it happens in matters of state; for knowing afar off (which it is only given a prudent man to do) the evils that are brewing, they are easily cured. But when, for want of such knowledge, they are allowed to grow so that everyone can recognize them, there is no longer any remedy to be found."

The shape of some future events can be calculated from trend data. But, as with a practical decision mentioned earlier, there is usually an information gap that has to be bridged, and one must cultivate the conditions that favor intuition. This is what Machiavelli meant when he said that "knowing afar off—which is only given a prudent man to do." The prudent man is he who constantly thinks of "now" as the concept in which past, present moment, and future are one organic unity. And this requires living by a sort of rhythm that encourages a high level of intuitive insight about the whole gamut of events from the indefinite past, through the present moment, to the indefinite future. One is at once, in every moment of time, historian, contemporary analyst, and prophet—not three separate roles. This is what the practicing leader is, every day of his life.

Living this way is partly a matter of *faith*. Stress is a condition of most of modern life, and if one is a servant-leader and carrying the burdens of other people, going out ahead to show the way, one takes the rough and tumble (and it really is rough and tumble in some leader roles). One takes this in the belief that, if one enters a situation prepared with the necessary experience and knowledge at the conscious level, *in the situation*, the intuitive insight necessary for one's optimal performance will be forthcoming. Is there any other way, in the turbulent world of affairs (including the typical home), for one to maintain serenity in the face of uncertainty? One follows the steps of the creative process which require that one stay with conscious analysis as far as it will carry one, and then withdraws, releases the analytical pressure, if only for a moment, in full confidence that a resolving insight will come. The concern with the past and future is gradually attenuated as this span of concern goes forward or backward from the instant moment. The ability to do this is the essential structural dynamic of leadership.

The failure (or refusal) of a leader to foresee may be viewed as an *ethical* failure, because a serious ethical compromise today (when the usual judgment on ethical inadequacy is made) is sometimes the result of a failure to make the effort at an earlier date to foresee today's events and take the right actions when there was freedom for initiative to act. The action which society labels "unethical" in the present moment is often really one of no choice. By this standard, a lot of guilty people are walking around with an air of innocence that they would not have if society were able always to pin the label "unethical" on the failure to foresee and the consequent failure to act constructively when there was freedom to act.

Foresight is the "lead" that the leader has. Once he loses this lead and events start to force his hand, he is leader in name only. He is not leading. He is reacting to immediate events and he probably will not long be a leader. There are abundant examples of loss of leadership which stemmed from a failure to foresee what reasonably could have been foreseen, and from failure to act on that knowledge while the leader had the freedom to act.

Pericles, in the speech quoted earlier, said to the Athenians who had chosen him to lead, "You took me to be what I think I am, superior to most in foresight . . .".

How to achieve foresight if one is not born with it? One begins, I suppose, by recognizing the importance of it. And, if one does not have it, then stay close to someone who does have it. Maybe some of it will rub off. I doubt that the gift of foresight can be taught in a course.

Required, I believe, is that one live a sort of schizoid life. One is always at two levels of consciousness: one is in the real world of the present—concerned, responsible, effective, value-oriented. One is also detached, riding above it, seeing today's events, and seeing one-self deeply involved in today's events, in the perspective of a long sweep of history and projected into the indefinite future. Such a split enables one better to foresee the unforeseeable. Also, from one level of consciousness, each of us acts resolutely from moment to moment on a set of assumptions that then govern one's life. Simultaneously, from another level, the adequacy of these assumptions is examined, in action, with the aim of future revision and improvement. Such a view gives one the perspective that makes it possible to live and act in the real world with a clearer conscience.

WHAT GIVES STRENGTH TO THE STRONG?

What gives the strong their strength? The three preceding sections, "A Sense of the Unknowable," "Contingency Thinking," and "Foresight," suggest dimensions of the inner resources of a leader that support self-confidence and that build confidence in followers. Why would anyone follow the leadership of another unless one has confidence that the other knows better where to go? And how would one know better where to go unless one has a wider than usual awareness of the terrain and the alternatives, unless one is well ar-mored for the unexpected, and unless one's view of the future is more sharply defined than that of most? Also, one's confidence in a leader rests, in part, on the assurance that stability and poise and resilience under stress give adequate strength for the rigors of leadership. All of the above stand on a base of intensity and dedication to service that supports faith as trust.

Earlier it was suggested that faith might be viewed as communicated confidence that a mutually agreed-upon goal can be reached and is worth achieving, and that builds the sustaining will to persevere and contend with the inevitable vicissitudes. These may be subliminal things. And they may breed a feeling of trust by followers in the dependability of the inner resources of the leader as suggested in the preceding sections. Is not, then, *faith as trust* in a religious leader rooted in a firm sense of the dependability of the inner resources of one who influences or takes actions that rebind?

Could we say, then, that part of the religious leader's own faith is trust in his or her own inner resources? If one is to take the risks of leadership (and all significant leadership entails venturing and risking), one needs to trust one's inner resources, *in the situation*, to give the guidance one needs to justify the trust of followers. One cannot know *before* one ventures to assume leadership what the markers on the course will be or that the course one will take is safe. To know beforehand would make the venture risk-free. One has confidence that, *after* one is launched in the venture, the way will be illuminated. The price of some illumination may be the willingness to take the risk of faith. Followers, knowing that the venture is risky, have faith as trust in this communicated confidence of the leader.

Some may speculate on what lies beyond the inner resources of the leader, but leader and follower may or may not share these speculations. For faith as trust to be real, even in a religious leader, it suffices that the inner resources of the leader are known by both leader and follower to be dependable. The test: *a leader feels strong and is accepted by followers as stronger than most.*

I have listened in recent years to many in responsible positions in religious institutions as they have discussed what they called their leadership problems. The following are some of my impressions:

- change a few words, and they sounded no different from the harried executives in other institutions that I have been listening to all my life.

- most of what they called *lead* I would label *manage*, *administer*, or *manipulate*. I was not aware of much leading—as defined here.

- the main problem revealed was a lack of faith—as it would relate to leading. What they called faith seemed to me to be mostly belief in certain doctrinal positions. There was little evidence of deep inner resources—that they trusted and that others would trust—which would be the basis for confidence in their ability to attract and hold followers in a high risk venture. They were mostly "safe" people.

In short, too many of these good people seemed to lack enough faith to lead. As I once put it bluntly in an off-the-record session with such persons, "You seem not to believe your own stuff."

RELIGIOUS LEADERS IN ACTION

If we accept definitions like those given above, what can be said about the person who might be giving effective religious leadership today?

Anything said in answer to that question is indeed a speculation. Religious leaders in the future, like all sorts of leaders in the past, will probably be many different types of people. And they may evolve in ways that we cannot now foresee. They are more likely to emerge if there is an expectancy, and an awareness and acceptance of the probability that they may not resemble any type that we can now imagine. Let me select from the past, descriptions of two quite dissimilar examples of persons whose work has impressed me as I have reflected on the question above.

John Woolman

Leaders work in wondrous ways. Some assume great institutional burdens, others quietly deal with one person at a time. Such a man was John Woolman, an American Quaker who lived through the middle years of the 18th century. He is known to the world of scholarship for his journal, a literary classic. But in the area of our interest, leadership, he is the man whose great contribution was to help rid the Religious Society of Friends (Quakers) of slaves.

It is difficult now to imagine the Quakers as slaveholders, as indeed it is difficult now to imagine anyone being a slaveholder. One wonders how the society of 200 years hence will view "what man had made of man" in our generation. It is a disturbing thought.

But many of the 18th-century American Quakers were affluent, conservative slaveholders, and John Woolman, as a young man, set his goal to do what he could to rid his beloved Society of this terrible practice. Thirty of his adult years (he lived to age 52) were largely devoted to this. By 1770, nearly 100 years before the Civil War, no Quakers held slaves. His method was unique. He didn't raise a big storm about it or start a protest movement. His method was one of gentle but clear and persistent persuasion—largely one person at a time.

Although John Woolman was not a strong man physically, he accomplished his mission by journeys up and down the East Coast by foot or horseback visiting slaveholders, over a period of many years. The approach was not to censure the slaveholders in a way that drew their animosity. Rather the burden of his approach was to raise questions: What does the owning of slaves do to you as a moral person? What kind of an institution are you binding over to your children? Man by man, inch by inch, by persistently returning and revisiting and pressing his gentle argument over a period of 30 years, he helped to remove slavery from this Society, the first religious group in America formally to denounce and forbid slavery among its members. One wonders what would have been the result if there had been 50 John Woolmans, or even 5, traveling the length and breadth of the Colonies in the 18th century, persuading people one by one with gentle, nonjudgmental argument that a wrong should be righted by individual voluntary action. Perhaps we would not have had the war with its 600,000 casualties and the improverishment of the South, and with the resultant vexing social problem that is with us a century later with no end in sight. Some historians hold now that just a slight alleviation of the tension in the 1850s might have avoided the war. A few John Woolmans, just a *few*, might have made the difference.

Leadership by persuasion has the virtue of change by convincement rather than coercion. Its advantages are obvious.

John Woolman exerted his leadership in an age that must have looked as dark to him as ours does to us today. We may easily write off his effort as a suggestion for today on the assumption that the Quakers were ethically conditioned for this approach. The Quakers of Woolman's day were not pushovers on this issue. All persons are so conditioned, to some extent—enough to gamble on.

Nikolai Grundtvig

Nikolai Frederik Severin Grundtvig, whose adult life was the first three-quarters of the 19th century, is known as the father of the Danish Folk High Schools. To understand the significance of the Folk High School, one needs to know a little of the unique history of Denmark. Since it is a tiny country, not many outside it know this history, and consequently Grundtvig and his seminal contributions are little known. A great church dedicated to his memory in Copenhagen attests the modern Danish awareness of what he did for them—but he was not widely applauded in his time.

At the beginning of the 19th century, Denmark was a feudal and absolute monarchy. It was predominantly agricultural, with a large peasant population of serfs who were attached to manors. Early in the century, reforms began which gave the land to the peasants as individual holdings. Later the first steps toward representative government were taken.

A chronicler of those times reports, "The Danish peasantry at the beginning of the nineteenth century was an underclass. In sullen resignation it spent its life in dependence on estate owners and government officials. It was without culture and technical skill, and it was seldom able to rise above the level of bare existence. The agricultural reforms of that time were carried through without the support of the peasants, who did not even understand the meaning of them. . . . All the reforms were made for the sake of the peasant, but not by him. In the course of the century this underclass has been changed into a well-to-do middle class which, politically and socially, now takes the lead among the Danish people." (From The *Folk High Schools of Denmark*, by Begtrup, Lund, and Manniche, Oxford University Press, 1926.)

Freedom—to own land and to vote—was not enough to bring about these changes. A new form of education was envisioned by Grundtvig explicitly to achieve this transformation. Grundtvig was a theologian, poet, and student of history. Although he himself was a scholar, he believed in the active practical life, and he conceptualized a school, the Folk High School, as a short intensive residence course for young adults dealing with the history, mythology, and poetry of the Danish people. He addressed himself to the masses rather than to the cultured. The "cultured" at the time thought him to be a confused visionary and contemptuously turned their backs on him. But the peasants heard him, and their natural leaders responded to his call to start the Folk High Schools—with their own resources.

"The spirit (not knowledge) is power." "The living word in the mother tongue." "Real life is the final test," as contrasted with the German and Danish tendency to theorize. These were some of the maxims that guided the new schools of the people. For 50 years of his long life, Grundtvig vigorously and passionately advocated these new schools as the means whereby the peasants could raise themselves into the Danish national culture. And, stimulated by the Folk High School experience, the peasant youth began to attend agricultural schools and to build cooperatives on the model borrowed from England.

Two events provided the challenge that matured the new peasant movement and brought it into political and social dominance by the end of the century. There was a disastrous war with Prussia in 1864, which resulted in a substantial loss of territory and a crushing blow to national aspiration. And then, a little later, there was the loss of world markets for corn, their major exportable crop, as a result of the agricultural abundance of the New World. Peasant initiative, growing out of the spiritual dynamic generated by the Folk High Schools, did much to recover the nation from both of these shocks by transforming their exportable surplus from corn to "butter and bacon," by helping to rebuild the national spirit, and by nourishing the Danish tradition in the territory lost to Germany during the long years until it was returned after World War I.

All of this, a truly remarkable social, political, and economic transformation, stemmed largely from one man's conceptual leadership. Grundtvig himself did not found or operate a Folk High School, although he lectured widely in them. What he gave was his love for the peasants, his clear vision of what they must do for themselves, his long articulate dedication—some of it through very barren years, and his passionately communicated faith in the worth of these people and their strength to raise themselves—if only their spirit could be aroused. It is a great story of the supremacy of the spirit.

It may be that power, no matter what its source—whether physical strength, intellect, wealth, prestige, cunning—is only effective in building a better society as it liberates the spirit of the powerless and gives them a vision of greatness so that their native wisdom can function. Grundtvig's power of prophetic vision and persuasiveness seems to confirm this thesis.

And Now!

These two examples from previous centuries illustrate very different types of leadership for the common good. They are not suggested as general models for today, although some useful hints may be found in them. What these examples may tell us is that the leadership of trail blazers like Woolman and Grundtvig is so "situational" that it rarely draws on known models. Rather it seems to be a fresh creative response to here-and-now opportunities. Too much concern with how others did it may be inhibitive. One wonders, in these kaleidoscopic times, what kind of contemporary leadership effort will be seen as seminal 100 years from now, as we can now see the two I have described.

One thing is certain about these two men: they were both strong, assured, and resourceful. Both clearly knew who they were and had their guiding stars in focus.

WHAT CAN BE TAUGHT ABOUT RELIGIOUS LEADERSHIP?

It may be that leaders are "born and not made," but some things might be taught to those who are "born" to the role. The most effective formal teaching of leadership I have seen was with mid-career executives who, in somebody's estimation, had demonstrated the potential for becoming significant leaders. The course was taught by a wise and perceptive person—Professor John Finch, Chairman of the Department of English at Dartmouth College. His course had the alliterative title "The Language and Literature of Leadership." After some consideration of the structure of language, Professor Finch moved on to the principal subject matter of the course, the four Shakespeare "history" plays—*Richard II, Henry IV* (parts I & II), and *Henry V*. These were employed as case studies of the use of language by kings, with the language artistry of Shakespeare as the central focus. Most effective leaders of all sorts have a somewhat unique language artistry. (Not necessarily bizarre like Casey Stengel or history-making like Churchill and Roosevelt, but effective in terms of one's opportunities.)

After watching this unusual teaching of language usage to mid-career executives, I have wondered whether it might be possible to employ this approach with college-age people and whether such teaching might have the effect of bringing some young people to an awareness of their potential to lead and establish early their sensitivity to language as an art form for effective leaders.

Part of a religious leader's role as consensus finder is inventiveness with language and avoidance of a stereotyped style. One leads partly by the constant search for the language and the concepts that will enlarge the number who find common ground. The leader thus strives to bring people together, and hold them together, as an effective force. An experimental approach to language is a part of this skill.

Part of success in leadership toward consensus is faith, confidence that the language exists that will provide the needed common ground if one will persevere and communicate this confidence to all involved. I don't believe that faith can be taught in a didactic way; but it can be communicated.

Beyond language, what can be taught about leadership? I suspect not much in a formal way. But there is much to be learned by one who is inexperienced yet has the potential to lead. A better question might be, How can that learning be accelerated? Can useful formative circumstances for potential leaders be created?

At AT&T, I once made a study of the careers of the 12 executives who made up the top command of that huge institution at that time. They seemed to me to be able people, but not exceptional. What had happened in their careers that pushed them to the very top? All 12 reported that there was one early boss who greatly accelerated their growth as managers (managing and leading are not identical, but they are related).

The most significant finding was that 4 of the 12 had had their early formative experience under one mid-level manager. This person was one of 900 at his level and, as far as anybody knew, he had no more access to talented young people than other managers at his level. Yet a generation later he accounted for one-third of the top command. More than that, all over the business there were middle and upper managers who had their early formative experience under him. He was dead when I learned this, but clearly he was a fantastic grower of people. Further, he was something of an oddball who did not himself rise to the top; he stayed many years at the middle level where he had access to young people. But, as one of 900, he was probably the most influential manager of his generation. There is no way to make the judgment, but he may have made a greater contribution to the future of the business than the chief executives of his time. Among those who had their formative experience under him, there was no question about how he wielded his great growth influence.

He managed a good department—but the controls on the business required that. His uniqueness was that he had a passionate interest in the growth of young people—no less vivid term would describe it—and the controls of that time did not require that (nor do they now require it). Further, he sustained this passionate interest in the depth of the Depression; his able young people were running hard when others were dying on the vine all over the place. When the curtain of the Depression lifted and the business started to recover and had urgent need for able young people to advance, this man had people who were ready to move when few others had them. What was he like? Those who worked under him were agreed on the following:

He was a good intuitive judge of potential. He did not waste his limited opportunities on people who were not likely to profit from them. He watched closely the growth of his promising young people, and he saw to it that they were always challenged and busy. Sometimes this required some ingenious "made" work. He did not have unlimited latitude to do this, but he stretched the charter of his job to the limit in order to favor the growth of high potential young people.

He was friendly and freely available for consultation. But he was reserved, not folksy or chatty. The growth of his promising people was an evident serious concern that he communicated.

But, most unusual, he had a firm belief in the importance of error in the formative experience of young people. If one of his youngsters was getting along a little too smoothly, he would contrive an error so that he would fall on his face. And he would figuratively pick him up and dust him off and say, kindly, "Well, Bud, that hurt; but what did you learn?" And they would talk about what was learned. Error was never greeted with censure—unless it was repeated and then this boss would come down hard. All of this was carried on in an atmosphere in which able people were encouraged to grow.

Does the example of this extraordinary man have anything to say to the question of what can be taught about religious leadership? I think it has much to say. Anybody can learn, but crucial formative experience comes when one is young. It best takes place in a serving institution. And there should be influential people in that institution who have a passion for growing people—growth in the strength to lead.

SEMINARIES HAVE THE PRIME OPPORTUNITY

Where can growth in strength as religious leaders best take place? *In seminaries!* And what might a seminary be like when significant formation of this kind takes place there?

- Its priorities will be reversed. Whereas seminaries are now mostly academic and only incidentally formative, formation of religious leaders will be primary and academic teaching will be secondary.

- The staff of the seminaries will contain a strong element of those who have a passion for growing religious leaders—and are good at it. They may or may not be scholars in the usual sense.

- A major mission of the seminary will be to evolve, and maintain, a theology of institutions that deals realistically with the problem of how to recover moribund institutions as vital, effective, caring, and serving. This will not be a theoretical endeavor because it will be forged on the seminary's own experience as it builds itself into—and maintains itself as—the pivotal institution it is determined to become. Seminary students will be deeply involved in this continuous effort to build and maintain this theology. They will not just read and hear lectures about it.

- The primary mission of the seminary will be leading and serving churches and supporting them as strong influential institutions. Most of the learning of seminary students will result from involvement in this effort.

- There will be creative thinkers among its faculty who are developing and articulating a contemporary theology of what makes religious leaders, and the institutions they serve, *strong*. Students in the seminary will be deeply involved in responding to this with their own thinking.

- Such seminaries will become known as effective nurturers of able religious leaders, and they will attract a wide spectrum of strong young people in search of such formative development. Some of these students might find their career opportunities in churches, but the seminary will become a prime source of religious leaders for all segments of society. It will acknowledge that any institution where religious leaders predominate may effectively become a church.

If only one seminary achieves this status, it will, in time, have a significant influence on the quality of the whole society. I hope there will be more than one.

I can hear the anguished cry, "Where will we ever find the money and the people to do this!"

It begins with a vision that is translated into ideas and language. Then someone deeply believes in it, advocates, and perseveres despite obstacles. Finally the really tough test: someone has the leadership strength and skill to bring together and hold a following that will see it through.

Some of what might be learned about religious leadership—in a seminary—is discussed in the next section.

PITFALLS AND OPPORTUNITIES

Earlier, in discussing *strengthening the hands of the strong*, it was noted that one way to do this is to help such persons acquire an awareness of the pitfalls and the opportunities for those who would be servants of society.

As ours has become a society that is dominated by institutions large and small, to an extent quite different from the times of

Woolman and Grundtvig, some new problems have been presented. How does one sustain these institutions as effective servants? The answers to this question define some of the opportunities.

Some of the pitfalls lie in the temptation, when there is institutional pain, to reach for an aspirin, a quick fix, or to seek the help of an "expert" who will provide a reassuring "bedside manner" along with a remedy—perhaps an aspirin.

These problems present some unusual challenges to churches— as well as other institutions. These are discussed in the next five sections.

The Problem of Organizational "Gimmicks"

The opprobrious label "gimmick" is applied to any organizational procedure that is introduced with the hope of accomplishing what only better leadership can do, or that will not be effective, long term, because it is not in harmony with the prevailing quality of leadership. Such nostrums that claim to reduce institutional pain (which most institutions have some of) or boost organizational effectiveness are abundantly available. Too often the result is an "aspirin" effect—not the path to long-term health for either person or institution. Well-led institutions are not good customers for gimmick salesmen. These exceptional institutions either evolve their own procedures, or they learn from other well-led situations. They are not in the market for aspirin.

I hear the protest: "What does one do when the organizational pain is intense?" My response is, "Attend to the quality of leading, unless you want to spend the rest of your organizational life living on aspirin!"

In my work with American Telephone and Telegraph Company, I had the opportunity, almost from the beginning, to follow closely the "Hawthorne" researches that culminated in a landmark book in 1933, *Management and the Worker*, and, in 1966, *Counseling in an Organization, A sequel to the Hawthorne Researches*.

This research, and the employee counseling program that grew out of it, were done in the Hawthorne plant of Western Electric Company in Chicago. This was a huge factory with 25,000 workers that had a long record as a very productive place with fine human relationships. It had had the benefit of unusually able management for several years before the research started. The research revealed, among other things, that employee preoccupation with personal problems was a significant element in satisfaction and productivity with work. There ensued from this finding a substantial program of employee counseling, probably the most ambitious effort to serve an industry and its people in this way that has ever been undertaken. The report in *Counseling in an Organization* notes that there were 5 employee counselors on the staff in 1936. This number rose to 55 in 1948 and by 1955 it was down to 8—the last count. Why did this work rise and then decline? And why did the effort fail when employee counseling was introduced in several other Western Electric plants and operating telephone companies? The conclusion of close observers, including myself, was that it declined at the Hawthorne plant when the last of the succession of great managers retired in 1952 and new managers who had different ideas began to question the cost of it. The justification during the peak years was philosophical rather than statistical. It was simply one of the appropriate things to do in a factory that had had the exceptional leadership that the Hawthorne plant had long enjoyed. It "paid off" because it was part of the right way to run a factory (which is probably why the researches were done in the Hawthorne plant in the first place). It was not introduced as a gimmick. Rather it evolved in a natural way as an appropriate thing to do. When the counseling program was introduced at other locations with great care, sometimes using staff from the Hawthorne plant to head it, it was done with the intent of fostering the benign and productive circumstances at Hawthorne. It was a gimmick, and it was promptly rejected as an inappropriate skin graft in five other locations. It did not belong there.

Later, after I retired from AT&T and acquired a much wider

view of institutions, I noted that the occasional exceptional institution was usually free of gimmicks. Exceptional institutions, I concluded, are astutely administered and wisely led. They learn from other experience, but their procedures (and every institution needs them) evolve out of their own experience, and they are congenial to the local culture.

Physical technology is readily transferable; but organizational technology is culture-bound, and any institution imports it at its peril. My advice: any effort to improve organizational performance should begin with attending to the quality of leadership; then evolve organizational procedures that are congenial to the way that leadership operates. In organizational performance it is the quality of leadership that governs. Procedures are important, but they are subordinate to the way the institution is led. Avoid organizational aspirin!

When I wrote the first essay on "Servant as Leader," I discovered that I had given that piece a catchy title. I am grateful that the title gave the piece some circulation, but I am also aware of the danger: servant-leadership could become a gimmick. The top person of some ailing institution might try to insert servant-leadership as a procedure, as a general management idea, as a means whereby the institution might do better. Such a move might have a short-lived aspirin effect, but when that effect wears off, it might leave the institution more ailing than it was before, and another gimmick would need to be sought. The surer way for the idea to have a long-term good effect is *for the top person to become a servant-leader*. What that person *is* and *does* then speaks louder than what is said. It might be better if nothing is said, just *be* it. This, in time, might transform the institution.

In a discussion of this subject with the staff of a large religious institution, the head of the staff asked rather plaintively, as if he had had some sad experiences with gimmicks, "How do you tell a gimmick when you see one?"

My answer was, there is no *way* I know of, no gauge that you can slip over an idea and say with certainty that it is or is not a gimmick.

The problem is that what is clearly a gimmick in one situation may not be judged that way in another. The counseling program at its peak in the Hawthorne plant was not a gimmick; everywhere else it was tried it was an aspirin—or worse! There are some organizational ideas abroad that seem to me to have no merit anywhere; but that reflects a personal bias. And there are some institutions that are so poorly led that aspirin may be better than nothing. But one is not likely to achieve institutional health, ever, by aspirin—just temporary relief from pain, leading to use of another aspirin.

Religious leaders, being human and fallible, will occasionally sense institutional pain in what they are leading. If the first response to that signal is to ask "wherein is my leadership at fault, what can I do to improve it?" it is unlikely that they will be tempted to reach for a pill, a gimmick, and gimmick salespeople who infest our society will not find them good prospects.

One of my sad experiences has been to watch at close range as an important institution bought one gimmick after another. I have become fatalistic about it. Just as there are people who are addicted to aspirin, there are institutions that seem addicted to gimmicks. Neither seems healthy.

LEADING VERSUS STRUCTURING

One of the common responses to institutional pain is to tinker with the structure. Everything that is organized has some kind of structure, even if it is only an informal understanding of who will do what. The most common explicit structure is hierarchical (as first described in Exodus 18). This arrangement is coming to be seen as seriously flawed, but the authoritarian bias that supports it is so entrenched that it is difficult even to discuss alternatives.

Standing alongside most formal structures are informal ones whose function is to patch up the inadequacies of the formal ones. Even in the most rigid of institutions, there are usually acceptable deviations from and exceptions to the prescribed structures. They couldn't function without them.

The assumption here is that if an institution is well led, the nature of the formal structure is much less important than if it is poorly led. If leadership is exceptionally good, an institution sometimes operates without much reference to formal structure, even though it may have a well-defined one.

In a well-led institution, the need for structure may be minimal, but it is well to have some structure because even exceptional leaders sometimes falter and an understood structure serves as a "safety net." Also, able leaders may be succeeded by mediocre or poor ones, and that contingency needs to be provided for.

The ideal organization structure would probably be one that is redesigned each time there is change in the conditions the institution confronts—which may be every few days. Therefore, the need for stability suggests that the best that can be hoped for is a "best fit" for a range of conditions. This is not likely to be optimal for any one of them. The dilemma of all leaders of institutions is to accept that structure, no matter how well designed, will be awkward and inhibitive.

The above view suggests one of the inevitable ambiguities of life in all institutions, large or small, and defines one of the challenges to leaders who want to lead effectively so as to sustain what they lead at the level of exceptional. And it suggests to those who act as trustees that they should focus their energies, first, on themselves providing the best leadership they are capable of; second, on finding and supporting able leaders who will also administer; and, third, then designing a structure that is least inhibiting to good leadership.

In the context of religious leadership, tinkering with structure is not a first choice of means for building or sustaining quality in an institution. *Leadership is the prime concern!* And when leadership is effective, structure is not a significant concern. Just watch to see that it does not get in the way.

Beware! Preoccupation with structure could be a gimmick!

THE GROWING-EDGE CHURCH

Years ago I wrote an essay on "The Institution as Servant" in which I made a comment on The Growing-Edge Church. Such a church, I suggested then, is "one that accepts the opportunity all churches have to become a significant nurturing force, conceptualizer of a serving mission, value shaper, and moral sustainer of leaders everywhere." Since then I have not made a systematic study, but I have kept a close watch and I have not found a church that I think qualifies as a growing-edge church in these terms. I have wondered, why? Are the criteria suggested unrealistic, do any really want to be growing-edge churches, or is something standing in the way? I have concluded that it is the latter. If so, what is standing in the way?

As I get about among churches and church-related institutions, I am impressed by the extent to which they, rather casually it seems to me, employ commercial consultants to advise them and rely on procedures on which I would place the opprobrious label "gimmick." Both, it seems to me, are evidences of inadequate religious leadership. Well-led institutions are not good customers for either consultants or gimmick salesmen. If these are valid judgments, might they not account, in part at least, for the inability of churches to achieve the healing influence they might have on the two pervasive problems; alienation of persons and failure of institutions to serve? Why would one look to any church for moral and spiritual guidance if that church is seen, even to a small extent, as simply a broker between those in need and facilities that might serve that need which are abundantly available elsewhere? And, further, how can a church in this posture infuse religious leadership, a critically needed quality, into the fabric of society as a whole? If churches, in these chaotic times, are to *lead*, they must *originate* and not be seen as sponges for the fads of the day, and they should work from their greatest asset—inspiration.

A church might choose another mission than to become growing-edge by the criteria I have given. But if it aspires to that distinction, then I submit that recourse to consultants, as they are commonly used, and gimmicks will stand in the way.

Let me speculate on why some churches, because they are not clear about their missions, or have not thought through their implications, may have turned to consultants and gimmicks. Could it be that this diversion to do the "in" things and to look for "answers" from experts is an unconscious escape from the much tougher and more demanding course of nurturing seekers? Seeking is an opening to prophetic vision which could have disturbing consequences—and not many are likely to undertake it unless they are given exceptional leadership. And seekers are a resource that cannot be bought with money.

I have followed one thread of this diversionary influence in churches for 35 years. In the summer of 1947, I attended the very first group development conference at Bethel, Maine. This was to be the launching of a major research effort by Kurt Lewin, who came to this country as a refugee scholar in the 1930s. But Lewin died suddenly on the eve of this first session, and it was carried on by his students.

Lewin was a rigorous experimental psychologist, and I registered for this session on the urging of a close friend, an equally rigorous experimental psychologist, Carl Hovland, who was then chairman of the Department of Psychology at Yale, because Carl felt that this work might be a breakthrough of a great practical consequence—my prime interest.

Alas, in my judgment, Lewin's students who carried on his work were not of his careful scientific temperament and skill, a view confirmed by the abrupt termination of the tenure of Lewin's Research Center for Group Dynamics at Massachusetts Institute of Technology after his death. I have since often wondered where we would be today if Lewin had lived a normal life span (he died at age 47). I am quite certain that the cultish movement that took off from that session I attended in 1947 would not have materialized. I promptly dissociated myself from it. But some churches bought in on it in a big way. Sensitivity training has been one of the "in" things to do. Some of what is called the "human potential movement"—centering on self—had its origins in this work. There are other examples in recent years of church investments in diversionary activities, some of which have the flavor of gimmicks; but this is the one I have been closest to.

These are called "diversionary" activities because they divert churches from what I believe should be their central concern, *inspiration*, and divert them to techniques and procedures. Differing contexts of belief illuminated by a range of theological reflections suggest many meanings for the word *inspiration*. I doubt that any of those meanings would embrace techniques and procedures that have the flavor of gimmicks or the advice that most commercial consultants would give.

This is not intended as a diatribe against consultants—in my more active days I have been one myself, and later I will comment on an acceptable limited use of them. But, once I evolved the views I have expressed about consultants to churches—and their wares—I no longer accepted money for consulting service to a church. I gained some perspective on this from Alcoholics Anonymous.

AA received its unusual view of money from a wise and deeply concerned philanthropist in the 1930s. This very wealthy man had watched the slow evolution of this unusual group and, when they reached sufficient size and certainty in their approach, he convened them in his office to help them organize and clarify their principles. In the course of the discussion, he made a statement like this: "I believe I know from my experience something about what can be done with money and what cannot be done with money; and you have one of the things that cannot be done with money." The firm resolve that the essential work of AA, one recovered or partly recovered alcoholic helping to recover another, would not be done for money, was made at that meeting. The phenomenal success of AA rests in part, I believe, on strict adherence to this principle.

AA is a religious movement, an ad hoc church. All churches may do well to keep sharply in mind the question, "Are we trying to do something with money that cannot be done with money?" If it aspires to be a growing-edge church, as conceived here, it will harbor and encourage *seekers*. They are more likely than most to hear and evaluate the prophetic vision that is with us all of the time.

A church in which inspiration is the prime source of its guidance may safely pay a lawyer, accountant, or architect, or others rendering ancillary service. But if a church is uncertain about the inspiration that guides it, then it had best turn to seekers. What the world of institutions needs from churches is not preachment about leadership, but clear and convincing models, because every institution, within the scope of its mission and opportunity to serve, needs its own equivalent of seekers to keep it on a true course as servant and to assure its survival. And it is just as difficult to sustain such persons in a business or unit of government or university as it is in a church. Are other institutions likely to learn to evolve, support, and encourage these people unless churches hold up the model of them—in its purest form? Any church that offers a clear and convincing model as a harborer of seekers will, in my judgment, distinguish itself as a growing-edge church. Its effective religious leadership will be confirmed thereby.

The pastor of a church who is usually, but not always, a full-time professional may be paid. But the pastor's strongest role may not be as a seeker. Rather he or she will be the leader and nurturer of seekers who will not be paid.

The absence of evidence that churches are nurturing seekers, or aspiring to strengthen leaders, is one of the reasons I have not identified a growing-edge church. I come by my conviction on this point by reading the history of the Quakers. If George Fox, the great prophetic visionary who founded the sect in 17th-century England, had not been preceded by a lay movement known as "seekers," Fox might not have been heard. I firmly believe that for a prophet to be heard there must be seekers. When the Quakers, after the first powerful generation, ceased to harbor seekers, they "had it." What they "had" was, and continues to be, good; but they were no longer on the growing edge.

An interesting aspect of leadership is that, whereas administrative responsibility in institutions can be assigned, authority given, and resources allocated, *anybody can lead!* Anybody can lead who can bring together and hold followers as an effective force. While the logical place for leadership of churches may be in seminaries (as I have argued in essays published under the title of "Seminary as Servant"), in fact, such leadership may come from anywhere. *If one strong growing-edge church emerges, it may lead the seminaries of all denominations into the role of servant of the churches—from which position seminaries might evolve into significant leaders of churches (which they seem not to be now).*

THE CHURCH AS AN INSTITUTION

Earlier I opined that "any influence or action that rebinds—that recovers and sustains alienated persons as caring, serving, constructive people—is religious. And any group or institution that nurtures these qualities effectively is a church." Thus, institutions that have other explicit functions may also be churches, and those that are called churches usually have several roles. The concern here is only with a church's influence as defined above.

Churches, along with other institutions, have taken their lumps in recent years. They share the consequences of a general disaffection with all institutions. This comes about, I believe, not so much because of a feeling that the quality of their performance has declined, as because expectations have risen. More people, especially young people, believe that the institutions that serve them, including churches, could and should do better, much better.

In the early 1950s, an important book, *The Organization Man*, was published. It was a well-written and sharp criticism of those who lead or manage our institutions. It was an immediate spectacular success. For years it was required reading in college courses, and perhaps still is. College bookstores had stacks and stacks of them. I had a curious experience as a result of the popularity of this book with students.

One day the editor who had managed the publication of this book came to see me. He told me he had felt that this book would be a commercial success; but he did not anticipate that it would have such a great influence on young people; it probably was one of several factors in the student unrest of the 1960s, and he was deeply disturbed by this. He felt the book had done some damage to young people.

He was enough of a realist to know that no critical book like this one, however successful, would change our institutions or the people who manage them—only make them angry. The editor also knew that these young people, if they were to make their way in this world, would have to come to terms with the world as it is; and, if they were strong and worked at it over a lifetime, they might change it a bit. The editor also believed that, with the state of mind these students were then in, caught up, as so many were, in a zeal for instant perfection—partly as a result of reading this book—they were going to be set back, and some might be permanently harmed. Then he made a proposition. "You have made a good life out of being an organization man in a huge business," he said. "If you will write a hopeful book about how life can be made fruitful in institutions as they are, we will publish it and put all of our promotional resources behind it. Our aim would be to lay it down beside *The Organization Man* in every college bookstore in the country." He had a contract in his pocket. This was quite an offer from a big prestigious publisher, especially to one like me who had never had a book published and had no public reputation to exploit.

I turned it down, for reasons that I believe can be deduced from reading this piece. But a lifelong friendship with the editor, now dead, ensued. I have made this digression from the subject, the institutional church, because I feel that it helps illuminate the problem of churches as institutions that want to serve young people.

Another anecdote further illuminates it. In an off-the-record discussion, a high-level church executive, a sensitive and thoughtful person, made this observation in all seriousness, "I have come to believe, after long experience in my job, that an important passage of scripture should be rewritten as—When two or three are gathered in my name, there is bound to be a fight about something."

As I reflected on this observation, it occurred to me that many of the conflicts that plague our society and make "conflict resolution" such an active endeavor in churches, is the simple matter that "manners" have declined. The houses of Congress would not be able to conduct their businesses without strict codes of manners.

My estimate of the chief institutional problem of some churches is that they have put too high a priority on *preaching* and too low a priority on *being*. The churches of today will have more influence on the quality of society as a whole (which means, to some extent, the quality of the institutions that comprise it) if they think of their prime influence as *being*, through what they model as institutions. It may be that what a church *is* as an institution will have more impact on its own members than what it *says* to them. This is not to denigrate what is said, that is terribly important—just not *as* important as what it *is*.

As I reflect on my business experience in which I did much meeting attending and some speechmaking, it stands out in my memory that the few exceptional companies that I came to know after I retired from AT&T were rarely represented as speakers or attenders at meetings. They were too busy doing the things that make them exceptional. And they probably knew (what I now know) that too many of the people making speeches were either just spinning words or talking about what I have now come to label as gimmicks. What would an astute observer say of the church world in this regard?

As I reflect on my experiences with the radical students in the 1960s I despair when I think of the sea of words they were engulfed in. Where were the models they might have learned from? Faculties had taken advantage of the teacher shortage, in the years of expansion of higher education after World War II, to bargain down their obligations to teaching. By the time the sixties' generations of students came along, they realized that, too much, they were supporting faculty who used their positions as pads from which to do their own things. There were other causes for the unrest, but this one helped direct the venom of the disturbed students to the universities and colleges—*as institutions*. Students of that period simply did not sense a sufficient dedication of teachers to their calling. The result was disaster in some places.

The ultimate model of servant is one whose service is rendered in one's own personal time for which one is not paid. Students saw too little of this model in the 1960s. They still don't see much of it, I am told. This is what my book *Teacher as Servant* is about. I tried to describe what a dedicated university professor who accepts this premise would be like.

Churches, then, have the opportunity to be institutional models for the universities. Many of those who teach in and administer universities as well as those who shape policies in business, government, hospitals, etc. attend churches. Do they just hear words, or do they see a model—a model of strength and effective religious leadership? And what would the model of a serving institution be like—*any* institution?

I realize there is a problem with the word *institution*. It has an ugly sound to some. I have looked into the etymology of that word and it does have a rather checkered history; but tucked away among the many historical meanings is: "something that enlarges and liberates." Is there any other single word that has that connotation? Let me suggest a definition for our purposes:

"An institution is a gathering of persons who have accepted a common purpose and a common discipline to guide the pursuit of that purpose, to the end that each involved person reaches higher fulfillment as a person, through serving and being served by the common venture, than would be achieved alone or in a less committed relationship."

Not all who "belong" to churches may want, or be capable of, firm commitment to a purpose like that described at the opening of this section. Unless a church serves only a selected constituency, it may need to maintain separate programs for homogeneous groups. I suggest that if a church is to be influential in shaping the culture, now and in the future, it must shelter within its active members a group of strong, assured, resourceful people so that each of them "reaches higher fulfillment as a person, through serving and being served by the common venture, than they would achieve alone or in a less committed relationship."

Such a church will be seen as strong.

GETTING HELP AND USING MONEY IN A CHURCH THAT ASPIRES TO BE ON THE GROWING EDGE

In my essay "The Institution as Servant," I defined the growing-edge church as "one that accepts the opportunity all churches have to become a significant nurturing force, conceptualizer of a serving mission, value shaper, and moral sustainer of leaders everywhere." I now suggest an amendment which holds that such a church will get its strength from harboring and nurturing an active group of seekers who are open to inspiration. A church that aspires to be on the growing edge in these terms, in the absence of leadership and support from seminaries, may need some help that it will pay for.

If one conceives of a church as I do, as an institution whose primary opportunity is to sustain contact with inspiration and infuse a healing, building influence into the world, finding a helper for the process of building a growing-edge church may be difficult. A church that does not aspire to wield an influence in the growing-edge role may find the usual services of commercial consultants congenial and helpful. But continued reliance on that source of help may build dependency rather than strength. Churches that aspire to be on the growing edge need to be strong, and they should seek help that builds strength.

While I was writing this, I received a phone call from a man who introduced himself as the administrator of a large Catholic hospital. He had read something I had written on the servant theme and asked whether I had written anything on how to conduct a Christian disciplinary interview with an employee. He was in need of help. I told him that I had not written on such detailed procedural matters, and, after a few pleasantries, the conversation terminated. He is a ripe prospect for a gimmick salesman.

Later I reflected, since the advice sought was in Christian terms, I might have suggested that if Jesus were among us today and were asked that question, there is a good chance that he might respond, "Become the full stature of the caring, serving person you have the potential to become and all will come clear to you on such matters."

Then I reflected, "Where is this man's church?" Good question. Where is his church? Is it on the growing edge? Does it aspire to be? Is it striving to be of practical help to those it reaches as they do the work of the world—including managing church-related institutions?

And where are the seminaries—200 in the United States, 60 of them Catholic? Consultants and gimmick salesmen, mostly good, conscientious people, seem to be trying to fill the gap created by the failure of seminaries to lead. But it may be that seminaries will not have the incentive to lead as long as consultants and gimmick salesmen seem to be filling the gap and are eagerly sought by churches because there are no other resources. Something needs to change. A church that gets the vision of becoming a growing-edge church may initiate the change, and may need some help. They will do well to find a helper who is wise and judicious and who has the vision and the patience to help that church to evolve a powerful formative character that will favor the growth of strong, caring, serving persons. The following experience comes to mind.

Back in the days when Richard King Mellon and Mayor Lawrence were bringing off their renaissance of Pittsburgh, I asked an old and wise friend who was well placed in a city of comparable site and not too far from Pittsburgh, why could not his city achieve this? His prompt response was that the reason was simple: his city did not have a Richard King Mellon. They could produce a Mayor Lawrence if they had a Mr. Mellon. Then he said, "We don't have anybody as rich as he is, but we have a few who are rich enough. The difference is that Mr. Mellon cares intensely about his city. Our rich people do not have his kind of caring. It is as simple as that."

Reflecting further on my own experience: the few institutions that I know intimately which, under close scrutiny, impress me as being exceptional seem to be led by people who have come much closer to their potentials as caring, serving people than most of us. They, like Mr. Mellon, do not need a consultant to tell them how to *act* as if they were human. They *are* human—and they just act naturally. They may need help to do some things they do not know how to do, but not with how to be human and caring. Formative experience is required for that. Such people who are human and caring live with an awareness of good work that is in harmony with the ultimate values they embrace. Their incentive to be human comes out of their faith. The crying need of our times is for greater formative resources for the growth of such people, a work for seminaries to initiate.

While I accept, grudgingly, that, in the absence of leadership and support by seminaries, churches that aspire to be on the growing edge and provide this formative experience may need, with caution, to pay for some help, I long for the day when churches generally will hold inspiration as their highest value and will acknowledge seekers who are not paid as their most precious resource.

RELIGIOUS LEADERS: A NEW FRONTIER

I think of religious leading as a new frontier because, as an explicit goal, it seems not to have been prominent in the concerns of religious thinkers. What then is the new opportunity? Is it not to make of existing religious institutions—churches, synagogues, temples, mosques, seminaries—laboratories for preparing leaders for a more caring society? Will not the first step be to prepare strong leaders for the work these religious institutions have to do, and then to share their mature experience with institutions generally? How will we do that, the incredulous may ask? Let them begin with William Blake's dictum: "What is now proved was once only imagin'd." And what will nurture their imagination? Let me suggest three subjects for reflection that have been prominent in this essay.

Persuasion

The move from the "control" model, that comes down almost unchanged from Moses, in the hierarchic principle, toward the "servant" model about which much remains to be learned, might begin with cultivating the attitudes that will permit the shift from coercion and manipulation to persuasion as the predominant modus operandi in institutions generally—including churches. Elsewhere I have written that one is persuaded on arrival at a feeling of rightness about a belief or action through one's own intuitive sense—checked, perhaps, by others' intuitive judgment, but in the end one relies on one's own intuitive guide. One takes that intuitive step from the closest approximation to certainty one can reach by conscious logic (sometimes not very close) to that state in which one may say with conviction, "This is where I stand." And this takes time! The one being persuaded must take that step alone, untrammeled by coercion or manipulative strategems. Both leader and follower respect the integrity and allow the autonomy of the other; and each encourages the other to find an intuitive confirmation of the rightness of the belief or action. Persuasion, thus defined, stands in sharp contrast to *coercion*—the use, or threat of use, of covert or overt sanctions or penalties, the exploitation of weaknesses or sentiments, or any application of pressure. Persuasion also stands in sharp contrast to manipulation, guiding people into beliefs or actions that they do not fully understand.

The religious leader will be persuasive and, insofar as humanly possible, will avoid any taint of manipulation or coercion. This is suggested as an indispensable condition of trust by followers or colleagues. Unilateral actions by leaders in emergencies, with later explanations, are more likely to be accepted as appropriate if the relationship is predominantly persuasive. But, in an imperfect world, there will be exceptions, and, no matter how it seems to the leader, some may see manipulation or coercion when the leader thinks they are not there. Perhaps discussion of the realities, in which lapses are acknowledged as failures, may be the most open course. Persuasion, when exercised by a leader, is not passive. It is dynamic, sustained, and challenging; and it may repel some who might be followers of a less insistent leader. The leader will be prepared for rebuff and failure and will need a sustaining spirit. John Woolman had such a sustaining spirit. Read his journal!

Seekers

Earlier it was suggested that prophet, seeker, and leader are inextricably linked. Sometimes two or three are merged in one person. But prophet and leader are seen as seekers first, who later evolve into other roles.

The seeker contributes ever-alert awareness and constant contact with available resources: spiritual, psychological, and material. Also, the seeker helps guard the religious leader against becoming trapped in one of those closed verbal worlds in which one's influence is limited to those who share one's exclusive vocabulary.

Seeking is also waiting and expecting and working with a sustained listening group that is ready to receive a prophetic vision. The group will have prepared itself to make discerning critical judgments about what they hear. Seekers are religious in that they share a discipline which sustains them as persons who are always prepared to respond to a new (but carefully examined) rebinding influence. An important part of the role of religious leaders is to provide the expectancy that sustains seekers.

Prophecy

The prophet, in William Blake's term, is one who imagines what will later be proved. Seekers will be listening and hear and test the validity of the idea, and religious leaders will carry the new idea into the work of the world.

It should be noted that in the 19th century Danish experience, Bishop Grundtvig did not offer a model of the Folk High School, nor did he himself found or direct such a school. He gave the vision, the dream, and he passionately and persuasively advocated that dream for over 50 years of his long life. He also gave the leadership. The indigenous leaders among the peasants of Denmark were listening and responded to that vision and built the schools—with no model to guide them. *They knew how to do it!* They were, in effect, the seekers of their time and place. Grundtvig gave them the prophetic vision that inspired them and communicated his confidence in their ability to act on what they knew.

Our restless young people in the 1960s wanted to build a new society too—and some still do; but their elders who could have helped prepare them for the task just "spun their wheels." They did not listen and gave little leadership. As a consequence of this neglect, a few of those young people simply settled for tearing up the place. And, in the absence of a new prophetic vision to inspire the effort to prepare our young people to build constructively, and leadership to help them do it, some of them may tear up the place again! Do not be surprised if they do just that. The provocation is ample. Among those in the older generation are some who could prepare today's young people to live productively in the 21st century. They know how to do that as well as 19th century Danish peasants did.

We live amidst a frightening shortage of ideas in all of our institutions, partly, I believe, because of the almost universal obsession about money. The nonprofits are so desperate for money that they can't produce the ideas that would make getting money easier. And businesses, financed as they are by the gigantic craps game that our society prescribes and in which our "best people" participate, are so eager for a quick buck that they can't produce the ideas that would give them a sound long-range future.

The serious deficiencies of our times may be in prophets who are not sufficiently realistic and inspired; in seekers who are not sufficiently humble, open, and dedicated listeners; and in enough religious leaders who are strong. As a consequence, ours is a poorly served society.

WHAT AND WHO SPEAKS TO
YOUNG POTENTIAL LEADERS?

Some effective religious leaders in every generation should be able to speak persuasively to potential leaders among the young—as Grundtvig and those who worked with him were able to do in 19th-century Denmark.

My principal experience with such young potential leaders, in my later active days, was with the radical students of the1960s. Colleges and universities of that period, when measured against the opportunities they had to help these able students mature into strong religious leaders, seemed not to have served those students well. I gather that their influence today in this regard is pathetically meager. Not much seems to have been learned from those trying times in the sixties—probably because of a paucity of seekers among faculty, administrators, or trustees.

What (or who) speaks to young potential religious leaders? I believe it is those who do what they can with what they have from where they are to build a better society. This communicates hope. Far too many of our able, well-meaning, well-placed contemporaries just spin their wheels. This communicates despair.

Small wonder that alienation is so widespread. Too much despair and not enough hope is being communicated!

LEADING VERSUS GOVERNING

We live in an age in which there is much talk about leading. Institutions in which there is little urge to do other than what they have done before, usually do not need leaders; able governance will suffice. But if, either out of necessity for survival or because they wish to serve better or more creatively, they want to do something that neither they nor others have done before, then leaders who are capable of venturing and risking—prudently—must emerge.

If followers are to respond voluntarily and with spirit, these leaders will do better if they have the dedication to persuasion and the language skills that will elicit this response from followers. People respond voluntarily and with spirit when something from the deep inner resources of the leader comes through to them. Competent and inwardly strong leaders who are by nature servants, and who are inspired by *religio,* can be the most influential of all when they have the gift of appropriate language *if,* in these times, they will address forcefully the interlocking problems of alienation and the failure of institutions to serve.

The need for many such religious leaders is urgent.

This is written as a sharing with those who aspire to be part of the vanguard of the effort to grow more religious leaders.

POSTSCRIPT

My perspective on the subject of religious leaders, as I said at the outset, is that of a student of organization, not of a theologian or scholar. From this perspective, I was prompted to state the central idea of this essay as *work! Do something! Work to increase the number of religious leaders who are capable of holding their own against the forces of destruction, chaos, and indifference.* Those who are in the vanguard of this effort will find ways to strengthen the hands of the strong who will become religious leaders. Such strong religious leaders will be an elite, one of the many kinds of elites. One of the blights on American life is our inability to face the fact that elites can serve. We have allowed *elite* to become a pejorative term. We need to be liberated from such constricting ideas. We must strengthen the hands of the strong who will be servants because only they can cope with the strong who are destructive and exploitative and who, unfortunately, are quite numerous. Increasing the number of religious leaders is not the only thing that needs to be done to make ours a better, nobler society; but unless we do that, other society-building efforts may not avail us much.

We do not need a new revelation to accomplish this. The machinery to move toward increasing the number of religious leaders (and I mean *large* numbers) is already in place: seminaries, to churches, to individuals, to "operating" institutions—governments, businesses, schools, social agencies. But this machinery is not working, not nearly well enough. Why is the machinery not working? I believe it is because seminaries that occupy the originating spot are not supplying the ideas and the language—the leadership—that they are best placed in the scheme of things to provide; and, without that leadership, churches are not likely to move forward in influence from where they now are. Furthermore, as long as seminaries occupy that spot and do not produce the ideas, and the language, and the leadership, it will be difficult for any other agency to do it *because* if the churches are to move, the effort must be supported by an appropriate theology.

It is a truism regarding any complex sequential process, social or mechanical, that if a vital link fails, the whole process fails. This is especially true if the originating point does not function. To get a steam engine to move, someone has to turn on the steam. If an institution, or a complex of institutions, is to move, someone has to lead.

Why do not the seminaries lead in a way that will help churches nurture religious leaders? Seminaries are staffed by able, thoughtful, conscientious people; why do they not give the needed leadership? I believe it is mainly because they do not see it as their role and, when pressed, they tend to say it is someone else's role—such as denominational bodies. And they have not prepared themselves to do it.

From my bias, the answer is simple: they do not have among their trustees, faculty, or administrators enough people who think in terms of how things get done in complex institutional arrangements. These people are a little rare, and I doubt if just one person—faculty, administrator, or trustee in a seminary—would survive if he or she tried to wield this influence alone. And it probably would not help just to give seminaries the idea, such as handing them this document. They need help, but probably a rare and special kind of help *from the outside*. They need help that is both persuasive and enduring because of the magnitude of the expected change. It is not that seminaries will need to abandon anything they now do; I am not judging that. But what they will need to add will make them radically different places because they will become primarily formative in their influence.

They need the kind of help that only a modern John Woolman is likely to give, because seminaries are tender, fragile institutions (all institutions, being collections of humans, are tender and fragile, but seminaries are a rare and special kind), and they need help in the spirit of great loving care. They not only need it, as everybody does, but help will not be effective without it.

John Woolman was passionately opposed to slavery, but this was shared with others who were so vehement in their opposition that, in the judgment of some historians, they helped make the Civil War inevitable. What made Woolman's persuasion effective, with no harmful side effects, and helped free the Religious Society of Friends of slavery 100 years before the Civil War, was that he loved the slaveholder with equal passion. He understood his dilemma, he was the slaveholder's friend, and he was willing to spend 30 years of all the time he could spare from earning his livelihood (he supported a small family) in visiting slaveholders over and over as he pressed his gentle but firm argument. In my judgment, this method will be effective with most reasonable people, including trustees, administrators, and faculties of seminaries who might be persuaded that they should enlarge their missions to include leading the churches as they wield their influence on people and institutions through the diffusion of religious leadership.

If the above is a reasonable assumption about the need and how to serve it, where are the Woolmans of this day, men and women who will understand and love and serve seminaries and the people who are in them? There are 200 seminaries in the United States, and I estimate that it will take 50 such able committed volunteer persons many years to give this service—each working with four seminaries. The 50 would be one in several million of the adult population. I think it a reasonable assumption that these 50 men and women exist and that they would rise to the opportunity to enrich their lives by giving this service—gratis. *And* I have confidence that some seminaries would, in time, respond to their service. The big question is how to find and prepare these 50 people—and finance it.

I went to sleep with this question on my mind and, as so often happens when I do this, I dreamed about it. (I am not a lawyer, but many years ago at AT&T, I was a member of a task force that was preparing an important law case for litigation. We had worked for six weeks and had not found a satisfactory basis to present our case—and trial time was nearing. We were under pressure. Then one night I had a dream in which we were in court. *I* was the lawyer pleading our case and I was arguing the very structure we needed. The case went to trial exactly as I dreamed it; but I never admitted to my colleagues how I got the idea.) I am now at the age when I am not as circumspect as I used to be, so I will share this one.

In my waking reverie the next morning, I was given a quite complete answer to the question of how can we find and prepare these 50 people—and finance it. After breakfast I went to my desk and wrote a fable [*Editor's note: published as "Fable," in* Seeker and Servant, *Robert Greenleaf, published in 1996 by Jossey Bass.*] in which I looked back from the year 2000, at which time a large number of churches in the United States had become strong influential institutions, alienation had declined, and the number of extraordinary serving institutions in the United States had increased. It is not a very good fable, but it does outline the steps that were taken to locate and prepare the 50 choice people whose persuasion caused enough seminaries to enlarge their programs to bring this about. I will send this fable to any who ask for it *if* I am assured that the asker aspires to be in the vanguard to which this paper is addressed.

What is now proved was once only imagin'd.

William Blake

6

Seminary as Servant

INTRODUCTION

The essays that follow were written in recognition of two pervasive social problems: (1) widespread alienation in all strata of the population, and (2) the inability or unwillingness to serve on the part of far too many of the institutions that make up our complex society. Each of these problems may be a contributing cause to the other, and neither is likely to be healed without coming to terms with the other.

I believe that new religious insight is needed to deal with the dilemma that this reciprocal dependency presents (*religious* in the root meaning of *rebind*). Such insight may come as a gift to any earnest seeker, but its availability to the many whose lives may be enriched by it will be greatly enhanced if seminaries embrace it, put it in

169

a context so that churches may mediate it, and give sustaining support to churches as they do their work. Any seminary that performs well in this role will be truly a servant in our times. But, as I argue later, this achievement is unlikely to come unless the stated missions of seminaries require it—mission statements that have clarity and power and the ring of contemporaneity. Such mission statements are not likely to emerge until seminary trustees give a character of leadership that is not yet generally accepted.

The three essays were written to encourage a few seminary trustees to use their influence to bring *one* seminary to the position of greatness as servant, both as a seminary and as a model of institutional quality that will be a powerful leaven in the culture. If one seminary will achieve this, the less venturesome may take courage and try.

The three essays were written in 1980, 1981, and 1983 at the suggestion of Dr. Robert W. Lynn, (then) vice president for Religion of Lilly Endowment, with whom I share a concern for enlarging the contribution of seminaries of all faiths to the enrichment of American society and to whom I am deeply indebted for helpful criticism of early drafts of these pieces. I am grateful for the incentive to write these because this work caused me to probe deeper than I might otherwise have done into facets of my long-held interest in institutions, large and small, and the place of trustees and directors, particularly their chairpersons, in assuring the optimal performance of these institutions.

Out of my probings, the idea of a *hierarchy of institutions* evolved. In this hierarchy I see, at the top, seminaries and foundations. Foundations are in that oversight position because they have the resources and the opportunity to gain perspective that enables them to provide conceptual leadership to colleges and universities, some of which seem in want of new directions which they are unable to find for themselves.

Seminaries are in a strategic position to give similar support to churches, whose needs are also urgent. In turn, both churches and universities are well placed to give nurture and guidance to individuals and to the whole range of "operating" institutions: governments, businesses, schools, hospitals, communities, families. Any effort to aid our ailing society might well start with a consideration of how the leadership of foundations and seminaries, each from its respective strategic position, might be made more effective.

In writing these essays, the role of trustees of seminaries and foundations received fresh scrutiny. I had written earlier on this subject ("Trustees as Servants"—Chapter III of *Servant Leadership*, Paulist Press, 1977), but in reflecting on the nature of this role in seminaries and foundations some new insights came. These two institutions, standing as they do at the top of the hierarchy of institutions, are in a precarious position (in their roles of servants of society) because they have little sheltering support available to them from other institutions. Since not many people are able as trustees to provide the constant regenerating influence that all institutions need if they are to serve and prosper over a long period of time, the durability of society rests on a few institutions (such as seminaries and foundations) acquiring self-regenerating capacity. These three essays are premised on the assumption that foundation and seminary executives and staffs, on their own, are not likely to provide this self-regenerating influence. It is for exceptional trustees to provide. "Exceptional" trustees are not necessarily high-status persons by other standards. The ablest trustee chairperson I have seen, in considerable involvement with trustees in a range of institutions, is a low-status person by other standards—but truly great as a trustee and in the chair.

Since exceptional trustees, by definition, are not common, if some of this small number can be drawn into the care of foundations and seminaries, these two can then spread the influence of their exceptional trustees to all institutions. I see no better way for a needy society (as ours is) to be well served by its ablest citizens. But seminaries and foundations will need to rise to this view of their opportunities and bring such exceptional trustees to their service, or inspire with new vision those they now have. Addressed here are the opportunities for seminaries. Elsewhere (chapter VI of *Servant Leadership*) I have discussed the opportunities available to foundations.

In the three essays that follow, I note that the perspective from which I approach the subject of seminaries and their missions is that of a student of organization, how things get done, not as a theologian or scholar. Included in my perspective is a longtime immersion in the writings of Machiavelli. It is my view that, while manifestations differ, joustings among contemporary power seekers (of whom there are plenty) are little different in their essentials from what they were in 16th-century Florence. Since I am now retired and no longer in the fray, I turn to Machiavelli periodically as a means for keeping myself refreshed about the nature of the society in which all live and do our work. I find no other commentator, ancient or contemporary, who is as clear, realistic, or insightful on the use of power in society as Machiavelli. Also, I find in his writing much wisdom that is useful to a person or institution that would be a servant in our time.

Against the dismal view of human nature that one gets from reading Machiavelli, I place the religion of hope (*religion* again used in its root meaning of *rebind*). I could not read this coldly realistic Florentine, and keep my sanity in this chaotic world, unless I had hope. Not hope that some miraculous intervention will banish evil so that good will prevail; I am not sure that I would be happy in such an aseptic place. My expectations are really modest: that a few able people who think of themselves as "good" will become more dedicated servants of society and will work a little harder and more astutely at it than some who think of themselves as "good" are now accustomed.

My short-run hope is that some of these able, good people will become trustees of seminaries and do what only inspired trustees are likely to do: work to give their seminary a vision of greatness that will lift it clearly out of the bureaucratic mold that engulfs so many institutions and set it on a course that will assure that it becomes the influential force that its top-of-the-hierarchy position makes possible.

My long-run hope—as expressed in the essay on "Mission"— is that, as the result of seminaries establishing their claim to this position, institutions whose primary motive is caring for persons and are governed by persuasion will rise to dominance in the culture over those that seem now to dominate: institutions that are governed by coercion and whose primary motive is private gain and survival in the competitive struggle.

It may be said that the quality of contemporary society is determined by the quality, as separate entities, of the legions of institutions that comprise it. The seminary will be an effective force in this composite as it wields its influence, through the churches, on both individuals and the institutions which they both govern and are governed by.

These three essays, addressed to seminary trustees, are made available for wider distribution because I feel they may be of some interest to those who share my concern for the quality of institutions generally. Further, one who is trustee of a quite different institution from a seminary may be stimulated to produce insights of immediate relevance to one's primary trustee obligation. Then, from my perspective, all institutions are drawing closer together when judged by the challenges they present to their trustees and directors. In the interest of furthering discussion of areas of common ground, these three essays on seminaries and their trustees and chairpersons are offered to all trustees and directors of institutions of all kinds.

The three essays, while having different emphases, are not three distinct chapters. They are three discussions of the same subject written a year or two apart. The second and third reflect growth in thinking after the first. They are offered now, not as a definitive treatise on either seminaries or trusteeship, but rather as a sharing of introspection on what I believe is a common interest with the reader: Where can one best put one's effort to build a better society? I see a "good" society as one in which there is widespread *faith as trust*, a quality that encourages people to become constructive influences in the world as it is—violent, striving, unjust as well as beautiful, caring, and supportive.

Caring for persons, the more able and the less able serving each other, is what makes a good society. Of all the institutions I know about, I would put the most stringent test of caring on seminaries because I believe that they hold, potentially, through the churches, the greatest leverage to influence the caring, serving quality of the whole society.

These essays are offered in the hope that they will encourage trustees of just one seminary to give leadership to theologians who will generate similar ideas about how our low-caring society might do better, who see things whole; and who have the gift of language so they can tell ordinary mortals what they think and see—folk who, by what they do or refrain from doing, make or break the society.

The Seminary as an Institution

I venture to discuss the seminary as an institution, not as a theologian, but as a student of organization. I hope that what I have to say from this perspective will be of interest to all constituencies of seminaries, but my primary concern is to speak to trustees, particularly the chairpersons of trustees, who may not have been trained in a seminary. It may be helpful if I share how I came by my interest in organization and what leads me to a special concern for seminaries.

Up to 20 years ago, most of my concern about organization was directed toward one large business where I had my major career: American Telephone and Telegraph Company. In my later years there, I held the position of Director of Management Research. With the help of a professional staff, and within a broad charter, I was both involved and detached so that I could study and advise regarding the management of this huge institution (over 1 million employees) immersed as it is in sophisticated technology, elaborate human organization, and regulated public service. I was concerned, among other things, with its values, its history and myth, and, intimately, with its top leadership. I learned the hard way about the profound influence that history, and the myths of institutions that have considerable history, have on values, goals, and leadership. And I was painfully aware of the cost in those terms of any insensitivity to history and myth—especially among the top officers.

This experience at AT&T gave me a good perspective and the impetus to venture, in my retirement years, into a close working relationship with a wide range of institutions: universities (especially in the turbulent sixties); foundations (both as trustee, consultant, and staff member); churches (both local, regional, and national) and church-related institutions; professional associations, and businesses—in the United States, in Europe, and in the Third World. This brought me, in time, to a realization of the crucial role of trustees in the performance of any institution, anywhere, and the strategic leadership opportunity in the position of chairperson. This led to writing a monograph on "Trustees as Servants" [available from The Greenleaf Center].

In my later years, as I have had more time for reflecting and writing, and as I have become more aware of the fragile nature of our whole society, I have asked myself the question, where, in the vast range of institutions that serve us, is there the greatest unrealized potential—potential for constructive influence on the whole society? My answer is, of course, a subjective judgment, but I have concluded: *seminaries*, seminaries of all faiths, particularly in our country. Simply in terms of the prudent use of resources, I believe that more can be done to raise the quality of our total society than in any other one way, *if* seminaries of all faiths could move closer to their full potential as servants. (The word *servant* has special significance to me; but rather than attempt to define it explicitly at this point, I would prefer that the meaning that word has for me be permitted to evolve as one reads further.)

I have had a fairly long contact with seminaries because, in my AT&T role of concern for values of that institution, I sought a relationship with professors of ethics in Protestant, Catholic, and Jewish seminaries. Some of these developed into lasting friendships which endure to this day. I invited some of these professors to meet with my AT&T colleagues, and I arranged for them to lecture in programs for executives. My relationship with them was close enough to permit me to have an insider's view in several seminaries. Then, later, I served six years on the Visiting Committee at Harvard Divinity School. More recently, I have read some of the history of seminaries and have talked with historians about the implications of this history.

Even without this involvement with seminaries, out of work with churches and church institutions and my later introspection about the structure of society, I believe that I would have come to my present view regarding the crucial role available to seminaries. I hold this view because of the strategic space seminaries seem to me to occupy, or could occupy, in the hierarchy of institutions in which seminaries have the opportunity to give sustaining support to churches, and churches, in turn, can give religious nurture and moral guidance to individuals directly and support (as conservers of traditions and advocates of values) the whole gamut of "operating" institutions: governments, schools, businesses, hospitals, social agencies, philanthropies, families, communities. The strength and durability of our democratic institutions rest on the wide acceptance and practice of a common moral code. And I see the seminaries as having the potential to hold the prime position of supporting the churches as they work to foster religious concern and to strengthen the moral basis of society.

When I say that seminaries have the opportunity to give sustaining support to churches I mean much more than training their pastors, important as that service is. I see the opportunity for the seminary to stand as a constant source of intellectual rigor and prophetic vision, of spiritual energy and as the support and inspiration for strong leadership and society-shaping influence in the churches. One of the simple truths that survives from my business experience is that it is possible for able conceptual leadership in a central staff to sustain exceptional performance in an almost unlimited number of local operating units which, on their own, would be quite ordinary. Further, in my experience, this exceptional performance is best achieved by persuasive conceptual leadership, without coercion or authority. At the core of this unusual business is an assembly in basic science that has been called the closest thing to a university outside the university, and that has produced, in its time, seven Nobel Laureates. This, I believe, is the source of the strong conceptual leadership that I experienced. If a business can make this principle viable, a seminary also has the opportunity to do it—and better. *Please note that I have only said that the seminary has the opportunity, because of its place in the hierarchy of institutions, to give this leadership. If it is to exploit this opportunity, it must generate sufficient leadership power—with its own resources.* (Foundations have a similar opportunity, largely unexploited, to serve colleges and universities.)

As I see churches today—churches of all faiths—they are struggling to shore up a deteriorating society without much sustaining support—from seminaries, or, with few exceptions, from anywhere else. This brings me to the observation that seminaries (from the perspective of a student of organization), in general, and as they now stand, are marginal institutions. They are judged marginal because, in our highly institutionalized society, they do not carry the weight of influence and leadership that their place in the scheme of things makes possible. I sense that they are marginal in their own self-image, in the eyes of their principal constituency, the churches, and in the public view. While seminaries perform an acknowledged necessary function, the training of pastors, they do not generally provide the sustaining support and prophetic leadership for churches, for which they are correctly positioned and of which I believe they are potentially capable. The gap between seminaries and churches is not likely to be healed by a reach from the churches. The initiative rests with seminaries.

In saying these things, I am not suggesting for seminaries an unrealistic utopian achievement. What is reasonable and possible with available resources, human and material, is the standard I would apply. I would like to see all seminaries, seminaries of all faiths, reach from where they now are to attain much more of the reasonable and possible—each seminary with its own resources and within its own vision of what it ought to do and to be. I am confident that any seminary that makes this reach, and thereby moves from the marginal stance toward a central and crucial role, will find a much more rewarding institutional existence than what many now enjoy. And I believe that the typical seminary can make this movement, over time, by a series of prudent steps—prudent, but not necessarily comfortable. Prudent, because each seminary will build from its own resources, human and material, with understanding and respect for, and within the vision defined by, its own history and myth. It will not be simple or easy, and it will be a major creative challenge. The first step for a seminary may be to accept that, next to survival, building leadership strength—to lead the churches—may be its first priority in these times.

Premise

Occasionally institutions of all categories (including seminaries) rise to the exceptional under the long-term direction of an unusually able administrator. But, usually, when that administrator leaves, the institution lapses, in time, back to the ordinary. There are not enough of these exceptional administrators around to fill all top administrative posts of all institutions with such persons. Even if, potentially, such gifted administrators were abundant, the common wisdom does not yet provide a way to bring them all into top positions. Able top administrators, with occasional exceptions, have always been, and probably always will be, just ordinary, good people. The challenge is how to bring an institution to exceptional performance with ordinary good people to administer and staff it. The premise here is that ordinary good people as trustees, and with such a person chairing the work, can do it—*if* they are sustained by a concept of greatness as their goal; greatness as servants of society—in the case of a seminary, greatness in service to churches and through churches to society. What kind of belief builds confidence in this premise?

    For one who grew up in the Christian tradition as I did, the roots, of course, are biblical—"whoever would be great among you must be your servant, and whoever would be first among you must be your slave"—(Matthew 20: 26 and 27). The choice of the word *slave* for the one who would be first suggests that the trustee chairperson will have an unusual dedication and caring concern. My own personal credo is stated thus:

I believe that caring for persons, the more able and the less able serving each other, is what makes a good society. Most caring was once person to person. Now much of it is mediated through institutions—often large, powerful, impersonal, not always competent, sometimes corrupt. If a better society is to be built, one more just and more loving and providing opportunity for people to grow, the most open way (and the most effective and economical course, while supportive of the social order) is to raise the performance as servant of as many institutions as possible by voluntary regenerative actions initiated within them by committed individuals: servants.

Part of the human dilemma in our times is that there is little in our biblical tradition, or anywhere else, that suggests what makes a servant—or a serving institution—in our highly institutionalized society. There is evidence that ours is a low-caring (poorly served) society, and concern for this condition has resulted in large-scale actions by government (1) to provide money to alleviate suffering and correct injustice, and (2) to give rewards and penalties to compel both individuals and institutions to behave in more socially constructive ways. In an imperfect world, some of these actions will always be needed. But compulsion is of limited use except to restrain destructive behavior and encourage conforming acts, and money does little other than cushion suffering and injustice. Neither compulsion nor money has much utility in causing institutions to be reconstructed as more caring and more serving. Only the voluntary actions of people inside an institution can accomplish this.

There is a stirring within some institutions today to improve their serving qualities. But this seems to be mostly exhortation or tinkering with procedures, "gimmicks." Much of it is a sort of "aspirin" treatment that produces a short-lived easing of the pain, but little fundamental change may result from it. However, these efforts have produced a burgeoning literature. The occasional institution that achieves high servant stature under the direction of a gifted administrator who has such a goal is usually conspicuous by the absence of the common "gimmicks" (such as those that are promoted under such labels as "Management by Objectives," "Planned Program Budgeting," etc.). A strong, healthy institution, as with a person, is not built by the aspirin treatment.

I cite these conditions not to pronounce a jeremiad on our society (although such may be warranted). Rather, I simply contend that there is little to date in our collective experience with institutions that trustees of a seminary may draw on as they seek to raise their seminary to greater servant stature. If the assumption of the hierarchical arrangement (seminaries to churches, and from churches to individuals and to operating institutions) is a valid one, it may be that other institutions will follow, rather than set models for, seminaries. How to produce an exceptional serving institution with ordinary good people to staff and lead it is the goal. If a few seminaries can demonstrate how, other institutions may be encouraged to try.

How to Do It

If, as has been suggested, seminaries have the opportunity to provide strong leadership to churches, and churches, in turn, can provide it to both individuals and to the many operating institutions, then, in concept and vision, a seminary needs to be wholly self-regenerating. No other institution stands as an available resource for seminaries. This means that a seminary, of all institutions, needs the caring support of able and dedicated trustees who are led by an unusually strong chairperson. And these trustees will need to find their way to a constructive role in helping to move the particular seminary from marginal status toward its optimum as a servant of the churches—and society. The question is, how to do it?

The answer to this question will need to be discovered for each seminary, for itself. Most seminaries have considerable history. There are doctrinal differences between schools and within faculties. Their faculties and administrators are unique individuals, they vary in age and adaptability, and most have quite firm, and probably differing positions regarding what a seminary ought to be. Financial resources differ. There are widely varying patterns of relationship to constituencies. All of these aspects combine to give the particular seminary its individual character, and the critical aspects need to be taken into account by trustees who wish to give the seminary new leadership. If trustees are to give new leadership, one generalization is risked: New seminary leadership from trustees is not likely to be asked for by faculty or administrators; nor is the overt offering of such leadership apt to be welcomed. But, then, rarely is leadership asked for or welcomed in any situation short of a condition of overwhelming confusion or imminent disaster. *Leadership* is one of the most talked about and least understood ideas in contemporary discussions. At its best, leadership is a subtle process. As the ancient Taoist proclaimed: "When the leader leads well, the people will say 'we did it ourselves!'" Leadership needs to be offered, and, if effective, it is voluntarily accepted.

Trustees of a seminary who choose to assert constructive leadership are confronted with an anomaly: they are charged by law with *managing* the institution, and they stand in the position of ultimate responsibility. They possess coercive power, and all who hold coercive power find their ability to lead is clouded by that fact, because leadership rests mostly on persuasion and the responses to it are voluntary, not coerced. And when any person who holds coercive power attempts to lead, there is apt to be the unasked question, "Where is the hidden agenda?" Further, while trustees hold legal power, faculties, by long tradition, have evolved a de facto power that is probably more potent. Evidence of the effectiveness of new constructive leadership by trustees may be the emergence of new transforming leadership among faculty and administrators, and *this* is the leadership that will move the seminary from a marginal to a central or crucial role.

What can be said at this point, in advance of experience to

confirm the above assertions, about the distinguishing characteristics of constructive trustee leadership in a seminary?

Constructive Trustee Leadership

Constructive trustee leadership begins with continuing to do well what trustees generally do now, such as: serve as legal cover and public image builder for the institution; raise money; authorize and audit the use of money; render gratis consulting services; take those actions required by the charter and bylaws; appoint or dismiss administrative officers; and stand as the court of last resort if internal administration and staff reach an impasse. These are all useful services that help keep the institution viable, but they are maintenance functions; they do not constitute *leadership*, in the commonly accepted meaning of *lead*, to go out ahead to show the way.

Parallel with these usual activities, and perhaps independently, trustees will start the search for the most constructive leadership role for themselves, for this seminary, and in these times. What is sought, it is hoped, is a prudent evolutionary movement that is congruent with the seminary's development up to now. What might be the direction of this movement?

The idea of trusteeship goes back to the person who was entrusted to manage the affairs of another. The concept of a governing board of trustees of an institution is relatively new because the vast structure of institutions that serve us now is rather recent—in the last 200 years, with much of it in this century. Two hundred years ago there were governments, armies, churches, and a few universities. But the common lot was life in families and simple communities with most people partly or wholly self-sustaining with the support of modest commerce. To the extent that lives were guided by a theology, it was a theology of persons.

The American constitution makes no mention of the common form of institution, the corporation, because they scarcely existed when our constitution was written. Corporations get their legal status because of the willingness of the courts to construe them as persons. Likewise, our available theology usually turns out to be a theology of persons, and there is little to turn to in our theological resources for guidance as to how institutions shall be brought under the shelter of theology—and thereby be made more humane and more serving. If one views *all* institutions, large or small, as I do: as intricate webs of fallible humans groping for meaning, order, and light—then, at the core, the problem of all institutions is, has always been, theological. Seminary trustees who seek a more constructive leadership role may find that the best basis for eliciting a new transforming leadership from faculty and administrators will be to start the deliberations leading to a new theology of institutions which the seminary, with the involvement of all of its constituencies, will labor to bring forth, and with the seminary's own institutional development as the laboratory.

The terms *theology of persons* and *theology of institutions* are not in common parlance. They are used here to suggest that, to a nontheologian like myself, who is concerned about the crucial role that seminaries could carry, there is a question about the adequacy of the theological resources of seminaries to support churches so that churches can be of greater help to legions of people who are immersed in the mass of institutions that make up contemporary society. Trustees may want to raise the question, "Are the theological resources of the seminary—whatever they are—adequate for this particular support?" Whatever the answer is, there is an opening for dialogue between trustees and faculty and administrators on what may prove to be one of the more important issues of the late 20th century—important for seminaries, for churches, for all of us.

If a seminary trustee is, as I am, a nontheologian, she or he will venture with caution in raising a question about the adequacy of theology. Yet, as a trustee, the issue must be faced—just as a layman who is trustee of a hospital must be prepared to question the practice of medicine, or the lay trustee of a university must be prepared to question the process of education.

The adequacy of any theology is tested, ultimately, by examining what it produces in the lives of people who have its implications interpreted for them through the mediation of churches. The issue of the adequacy of the available theology of institutions is an appropriate concern for seminary trustees who are searching for their most constructive role because *this* theology addresses both institutions in general and *this* seminary as an institution, in particular.

It is an interesting question. Anyone can make a contribution to theology; but established theologians are best positioned to originate and advocate a new theology of institutions—*and be heard*. However, nontheologians who are keeping a close watch on our institutions will make the ultimate judgment on the adequacy of that theology. One test they will apply is: What comes through to trustees and directors of institutions of all sorts, for profit or not for profit, that induces them to take and sustain initiatives that result in the institutions they hold in trust becoming substantially more serving than most now are to all the persons they touch? Other nontheologians will make other tests of the adequacy of other theologies—in terms of their ultimate consequences in the lives of people.

Constructive trustees of any institution will listen carefully to those who make the ultimate tests of adequacy of that institution's service. What makes seminary trusteeship especially interesting and challenging is that the seminary has the potential for influencing such a wide gamut of human affairs.

Preparation for Trusteeship

How can seminary trustees initiate the move toward a more constructive role for themselves, and give the new leadership that helps bring the seminary to optimal strength as a servant of society?

They might first seek to clarify for themselves, and for all constituencies, what the history and myth of their particular seminary is, and they may find much of it is not written and that no single person knows it all. (*Myth* is used in the sense of a story that relates historical events and that serves to explain some practice or belief.)

Then they might gather and study the literature on seminaries in general, which is considerable, and of varying quality, and encourage other constituencies to do the same. There have been studies, some recent, by individuals and groups that raised the issues about seminary purpose and the content and method of theological education.

Trustees, particularly their chairperson, will need to take the time to meet and discuss with faculty, administrators, students, alumni, church representatives, and denominational officers—if it is a denominational seminary. Trustees might attend faculty meetings, student assemblies, and occasional classes in rotation—all if invited. Also they could meet with students in small groups where issues in the seminary are being discussed. While this work may be shared, seminary trustees will do well to accept at the outset that their role with this unique kind of institution will make a large claim on their time.

Out of these discussions, the trustees will discover that seminaries, in the course of their history, took on the values of universities and that their faculties tended to assume the characteristic university position, "the faculty is the university." This position in both university and seminary may have come about by default. No one else, trustees for instance, concerned themselves with defining the institution, so faculties, with their large career stake, defined it as themselves. The first concern of seminary trustees in search of a new leadership role may be to search for the idea, the unifying vision, that will define the seminary.

Conceptual leadership by trustees may best be manifested by questions. The trustee is the asker, not the answerer of questions. *Whom and what purpose should this seminary serve?* This may be the prime question to be asked of all constituencies of the seminary. The faculty contribution to answering that question will be very important, but not the only source. Gradually, faculties may be led to accept the *servant* role: that their best part is to serve whatever purpose evolves from the deliberate search conducted by trustees, a search in which they have had a majority but not exclusive role.

I suggest that the key to greatness, in a seminary or in any other institution, is the quality of the dream, the vision, and the primacy of that dream as the ultimate government. Every person, every constituency, stands subordinate to the dream. Helping the dream to evolve and nurturing it is the first consideration in trusteeship.

Trustees, in giving leadership, should be ever-mindful of the sensitivity of faculty members to the faculty role in governance and of their apprehension about the trustees' use of their power. Faculty will be concerned that trustees have a sufficient understanding, in depth, of the faculty's perception of the nature of a seminary.

Seminary trustees might also be aware, as they pursue the search for the answer to the question of purpose, that they will never answer it, definitively or for all time. Yet, at any one time, the seminary should be proceeding with assurance to serve a clearly identified constituency with a firm purpose in mind. Part of the art of trusteeship is to maintain a balance between *order* and *stability* and *search*. Search, for any institution or any person, should never end. Balance between the two is important, because, in any institution, there is an optimum tension between order and search. Either too little or too much tension is destructive. Further, except for the rare seminary that has funds at its disposal to engage new staff for new programs, trustees will acknowledge that their seminary can undertake only what they, the trustees, can persuade the existing faculty to accept.

Once a workable answer, for the present, has been achieved for the question, *Whom and what purpose shall this seminary serve?* the next question for trustee concern might be: *What shall be the content of the teaching and how shall it be taught?* Here, again, the trustee is the asker, not the answerer of the question. The aim is to find the best possible curriculum and method to implement the goal established in answer to the first question. Again, faculty opinion will be important, but not necessarily governing. And, again, unless there is money for new staff, the seminary can undertake only what the trustees can persuade the existing faculty to accept and *learn to do*. Two further questions may be asked by trustees: *How can the semi-*

nary best support churches? How can the seminary be a constant source of prophetic vision?

When Karl Marx sat alone in the British Museum evolving the theories that would shape so much of the 20th-century world, was he not filling a void that resulted from failure of the churches of his day to come forth with a new prophetic vision that the conditions of the industrial revolution made imperative? But Marx apparently did not foresee the institution-bound society that was evolving as he wrote. And Marxist nations, today, are plagued with the same problem we are: how to make their complex institutions more serving. Thus there is now another void, worldwide—a crisis of institutional leadership. Who will produce a new vision to fill *this* void?

Thoughtful people today are complaining about ours being a "media-dominated" culture, to our detriment. Could it be that, in the absence of an adequate theology of institutions, the media are simply filling the void?

This question helps define the opportunity for new trustee leadership in seminaries.

Persuasion—Prime Art of Trustee Leadership

Trustees, if they are to lead constructively, will understand the meaning of, and be gifted in, the art of *persuasion*.

One is persuaded, I believe, on arrival at a feeling of rightness about a belief or action through one's own intuitive sense—perhaps checked by another's intuitive sense but, in the end, one's own intuitive feeling will govern. One takes an intuitive step from the closest approximation to certainty to be reached by conscious logic (sometimes not very close) to that state in which one may say with conviction, "This is where I stand." The act of persuasion will help order the logic and favor the intuitive step. And this takes time! But the one being persuaded must take that intuitive step alone, untrammeled by coercion or manipulative stratagems. Both leader and follower respect the integrity and allow the autonomy of the other; and each

allows and encourages the other to find his or her own intuitive confirmation of the rightness of the belief or action.

If persuasion is ever to rise over coercion and manipulation as the
prevailing modus operandi in our violence-prone society, then the
clear model of an institution that is led by persuasion alone needs to
emerge in the most influential spot possible. I believe that some seminaries have the potential to occupy that spot—to be influential models for other institutions, to *be the civilizing models!*

In summary, trustees have the opportunity, by astute and persistent questioning and persuasive leadership, to encourage the seminary to: (1) *Evolve an adequate theology of institutions for these times.* (2)
*Define in contemporary terms whom and what purpose this seminary can
best serve.* (3) *Find the best curriculum and method to serve those people and
that purpose.* (4) *Give effective support to churches in the full scope of their
missions.* (5) *Become significant sources of prophetic vision, places that are
looked to for guidance and light.* A seminary that can achieve these
through its existing staff and with its present resources will become a
model for the regeneration of all kinds of institutions.

Glittering innovations can always be produced by new people
and new money. How can we do better with the people and the
money we now have? This is the urgent plea of so many who would
become constructive trustees or directors of the all-too-many low-
serving institutions of our times.

What guidelines might be useful to the seminary chairperson
who would like to make the first move—to do better, much better,
with the money and the people the seminary now has?

The Chairperson

All leadership positions are to some extent lonely posts. The chairperson of seminary trustees is no exception. Even if, among fellow
trustees, there are close friends, some detachment is required. One's
leadership strategy, whatever it is, should involve one with all trustees
on the same terms. While there will be occasional conversations with

individual trustees, there should be no grounds for suspicion that some trustee responses are prearranged. I know this contradicts the perception of some experienced trustees; but I am postulating here some conditions for a level of trustee performance that most have not experienced. The chairperson's role *should* be a lonely one. The trustee is what the title implies, the bearer of trust. And the chairperson, if well chosen, stands tall among colleagues in this dimension.

If the above is a reasonable assumption, and if the chairperson of a seminary wants to give leadership to trustees who will have a chance of being the constructive influence described earlier, then a confidant or coach for the chairperson should be sought. This should be someone who is completely uninvolved in the seminary. Every person who carries a difficult or sensitive role needs a confidant or coach. The administrators of the seminary may need such help. But the need of the chairperson is perhaps the most difficult to serve.

In choosing to relate to a confidant or coach, the chairperson is acknowledging that if the seminary is to move toward its higher potential as a servant of society the one who occupies the chair must be the first to become a learner. But since there is no clear body of knowledge about how to chair effectively, the one who occupies that spot must evolve the strategy for giving new leadership out of one's own experience through interaction with a coach.

All trustees should, as individuals or through committee participation, have some firsthand relations with all constituencies—especially faculty and students. There should be sufficient interaction so that, in their official deliberations, trustees have an experiential basis for good intuitive judgment on matters of trustee concern. The chairperson should have, in addition, a close relationship to administrators so that there is encouragement for dynamic leadership by all administrators. Also, the chairperson will want to help other trustees gain perspective for their evaluative judgment about administrative performance. This is a subtle process: to be close enough to administrative action to be helpful and encouraging, and to be critical and evaluative, but still to be detached enough so that administrators have sufficient scope for initiative and creativity to carry their roles with spirit. The chairperson should instruct the coach and confidant to be particularly watchful over this relationship between the chairperson and administrators.

All trustees should participate in evaluating administrators. But the chairperson should be prepared to provide more extensive data about administrators than any other trustee is likely to have.

The chairperson also has the obligation to build respect for trustee judgments among all constituencies. Trustees, by law, have the power to govern. But like all such power, its value is inverse to the extent of its use. It is important that the power be there, but *influence*, growing out of respect for trustee judgments, is the critical trustee asset. The chairperson, in consultation with the coach-confidant, should develop a clear strategy for building and sustaining trustee influence. This influence will depend on the evident trustworthiness of trustees as demonstrated by: *(1) The quality of greatness of the dream that evolves for the seminary and what it might become as a servant of society. (2) The dedication of trustees in terms of their investment of time and their caring for people—all of the people in the seminary. (3) The adequacy of their information about the seminary. (4) Their ability and disposition to persuade. (5) Adherence to collegiality and careful group process in reaching their judgments—a process that is understood by all constituencies.*

Trustworthiness, in the above terms, augurs for confidence in trustee judgments by all who are asked to accept them. The chairperson will be aware of elements like these that build trust, and will be watchful and diligent to encourage their optimum manifestation among seminary trustees. This, it seems to me, is the essence of leadership from the chair.

Not all persons who have a talent for leadership are effective in all situations at all times. If the seminary chairperson finds, after a reasonable time, that his or her leadership is not adequate for this institution at this time, then they should quietly step aside so that someone else can try. Every seminary, every institution, deserves an effective leader in their chairperson—all of the time.

Summary Comment

Three words are commonly used in reference to the oversight of an institution: *manage, administer,* and *lead.* Manage (from *manus,* hand) connotes control. *Administer* (from *administrare,* to serve) has the sense of "care for." These two, manage and administer, may be seen as the maintenance functions, terribly important but concerned mostly with conservation and perpetuation.

Lead is a word of less certain origin. Whereas management and administration usually derive from delegated authority from trustees, *leading* in the commonly accepted meaning of going out ahead to show the way, can be undertaken by anybody. The only test of leadership is that somebody follows. Following, as distinguished from compliance, is voluntary. Thus *strong* leadership can bring unity and clarity of purpose and uncertain leadership can bring disorder and chaos. The latter was conspicuous in the university world, including some seminaries, in the late 1960s.

Those who manage or administer in a seminary can also lead—and most do some leading. But consider the five basic questions cited above. *Are the theological resources of the seminary adequate? Whom and what purpose does the seminary serve? What should be the content and teaching method of the seminary? How best to serve the churches? How can the seminary be a constant source of prophetic vision?* These are questions that are best dealt with if there is at least supporting leadership from trustees. Trustees, in their more detached position, can afford to be persistent questioners and visionaries. Administrators, to whom have been delegated the essential maintenance functions, may find that if they undertake this type of leadership alone, it interferes with administrative obligations. Faculty may more readily respond, with transforming leadership of their own, to a trustee initiative than to some administrative initiatives. If trustees will take the risk of leadership toward a larger dream for the seminary, they may do it in a non-confrontational, persuasive way that elicits supportive leadership from other constituencies. Administrators may best give supporting leadership on some matters, if trustees will lead by questioning and persuading.

If a seminary is to move toward its full potential as harborer and nurturer of prophetic voices that give vision and hope, what is needed first is leadership that wants to take the risk of such a larger dream. And it is a risk. All leadership is nurturing and risking. Trustees and their chairperson are more expendable than able administrators. And some of the risks of leadership of a seminary, or any other institution, are best taken by trustees—partly because they can better tolerate the risk, partly because they are better positioned to assume some aspects of leadership.

Leadership does not "belong" to anybody, nor can it be bestowed on anybody. If trustees want to lead, they will need to build a role for themselves, including earning the trust that makes it possible. One of the contributions seminary trustees can make to our evolving society is to build the trustee role so as to make of the seminary a distinctive institution, a model for others.

Some respond to the thrust of this essay with these reservations: the hope expressed here for the role of seminaries is too idealistic; trustees are not available who will invest the time required; the money-raising role of the trustees has not been mentioned—most seminaries are poor; and the usual chairperson does not have the leadership skills that the role, as described in this essay, calls for.

Too Idealistic. What, in the end, will be judged too idealistic is that which is not achieved when the limits of the reasonable and possible with available resources, human and material, are reached. Most institutions I know about, including some seminaries, are so far from pressing the limits of the reasonable and the possible that the charge "too idealistic" has little force. The goals suggested here may be flawed on other grounds, but not on that one.

Not Enough Time. Most able people find the time to do the things that give them joy. In my experience with trustees, whether as participant or observer, I have found some of the proceedings so dull and unrewarding that only a strong sense of duty, a feeling of guilt, or a desire for the prestige of the office would hold a person to it. But the joy of creative achievement will elicit the investment of time—and care—that the full measure of trusteeship requires.

Who Will Raise The Money? How can trustees be expected to raise money when, in the usual seminary, they have only a maintenance role? Give them the kind of role described here, and they will want to raise money; not out of a sense of guilt or duty, which are not very good motives, but because they understand and believe in what the seminary is about. It is a matter of vital concern to them because they have given decisive leadership in bringing the seminary for the 21st century into being.

Inadequate Leadership Skills. Granted; the usual chairperson may not have developed the skills of leadership that the trusteeship function described here requires. Even though the incumbent may be potentially capable of acquiring those skills, they are not likely to emerge at a high level of accomplishment because they are not expected. The almost universally accepted casual performance of trustees in all sorts of institutions assures that the full maturing of these skills will be rare. Since leadership is a prime concern in the churches, should it not be a central issue in seminaries, both its theological implications and its sensitive practice? Let me restate my personal credo:

I believe that caring for persons, the more able and the less able serving each other, is what makes a good society. Most caring was once person to person. Now much of it is mediated through institutions—often large, powerful, impersonal, not always competent, sometimes corrupt. If a better society is to be built, one more just and more loving and providing opportunity for people to grow, the most open way (and the most effective and economical course, while supportive of the social order) is to raise the performance as servant of as many institutions as possible by voluntary regenerative actions initiated within them by committed individuals: servants.

Too much of the effort to care and serve is directed to easing the hurt of the "system" that is grinding people down faster than the most valiant rescue effort can help them; and too little caring effort is going into rebuilding the "system" (institutions) that will give greater assurance that those being served grow as persons; *while being served*, they become healthier, wiser, freer, more autonomous, more likely themselves to become servants.

If the *performance as servant* of as many as possible of our institutions is to be raised (a necessary condition if ours is to become a more caring society), then somewhere there must be an initiative that starts the movement toward this end. If my premise regarding the hierarchy of institutions—seminaries to churches to individuals and operating institutions—is a valid one, then seminaries are best positioned to take this initiative.

Whoever takes this initiative (and I hope it will be seminaries) will accept the challenge to bring into being a new teachable art of chairing—beginning with the chairperson of the seminary itself.

Then, drawing on its own experience, the seminary may find that it is in possession of the stuff for a prophetic vision for these times. This is my hope for the seminary as an institution.

"What is now proved was once only imagin'd."

William Blake

MISSION IN A SEMINARY

One of the easiest to ask and hardest to answer of all questions is, *What are you trying to do?*

It is hard enough for an individual to answer that question. But it is much more difficult for an institution to answer, and most difficult of all for an eleemosynary institution that has both the momentum of tradition and the support of sentiment to sustain it. There is always the possibility (and the temptation to hope) that enough sentimental support can be stirred so that the tough question can be avoided: *What are you trying to do?*

This essay explores the problem of dealing with this question of "What are you trying to do?" by trustees of a seminary, with particular reference to the strategic position that seminaries occupy in the culture and the great, but largely unrealized, potential influence in that position.

Who Dominates the Culture?

From my perspective, ours is a business-dominated culture. The business influence is there, not so much because of the magnitude of the business presence, nor because businesses are more committed than others to serve society, but because the missions of businesses are usually better defined than in other institutions. And they get that way partly because business executives usually have more coercive power to govern than do executives in eleemosynaries, partly because the pursuit of private gain and the need to survive in the competitive struggle require that missions be clear and forceful.

I am writing this essay because I believe that dominance of the culture by elements like coercive power, private gain, and survival in the competitive struggle do not make for the quality of society that is reasonable and possible with the resources we have. Criticism of business and restraining its influence by government will not, in my judgment, produce the quality of society that is realistically possible. What will build a better society I believe, and what is well within our resources to do, is to bring to prominence in the culture those institutions whose primary motive is caring for persons and that are governed by persuasion. My hope is that, in time, such predominance will wield a meliorating influence on the harshness of both business and government. A necessary first step is a statement of mission for all eleemosynary institutions that is clear and powerful and that puts a high priority on the contribution of each institution to the quality of society because of what it is, what it does, and how it is governed. In my view, the best placed institutions to initiate a definition of their missions in these terms are seminaries and foundations. This essay will be concerned with seminaries.

The test that I would put on the adequacy of a seminary statement of mission is: What does it promise to contribute, through
leadership of and service to churches, to building and sustaining a
good society? A good society is one in which there is widespread *faith
as trust*, a quality that can encourage large numbers to become constructive influences in the world as it is—violent, striving, unjust as
well as beautiful, caring, and supportive. Others might postulate
other tests, but this one suggests the premise on which this essay is
based.

Statements of mission in a seminary in addition to giving clear
guidance to informed constituencies, also need to be persuasive to
people unversed in the technical language of theology, particularly to
those who fund seminaries. If contemporary seminaries were all adequately funded, if churches were receiving the sustaining leadership
they should have from seminaries, and if seminaries attracted the students they should have in order to provide churches with able professional leadership, I could not make a case for the need for new
statements of mission for seminaries. But the need is urgent on all
three counts.

In addressing the subject of "mission in a seminary," I have a
concern for two pervasive social problems: widespread alienation in
all strata of the population and the inability or unwillingness to serve
of far too many of the institutions that make up our complex society.
Each of these problems may be a contributing cause to the other, and
neither is likely to be healed without coming to terms with the other.

Whom and What Purpose Shall This Seminary Serve?

In the earlier essay, "The Seminary as an Institution," I suggested
that the first question from trustees who want to be effective in their
roles is: Whom and what purpose shall this seminary serve? This
could be the first question that the trustees of any institution might
ask because the answer to it defines the mission. If this question
is asked of all constituencies of the seminary, and if trustees work

patiently and sensitively for consensus, a mission may be defined that not only helps finance the place and brings the students the seminary should have, but it becomes a vital element of the ultimate government of the seminary—by guiding and assuring those who govern—thereby adding greatly to its strength as an institution.

Every person in whatever relationship, whether administrator, faculty, student, or staff, is the *servant of the mission*. All have appropriate and clearly defined roles as servants of the mission. Every significant policy or decision, every act of teaching, the formation of every influence from or to any constituency, is made with reference to that mission. There will be problems, of course, but clarity and power in the statement of mission will help resolve them. While primary power in the seminary is lodged in the commonly acknowledged mission, people in the seminary—administrators, faculty, and students—also have power, but that power is subordinate to the governing idea. When the mission is clear and compelling, people in the seminary do not ask (as I heard them in one instance) "who has the power?" The seminary in which the power of the mission is primary stands among other institutions as a model in which issues are met in creative fashion with reference to "what does the mission require of us?"

In any institution (including seminaries) that is comprised of fallible humans, it is important that the legal power to govern be clearly assigned. But the quality of the institution will be inverse to the use of that legal power.

What Is Worthy of Survival?

One of my sharply etched memories from the now distant past is a view from my office window, high above the east bank of the Hudson River in lower New York with a commanding view of the harbor. Much of the busy river traffic was made up of tugboats with groups of barges in tow. This scene was most interesting, sometimes frightening, when the tide was running out, perhaps with some wind behind it, and a tug was taking its group of barges downstream. The problem for the tug, under these conditions, was to sustain enough pull on the cables to the barges to keep them in orderly movement toward their destination. Under these adverse conditions, any slackening of that tension could result in chaos.

The memory of those scenes on the river came vividly to mind in the 1960s when I watched at close range as several venerable universities lapsed into chaos and seriously damaged themselves. When destructive forces were unleashed (and such are always latent in any institution) the power of the sense of mission in the university, like the pull of the tug on its barges, was not enough to keep a guiding tension on the several constituencies of the university. The answer to the question, "What in the institution is worthy of survival?" was not clear. There was not enough power in the governing ideas.

If either is faced with potential chaos, there is a parallel between the position of the skipper of the tug and the executive of any institution. The power to prevent chaos does not reside with either. That power is in the *engine* of the tug and in the *mission* of the institution. An able skipper or executive will better manage the chaos than inept ones, and thus render it less damaging. But given sufficient adverse conditions and not enough power in engines or mission, neither executive nor skipper holds the power to prevent chaos! All they can do is try to manage the chaos as best they can; but it is still chaos.

To the owner of the tug, I would say, "Don't dispatch that tug downstream when the tide is running out unless there is enough power in the engine to handle potential problems." To the trustees of any institution I would say, "Use what influence you have to get accepted a powerful governing idea (mission). If, after a reasonable effort, you conclude that you can't make it, find yourself something better to do. *It is a breach of trust to hold the position of trustee of any institution and to acquiesce in an inadequate statement of mission.*"

A great contemporary idea of what a university should be doing would make a better university at any time—before, during or after the 1960s. Some university missions may have been inadequate for a long time, but in that critical period of testing, some were found to be inadequate—by the simple test that their missions at that time did not have the power to hold against the forces of chaos. There is much to be learned from those traumatic experiences. Has it been learned?

What is worthy of survival? *An institution with a great mission!*—particularly a seminary with a great mission.

Why Is Mission Important in a Seminary?

It is important to avoid chaos because it wastes resources and hurts people. But that is but one of the benefits to be derived from a strong sense of mission in the seminary—or in any institution. Clear and powerful mission is important because it provides the substance of common purpose that all constituencies might be persuaded to accept. Once accepted, common purpose helps to heal, for all involved within the seminary the pervasive alienation of our times; it helps keep priorities in order; it builds organizational esprit; it clearly signals who should and should not be in the seminary—as students, faculty, or staff as well as the qualities needed in the administration; it provides the basis for resolving, on a reasoned objective basis, the many issues that arise in the course of any institution's life with a minimum of reference to assigned power; and it provides the stimulus and direction for the optimal performance of the seminary as the servant of all who are touched by its program.

These are qualities that are of great value to all institutions that have the potential to be influential—like seminaries—in order to assure a reasonably civilized society.

There are several ingredients of a healthy viable institution that mission alone will not provide: among these are, astute leadership and consistently able management. Machiavelli observed: "It is an infallible rule that a prince who is not wise himself cannot be well advised. . . ."

Mission and Trustee Strategy

Most trustees that I know have some awareness of what is stated above. But they believe that a clear and compelling mission, a great governing idea, is best achieved by installing and supporting an able executive. Able executives are always important, and they should be supported, but I suggest that the executive, with rare exceptions, can only manage what is there. If the executive tries, alone, even with the assurance of support of trustees, to lead the seminary to the influential role that it might occupy, his or her tenure as the executive may be short. The rare executive may make it, but it is a gamble against unreasonable odds for a trustee to assume that the executive will make it alone. And there is damage to the institution when the executive tries to give this leadership *alone* and fails.

One of the distressing incidents of the recent past was the appointment a few years ago of an able 28-year-old person as president of a college with the explicit charge from the trustees to give the place new leadership (which apparently was needed). However, the trustees took no action on a statement of mission that would require that leadership, nor did they seek acceptance of the need for it from the several constituencies. The result: early resignation of the new president with damage to both the person and the college.

A prudent seminary trustee, one who would like to see a clear and compelling mission for the seminary, will accept that *it is the trustee's role to make the first move toward a clear definition of mission and secure wide acceptance of it, and then to support prudent efforts by the executive who endeavors to lead the seminary to achieve that mission.*

What would such trustee leadership comprise, and where does the executive fit into it? In *The Seminary as Institution,* I suggested that trustees are most effective as askers of questions, and that the first question might be, Whom and what purpose shall this seminary serve? But this is an "umbrella" question, and other more penetrating questions will need to be asked—questions that imply criteria that trustees may have in mind for evaluating answers from various constituencies.

The first requirement is a trustee chairperson who has an understanding of, and skill at achieving, consensus. If a seminary does not have someone in the chair who has that skill and is willing to work long and patiently at using it, or if some other trustee will not endeavor to perform that function (in which case *that* trustee may effectively be the chairperson without benefit of title), that seminary will do well to make the best of its present role until it can find such a person to chair its trustees. Adequate mission, a widely accepted great governing idea, is not only unlikely to be achieved without that skill in the chair, but (as said above) the seminary may be damaged by trying to achieve it. I see the ability to find consensus as the prime skill in the art of chairing, both in defining mission and in presiding over the ongoing governance of the seminar): as it works to fulfill that mission.

Trustees whose chairperson has this skill are in a position to pursue the question, whom and what purpose shall this seminary serve? I see six subsidiary questions that might be asked in such a way as to suggest the criteria by which trustees will judge the adequacy of the answers. These questions do not define wholly separate and discrete areas and, to some extent, they overlap. But they may suggest to trustees a basis for initiating a dialogue with the several constituencies of the seminary out of which a clear and powerful statement of mission may emerge.

1. Does the Seminary See Itself as a Model for Other Institutions?

Does the seminary accept its place at the top of the hierarchy of institutions in which the seminary is the resource institution for churches, which, in turn, serve as support resources for individuals and for the whole range of "operating" institutions: governments, businesses, schools, hospitals, social agencies, families, communities? In asking this question, the trustees will be suggesting that the seminary should have a concern for the missions of churches and help churches to clarify their own separate missions, thus preparing themselves for a much greater society-shaping role than most churches now enjoy—society shaping by leading, not by manipulation or coercion.

This will be a most difficult concept for some seminaries to accept: that they will be models of institutional achievement and influence society, through the churches, more by the example of the quality of life within the seminary than by preachment. If the seminary can reach even a modest achievement as a model of "power in the mission" and can clearly demonstrate the effectiveness and strength in an institution that moves on this principle, it could, in time, influence the quality of the whole society.

2. Is Critical Thought a High Priority in the Seminary?

Critical thought is not necessarily identical with scholarship and the writing of books and papers that establish a scholar's reputation with peers. Scholarship is a necessary condition for critical reflection, but it does not automatically produce it. Critical thought is a fulfillment of the root meaning of seminary: *seminalis*, seed. It is the reflective thought that produces seminal ideas—ideas that become new visions in both ministers as persons and churches as institutions; ideas that support ministers and churches as they nurture *servants* who may shape the institutions that dominate the lives of all of us.

The adequacy of critical thought in seminaries is tested ultimately by ordinary folk who have its significance in their lives made real through their participation in churches. The incremental actions that build the serving quality of society, or maintain such as it has, are taken by legions of people who get inspiration and guidance from somewhere, mostly from churches—directly or indirectly.

We lack a theology of institutions for these times. I do not fault seminary theologians for this; their trustees are failing to do what only trustees can do: ask the penetrating and persistent questions that ensure the adequacy of critical thought in the seminary.

3. Does the Image Created by the Statement of Mission for the Seminary Suggest a Strong Contemporary Institution?

The nature of any seminary closely identifies it with its own history and tradition. It is precisely that tradition that frees the seminary to be always effective in contemporary society.

It is important that the mission suggest that the seminary, through the churches, is serving this contemporary society and is moving with that society into the uncertain future. Particularly, it should be clear that the seminary is supporting the churches—with the stuff to be strong—as they serve both individuals in their private and family lives and as they prepare, support, and inspire those who mold and shape modern institutions. Seminaries should be seen by informed people as critically important, strong, and useful contemporary institutions. The implication of the word *strong* is that seminaries are an influential society-shaping force because of the leadership they give to churches. But it is important that both the language and concepts of the statement of mission create the image of contemporaniety—it is the quality of *this* society that is the seminary's prime concern.

One of the important learnings from the university debacle of the 1960s may be that more attention to their history might have saved some universities from harm in that difficult period. Clearly, a mission concept that was adequate for 1900 did not suffice in the 1960s. A sense of history keeps one constantly aware that a mission statement that was adequate yesterday may not serve well today.

4. Does the Seminary Attract Students Who Have the Potential to Become Influential Leaders of Churches and Church Institutions, and Does It Attract Faculty Who Are Capable of Training Such Students?

Those who are attracted as students and faculty are influenced by the image discussed above. They are also attracted by what they know, from informed people, is really there. Is the seminary really strong? Does it prepare people for effective leadership of influential churches and church institutions? Strong people as leaders make strong institutions—because those people have the intellect, stability, integrity, *and spirit* required to generate *trust* in those who might respond to their leadership. *Leader* is used in the common meaning of "go out ahead to show the way." The connotations of *lead* are quite distinct from those of *manage* (control) or *administer* (care for). Leading is venturing and risk taking. "The way is not clear. I will go out ahead to show the way. Follow me!"

Leadership is not a professional calling. In any church, anybody can lead who can generate trust in followers. One task of the seminary is to provide as many professionally prepared women and men as it can, persons who have the ability to generate that trust in churches and church institutions so as to give them great influence.

There may be a place for a seminary that prepares pastors to serve weak or nominal churches. But if, as assumed here, a preferred role of the seminary is to prepare pastors as leaders who will build *strong* churches and church institutions, then the seminary must strive to admit those students who are most likely to qualify for that service. It is important that the mission attract those who want that kind of demanding life and discourage those who do not want it. One feature of any admissions process is self-selection by potential students and faculty—they tend to select themselves "in" or "out."

5. Does the Seminary Experience Develop Spirit?

The seminary, like other educational institutions, shapes and forms in ways that we but dimly understand. It is a community that has an ethos that is, in part, a consequence of its mission and how that mission is understood. There is a deeper issue of informing the life of the seminary community which suggests that the literary quality of the mission statement is important. Does it sing, does it carry spirit and inspire qualities of leadership and reaching that are spirit building? Part of the power in a statement of mission is the poetry of its expression that sets the seminary clearly apart from bureaucratic institutions.

Spirit is commonly defined as the animating force within living beings. In a seminary, I would want to add a value dimension to this definition: Is the person who is possessed of spirit disposed to be servant? Do those being served, *while being served*, become healthier, wiser, freer, more autonomous, more likely themselves to become servants? And, what is the effect on the least privileged in society; will they benefit, or, at least, not be further deprived? No one will be hurt.

Whether the seminary develops spirit, thus defined, seems to me to depend more on the quality of the seminary as an institution than on the precise design of its program. Has the seminary itself evolved as servant; deep down inside, is this what the seminary really is? One does not teach about spirit. One really is spirit.

Mission is a statement of how a seminary sees itself—at its very core. Is it, in its essence, spiritual? Does the statement of mission reflect this?

6. Does the Governing Idea (Mission) Have Power?

There is only one test: if the mission does not have power, it will not guide those who govern and people will be without purpose. The advantages of a powerful mission, enumerated earlier, will be only partly realized—if at all.

Earlier I suggested that ours is a business-dominated culture because the missions of businesses are usually better defined than in most other institutions. They get that way partly because business executives usually have more coercive power than do executives of others, partly because the pursuit of private gain and survival in the competitive struggle require it.

My hope for the future is that our culture will, in time, become less dominated by institutions that are ruled by coercive power, and motivated by private gain and competitive striving, and move toward a quality of society in which voluntary consensus and search for the good are a greater force than they are today. Could seminaries emerge as leaders of this movement by becoming institutions that are distinguished because of the power of persuasion and caring that comes in response to inspired trustee leadership whose primary tactic is penetrating questions?

These six questions are only suggestions for trustees of a seminary. Each trustee board will devise its own questions. If trustees ask such questions, and thereby give leadership toward defining a clear and powerful mission, what then is the role of the executive? It seems to me that the mission defines that role: it is to take those subtle steps of encouragement and discouragement that keep the seminary clearly centered on growth in achievement of its mission—with as close to consensus as possible.

Leadership—Going Out Ahead to Show the Way

Both the person and the institution are damaged if a seminary chews up its executives because they failed when they tried to give leadership in formulating a new and powerful mission. If the trustee chairperson tries to give this leadership to trustees—and fails, that chairperson can quietly withdraw with little damage to the person or the institution. In short, *chairpersons are expendable, executives are not.* Part of the reason for this difference is that the executive is a colleague of the faculty; the chairperson is not (or should not be). The executive has a career stake in the position; the chairperson does not (or should not have).

The head of the board who is not a seminary theologian (and should not be) can, by leading trustees to ask questions like those above, become a *public theologian.* The executive, who is a seminary theologian, cannot, on her or his own, ask questions like these. The executive's role is to lead the process of finding answers and to serve as interlocutor between trustees and various constituencies whose acceptance of the mission is necessary. This is a sensitive role.

With help from the chair, trustees may come to accept that the gap between potential and performance in their seminary is wide, but they can hold firm in their belief in the possibility for a great, powerful new mission for the seminary that will, in time, cause a dramatic reduction in that gap and move the seminary into the influential position that it should occupy. As matters now stand, seminary theologians, whether faculty members or executives, would have difficulty holding this view and carrying on with their present work. The seminary must be maintained as it is while its greater future is being worked out.

The best trustees, especially the one in the chair, will believe that a new clear and powerful mission can indeed result from dialogue that questions like the above will induce. Further, trustees will believe that mission will evolve in such a way that faculty and executives grow in the process. It is the kind of faith that people who move institutions of any kind have to have. There are such people available for seminary trustees, and every seminary trustee board should have at least one. That one, with the power of his or her faith, will lead the rest. And, if they fail, they will quietly retire so that someone else can try.

A seminary that is a viable contemporary institution will have at all times a person in the chair who holds this unqualified faith that movement toward potential greatness in the seminary is a realistically achievable goal. Such is faith in the power of a great idea. And it is contagious!

Reflections on the Relevance of Faith to Mission

What I have been writing the past ten years has brought me into close contact with churches: from local parishes to denominational bodies; and church institutions—hospitals, schools, and seminaries. Most of these involvements have centered on the servant-leader theme about which I have been writing. A major insight (to me) emerged out of this church experience two years ago when I met with an ecumenical group of high-level church executives who were convened for three days in a retreat house to consider the subject, "the churchman as leader." There were just 16 churchmen and I.

The first two days were taken by a candid discussion among the churchmen of their leadership problems, as they saw them—which were numerous. Change a few words and their problems seemed to me to be no different from those of the harried executives I have been listening to all my life. On the third day, I entered the discussion and made some comments based on what I had heard. As I prepared for that third day, a disturbing thought came to mind. Their main leadership problem seemed to be that they did not believe their own stuff—not as it applies to the institutional affairs of their churches. They are able, conscientious persons, but they lack the kind of faith that anyone who would lead anything in a significant way must have.

I did not share this observation with the church executives the next day, although I touched the edge of it—partly because I was not sure it would be helpful, partly because this was an insight that needed to be digested. If I were meeting with them today, I might share it because, as I have reflected further on my many experiences with churches, it seems to me that the inability (or unwillingness) to be guided by their religious beliefs in dealing with the human affairs of their churches may be the problem of the whole church establishment, and it may account for the failure of churches to give the leadership to this troubled society that they are in the best position to give. The one exception to this generalization that I would note is the Catholic Women's Religious Orders; but they seem troubled by their isolation and bewildered by the prospect that it may be up to them to lead. I wish they could generate more power to lead because they seem to have faith that people and institutions in this chaotic world can change for the better—and that inspired leadership by us ordinary mortals can bring it about. I would say that such faith is *faith as trust*. I once overheard one of the Sisters say, "There is no worse cynic than a religious cynic!"

What is the relevance of these reflections to the subject of this essay, "Mission in a Seminary—A Prime Concern of Trustees"? Is it simply this: to most people in seminaries, or who know intimately about them, the notion that any contemporary seminary could move from where it now is to the kind of institution described in this essay is one of those unbelievable things—a pipe dream. Only a person of truly great faith could accept it as a possibility to be seriously considered. That is why I said earlier that a seminary is not likely to move toward this vision unless it has trustees, particularly in a person in the chair, who are firm in that faith and who have the competence, tenacity, and fortitude that sustained and effective leadership to this end will require.

One would not have to be a cynic to say "I do not see any people on the horizon who might be such trustees for my seminary, especially one to chair it, people who have the faith, plus the necessary competence, tenacity, and fortitude to give the leadership that the achievement of this vision requires." I agree; I do not see them either. But I believe that they are not visible because they are not expected to be there—in fact, *they are not wanted by some.* A letter from a seminary executive, commenting on my essay on "The Seminary as an Institution," says, regarding the role outlined there for the chairperson, "The idea seems to suggest that a chairperson serves for a long time. In fact, at least among all . . . seminaries, and perhaps some others, the chairperson serves no more than two years and is, for all practical purposes, the presiding officer only. As I understand what you are saying, I reject it outright." This is a candid expression of what might be a quite general attitude. But such trustees seem to me to be little more than a legal front for faculty and administrators and for the denomination that has de facto control. For a trustee to accept such a limited role is clearly a breach of trust. Directors of a publicly held business corporation who accept this kind of role might be held personally liable in case of some default.

In our times, the heart of the matter of faith in the improvability of human performance—in institutions—may be *trust.* We have the misfortune to live in an era of low trust. I suspect we are in that state because, in relatively short time, we have moved from a society of individuals relating to individuals to a society in which most of us are involved in complex relationships with institutions. And a widely held basis for trusting people in institutions has not yet evolved. The visible basis for trust, fully functioning trustees, is conspicuously absent in too many institutions—including some seminaries. The first step to recover trust is to install trustees who are trustworthy.

Part of the opportunity to rebuild trust in our times is for trustees to become valid symbols of trust in their institution, and for the one who occupies the chair to stand tall among colleagues in building that symbol. But if there are no visible persons available for trustees, especially chairpersons as so conceived, this opportunity ranks with the unbelievable to many who are involved with seminaries.

I believe the opportunity is real and achievable because of my long experience with people who have demonstrated their ability to carry heavy burdens. Latent in many of these able men and women is trustee potential of the quality that seminaries need. I have had enough experience as an agent in the human transformation process to believe that this latent trusteeship ability can be brought to maturity as seminary trustees, even in some who are old.

Faith is required to do the unbelievable and to demonstrate that something can be done—for the first time. After it has been proven feasible; it will require great courage, strength, and competence to do it again—but it may not require faith. Where is the transforming agent with faith who will wield the formative influence that will produce trustees of this stature for seminaries? *Seminaries will do it for themselves.* Why should someone else produce these trustees for seminaries? Seminaries will produce their own trustees, and they will also render this service for churches and church-related institutions—a massive opportunity. A seminary that rises to this opportunity will grow conspicuously in stature.

"And how will we do that?" the incredulous seminary executive or trustee may ask. There is no easy answer to that question because that is what creative leadership is about. A seminary as it now stands, will find in its present resources the initiative to take the first step. A first order of business for any seminary that would operate with a great sense of mission may be to conceptualize the trustee role so as to make that role attractive to the people who would be the trustees that would give the leadership that would produce a great mission. Such trustees will then give the seminary the sustaining strength to operate with distinction within that mission.

The first question such a potential trustee might ask is "to whom will I be responsible?" The trustee is, of course, responsible to the closely related constituencies of the seminary, its students, faculty, staff, and administrators, and to the churches and other institutions that give it money, that employ its graduates, and that look to the seminary for both leadership and prophetic vision. Each of these constituencies has power—in one way or another and in varying degrees and sometimes in conflict with other constituencies—power to enforce its will on the seminary and on the character of its mission. The wise potential trustee, one who has the capacity to lead the seminary to a great mission, will know that as a trustee, these close constituencies will not be his or her primary responsibility. That primary responsibility will be to the society as a whole and to its needs. And he or she will want to know, "Can these close constituencies be brought to accept that this seminary exists primarily to serve the critical needs of society?" (I suggested two of these current critical problems at the outset: widespread alienation in all strata of the population and the inability or unwillingness to serve of far too many of the institutions that make up our complex society.) In order to bring this exceptional trustee to its service, any seminary as it now stands will need to give evidence that it is amenable to being led to acceptance of a great mission that is built around some definition of the public good, a mission that is accomplished through the churches that the seminary inspires, leads, and supports.

A great new seminary mission need not disturb present programs. A significant added dimension, concern for religious leadership, may be all that is required. If that new work is sustained by trustee support, in time, existing programs will accommodate to it. Serious concern in the seminary for religious leadership may stir a profound new area for theological reflection. What is hoped for is that religious leadership that originates in seminaries will find its way through the churches, to nurture values and inspire venturesome spirit in those who will: (a) build truly serving institutions and (b) generate in young people hope that they can become servants.

If one would lead *as servant*, one will first be open to being led by servants. Openness to leading by servants is a manifestation of *faith as trust*.

CRITICAL THOUGHT IN THE SEMINARY AND
THE TRUSTEE CHAIRPERSON'S ROLE

What kind of challenge does chairing the trustees of a seminary present?

A chairperson's answer would depend on how one sees the opportunities and obligations in that position, what one believes about the place of seminaries in society and their unrealized potential for service, and what one's personal feelings are concerning the assumption of leadership. One decides where one stands on issues like these. Then one chooses a role from a range of possibilities beginning, at the low end of the scale, with the seminary executive's view quoted earlier in which " . . . the chairperson serves no more than two years and is, for all practical purposes, the presiding officer only." Near the other end of the spectrum is one who believes that the seminary can be led by prudent steps toward the achievement of a much greater vision of service to society than most now aspire to, and who is disposed to take the risks of leadership to move it there.

What can be said to one who accepts the latter version of a chairing role and chooses to give leadership that will help move a seminary toward realizing a new vision of service to society by greatly strengthened churches? How can such a leader be helped?

There are ample resources for help on how best to carry out the important fiduciary aspects of all trusteeships. This essay will discuss the opportunity for unusual leadership from the chair when the effort is made to move the seminary, a unique kind of institution, from the marginal role that many now seem to occupy, to the pivotal position that is envisioned in the first two chapters.

The one who undertakes to give this leadership will need to be prepared to contend with the negative mind-set that disposes too many concerned and thoughtful people to write off seminaries as having little force in contemporary society. As matters now stand in some seminaries, this may be a valid judgment. But one who chooses to give new creative leadership to seminary trustees needs to believe firmly that we cannot afford to dismiss them since there are neither the time nor the resources to replace existing seminaries with more serving institutions that will give needed support to churches. Unless one wants to abandon the idea of building a better society through greatly strengthened churches, there is no feasible alternative to rebuilding seminaries that will give powerful new support to churches. The word *rebuilding* is used advisedly. No mere revision of the curriculum will do it. The acceptance of such a premise will be part of the armor of one who would lead the trustees of a seminary as, collectively, they lead the seminary toward a future of greatness as servant.

The discussion of critical thought in the seminary includes the following:

Critical thought is not necessarily identical with scholarship and the writing of books and papers that establish a scholar's reputation with peers. Scholarship is a necessary condition for critical reflection, but it does not automatically produce it. Critical thought is a fulfillment of the root meaning of *seminary; seminalis*—seed. It is the reflective thought that produces seminal ideas—ideas that become new visions in both ministers as persons and churches as institutions, ideas that support both ministers and churches as they nurture servants who shape the institutions that dominate the lives of all of us.

The adequacy of critical thought in seminaries is tested, ultimately, by ordinary folk who have its significance in their lives made real by participation in churches. The incremental actions that build the serving quality of society or maintain such as it has, are taken by legions of people who get inspiration and guidance from somewhere, mostly from churches—directly or indirectly.

I believe that the critical thought now emerging from seminaries generally is far from adequate for the urgent needs of these times. Too many churches are languishing for want of intellectual stimulus from seminaries. And seminaries are therefore not giving the vital leadership to churches that support them as they undertake to wield their constructive influence on society—leadership of ideas that give hope expressed in language that lifts the spirit. The premise here is that the need for more influential critical thought from seminaries is great.

Before discussing the implications of this belief, let us make a brief scan of history of seminaries in the mainline protestant denominations in the United States.

Seminary Leadership, a Historical View

There have been two approaches to critical thinking in and regarding seminaries: (1) about the seminary as an institution and (2) about the substance of theology itself. Such consideration of seminaries as institutions is more effective when it shapes the thinking of those who give the ultimate leadership to seminaries, their trustees. Theological ideas are more likely to be useful in building a better society if seminary theologians clothe them in persuasive reasoning and express them in language that gives them the power of prophetic vision. This vision will inspire and guide churches as they work to heal and prevent alienation and give strength and direction to those who will then build serving institutions of all sorts. I am not a close student of the history of seminaries but I have done enough reading to have some views about how to stimulate critical thinking about both the seminary as an institution and its theology.

The first protestant seminaries in the United States were Andover (1808–Congregational) and Princeton (1812–Presbyterian). In 1815, a remarkable new institution emerged that was called

American Education Society (AES). This was a group of strong and able people who effectively became trustees for protestant theological seminaries in the early 19th century. The AES's primary concern was not only for seminaries and churches but for the durability of the young republic, which was not assured at that time; and they believed that strong churches that were served by pastors who were both pious and learned were needed to give the society of their day the sinews of strength. Their strategy was to encourage the growth of seminaries on the Andover model of four years of undergraduate education followed by three years of seminary. They set out to accomplish this objective by raising funds for scholarships to subsidize the seminary education of students of any evangelical denomination that provided this solid scholarly three-year postgraduate program.

Until early in the 19th century, many pastors in protestant churches in the United States were trained as most other professionals were: by apprenticeship to an established practitioner. "Reading theology" was the common term. It could refer to an apprenticeship or to the final year in college. Meanwhile, others acquired the "gift" of ministry in less formal ways — by just starting to preach. The "circuit riding" pastors of frontier days needed only a few sermons, and this way sufficed for them. Both ways had the effect of producing pastors who were sometimes "pious but not learned."

With this AES support, the expansion of seminary resources on the Andover model was rapid. The AES continued for some decades as a powerful force, not only in increasing the number of seminaries but in sustaining the model of a three-year postgraduate curriculum whose chief components (relying on a prior study of classical languages), according to some observers, were "biblical studies, based on the original languages, sacred history, and didactic theology." There was vigorous opposition to this approach, but the founders of AES were strong enough to hold to their course. However, scholarly seminary preparation of clergy did not become the prevailing mode in the United States until well into the 20th century.

This spectacular development of theological education that AES sponsored was launched well before the radical social changes of the industrial revolution. The steam engine was there in 1800, but the first practical steam boat and railway locomotive did not emerge in the United States until near the middle of the century. The pastor who was trained in the older theological traditions could understand the total life of his parishioners because the conditions of life were not too different from biblical times, in which the theology of that day was firmly rooted. There was in that period little reason to question the adequacy of biblical theology as the quite complete preparation of a pastor.

But the character of American society was soon to change radically! By 1900, a powerful new voice had risen in William Rainey Harper, an eminent theologian and founding president of the University of Chicago. In 1899, he wrote a spirited article in *The American Journal of Theology* entitled, "Shall the Theological Curriculum Be Modified, and How?" It is a searching and provocative examination of curriculum design, and it contained a recognition of new conditions of society that needed to be addressed in the preparation of pastors. Some passages from Harper's article follow.

> Some adjustment must be found by which the curriculum will meet the demands that are made by the present peculiar social conditions. Reference has already been made to the inability of the ordinary preacher to make an impression on the lower classes. The evidence is quite conclusive that he is equally unable to influence the higher classes. The country is full of men who have become wealthy. . . . What is the attitude of the church toward this growing class of influential men? . . . Nothing has yet been proposed to provide a training which will enable the ministry to do successful work among the higher classes.

> If the student is to do his work in a democratic atmosphere, he must be filled with the democratic spirit and must learn to employ democratic methods. This is not the spirit, and these are not the methods, of the ordinary theological seminary.

The condition of the churches, both rural and urban is not upon the whole encouraging. Ministers of the better classes are not satisfied to accept rural churches; and yet these same ministers are not strong enough, or sufficiently prepared, to meet the demands of many of the city churches.

They (theological students) have little or no sympathy with scientific work. They utterly lack that point of view which will enable them to bring themselves into relationship with that greatest factor in modern civilization.

The great majority of American seminaries are located in out-of-the-way places and are not in touch with modern life.

The present scope of the theological curriculum includes practical preparation for only one kind of Christian work; namely, preaching.

The usual practice in theological seminaries of providing free tuition and rooms . . . cultivates in the very beginning of life a principle which in too many cases is applied throughout life.

The study of the Hebrew language should be made elective.

Much of the technique of a theological education could be put aside to advantage, if this time thus gained could be occupied by work in English Literature.

These quotes are just a sampling of Harper's essay. There was much more.

What Harper did not note in his essay in 1899 (and which seems even more apparent to me as a student of organization today) is that biblical theology was inadequate for the problem he described. And it is even more inadequate in our times, when the majority of us are enmeshed in vast bureaucracies—business, government, education, church—all of which have the same problems, and when the family farm that was dominant in Harper's day is largely gone. The fallacy (as I see it) that continues from Harper's day to this is that theologians assume that the needs of a radically changed (and changing) society can be met in seminaries just by revising the curriculum, and that this is all that is needed to make seminaries (and the churches that depend on them for intellectual and prophetic leadership) fully serving contemporary institutions. My cursory reading of history tells me that this may have been a valid assumption in the early days of AES. But by 1850, the conditions of the emerging society called for new critical thinking leading to a new theology—not repudiating the old, but adding what the new conditions required—and it was not forthcoming.

How can I justify these assertions? I have had more than 50 years of listening to and watching those who carry the leading and managing roles in institutions of all sorts, large and small. In all of this, I rarely hear reference to influence being wielded on these people's institutional roles by churches. And discussions of administrative problems by church leaders that I have listened to (and I have done quite a lot of such listening) sound no different from those of businesspeople. Yet the effect on the quality and character of contemporary society by the combined decisions these people make, people who are leading and administering American institutions, is the overpowering influence of our times.

A dedicated religious businessperson wrote:

> A speaker recently said in an address on the future of the church and evangelicalism, "Christian programs are not working at all in the business and professional world; the church is answering questions nobody is asking. 91.8% of 750 people in a survey said they would prefer talking with a fellow layman about spiritual matters.
>
> I wholly concur. Paid clergy are viewed by the business community as largely irrelevant. There is little to no business metaphor in church teachings or sermons unless as an object of criticism or derision. . . . The net result of this neutral or negative posture by the church is to overlook the condition of 100 million working men and women. . . .

I have no sense of how widely this harsh judgment may be held among thoughtful laypeople; but I suspect there is a disturbing amount of it.

The challenge today is the same in its essentials as that faced, and accepted, by the American Education Society in 1815: to produce able pastors who will lead influential churches that will add strength and quality to contemporary society. The difference is that in 1815 the available concept of the seminary, the Andover model, and the content of biblical theology were both judged adequate. Today neither seems adequate. New critical thought is urgently needed about both the concept of the institution and the content of its theology.

Those who founded the American Education Society in 1815 and gave such powerful impetus to early 19th-century theological education were motivated by an intense concern for the survival of the young democracy. The motivation that might move seminary trustees in the late 20th century may be similar—to heal and strengthen an ailing society. The means available for both seem to be the same: stronger, better-led churches. But the strategy for implementing those means may be radically different today from what it was when the protestant seminary movement started.

I have said that the strong group that made up the American Education Society were, in effect, the trustees of an important segment of protestant theological seminaries of that period. As I see it, the trustees of seminaries today, particularly their chairpersons, are best positioned to give the leadership that will produce the much needed critical thought about the seminary as an institution and the theology that both guides it and which it advocates as prophetic vision for churches.

If the chairperson accepts the risks of leadership that will be required to bring the seminary to become what it has the opportunity to become, and to produce needed ideas, a strategy for such effective leadership will be needed. Where is the relevant experience that the seminary trustee chairperson might turn to in devising this strategy?

Where Is the Relevant Experience?

If the trustee chairperson of a seminary resolves to give leadership that will help the seminary become a greater force in strengthening churches in our times, how does one proceed? What experience is there to draw upon to help one devise a strategy of leadership that will bring the seminary to become a great new source of critical thought—both about itself and as an institution and about the theology that it provides for churches?

Such a move in many seminaries would call for a substantial regeneration of the seminary as an institution. It would be a major undertaking that would not likely take place without astute and sustained leadership from the trustees, especially the one who chairs the board.

In the world of institutions, all can be roughly grouped in two classes: those designed so that they fail easily and live under the constant threat of failure, and those that are designed so that failure is difficult and rare. Businesses are generally in the first category, and nonprofit agencies and governmental units are in the second. Because of this sharp disparity, most of the experience with the process of regenerating moribund or low-serving institutions is in business. And the seminary trustee chairperson who is searching for ideas on how to give leadership to the school so as to bring it to greatness as servant with an abundance of critical thought as one of its distinguishing characteristics will be well advised to look to business experience as one source of ideas. I do not suggest that either seminary faculty or administrators should be concerned with the experience of business regeneration, but that their trustee chairperson take a close look at that experience.

My AT&T Experience as an Example

I had the good fortune to spend my active career in American Telephone and Telegraph Company, which had experienced a major regeneration shortly before I arrived in 1926, and some of the people who brought it through this great change were still around. From these people, I learned much about how that transformation was accomplished that may never get into written history.

The telephone was invented in Boston in 1876. The company was started in 1878 by Bostonians who lacked both vision and an adventurous spirit, and it remained in their hands until 1907, when J. P. Morgan the elder wrested control from them; installed a great builder, Theodore N. Vail (who earlier had been the company's first general manager), as president; moved the headquarters to New York; and gave it a vision and started it on an adventurous course. Morgan, who earlier had been instrumental in launching both General Electric and U.S. Steel, gave a powerful push to move AT&T from an ordinary to an exceptional institution.

In 1907, the company was a going concern, but it was burdened by four serious problems: (1) There was an acute employee morale problem. (2) The public reputation of the company was very bad. (3) There was a question about its financial soundness. (4) The available technology was insufficient to permit the development of the scope and quality of telephone service that we know today and that Vail and Morgan were determined to bring about. By 1920, when Vail died in the harness, all four of these were corrected, some seminal ideas about the institution and its technology emerged, and the company was a "blue chip."

I entered the company in 1926 and I immediately became interested in its history. The top question on my mind for a number of years was, how did this remarkable transformation come about? The answer was slow in coming, partly because it was so difficult to judge what Morgan's role was. Morgan, as he was then, would not only be out of style today, but he would be legally restrained. In the context of his times, however, he was a great trustee. He had and used great power, sometimes ruthlessly; *but he cared intensely about the quality of the business he controlled,* an extraordinary attribute for a person of great wealth early in this century. We cannot know how much of

Vail's genius as an institution builder should be attributed to Morgan. A safe assumption is to view them as a joint personality.

How did the transformation of AT&T come about? Very simple in concept; but awfully difficult to do. There were three basic strategies that I believe are universally applicable to the regeneration of any kind of institution at any time.

Strategies for Change

l. *Mission.* In his early period as the first general manager, Vail stated the mission thus: "We will build a telephone system so that any person, any place in the world, can talk to anybody else, any place else in the world, quickly, cheaply, satisfactorily." We aren't there yet, nearly 100 years after that goal was stated. But I believe we are much closer to it now than we would be if the man who piloted the company in those crucial years (1907–20) had not "thought big." In that later period, the goal was stated more modestly as "universal service"—perhaps because the company had lost a few tail feathers in its first brush with the antitrust enforcers in 1913. When I entered the business in 1926, there was still some of the feeling that we were "building a cathedral, not just laying bricks." It would be difficult in any institution to sustain the sense of urgency noted later if the commonly accepted mission does not require it.

The first step toward defining mission for one who chairs seminary trustees is to get an answer to the question, "Whom and what purpose does this seminary serve?" The chair should ask this question and stay with it until all constituencies—trustees, administrators, faculty, students, alumni—are agreed on a concept that the chair is willing to lead. If the constituencies, after long and patient urging either cannot agree, or if what they can agree on seems unacceptable to the one in the chair, perhaps that person should quietly retire and find something better to do. When Vail, the first general manager of AT&T, was unable to move the conservative Bostonians to become builders, he left the company and resisted later importunings to return when the company was in trouble. He did not return for 20 years until the Bostonians were ousted by Morgan, who was himself a great builder.

If the agreed-upon mission statement for a seminary is one I could accept if I were to undertake to lead the board, these are the answers I would prefer to see to the questions, Whom and what purpose does this seminary serve? *Whom?* Religious leaders, whether in churches or other institutions. *What purpose?* To provide churches with ideas and leadership to the end that churches become and are sustained as significant forces that heal and prevent alienation in people and nurture the leaders who will build serving institutions everywhere. The seminary might do some other things, but if I were to be the chairperson, this definition of mission—or one close to it— would be primary. Other chairpersons might view it differently. My advice to any such persons is: don't undertake to lead the board and the seminary in a direction you do not firmly believe in. Otherwise you will not be able to lead with spirit. Spirit will be needed.

2. *Obstacles to greatness are clearly identified* and the full ramifications of each is described. Then a capable staff person is assigned to each problem with the clear charge to find the means for turning it around and to persuade—to move—all of the people who need to act. As long as an obstacle to greatness remains as a problem, a capable staff person makes a high priority of finding a way to deal with it. If at any time it appears that the person assigned is either unable or unwilling to press for an answer, that person is replaced.

3. *A sense of urgency is created* and the move toward greatness is widely accepted as an imperative. It was my privilege to work at AT&T under the executive who, as a young man in 1907, was given the assignment of raising the morale and integrity of the women in the business—a difficult and essential task. By 1926 when I entered, the person who brought about this transformation had made an elite corps out of the department (switchboard operation) where most women worked. One of the by-products was that this department (in 1926) was producing a greatly disproportionate share of the top officers in the company (then all men). The man who piloted this

transformation (one of the most perfect gentlemen I ever met) accomplished it from a staff position entirely by persuasion. He was supported by the feeling of urgency that pervaded the business in that crucial period from 1907 to 1920.

From the soundings available about seminaries, I deduce that the principal urgency in some of them is the need for money to survive. In a seminary in which this is a valid judgment, could it be that one of the reasons for the primacy of money in seminaries is that there is not sufficient urgency felt regarding critical thought, the production of seminal ideas that are sorely needed in a faltering society?

When someone says to me, "You can't cause seminal ideas to emerge where they don't exist," my response is, "Oh, yes you can! (1) If you have a widely accepted mission for the institution that embodies a great dream of what it might become. (2) If you carefully identify all of the obstacles that stand in the way of realizing that dream and see to it that a competent person sets to work to remove or find a way around each obstacle. And (3) if you sustain a sense of urgency about the whole process of regenerating the institution."

Do these three things, and do them well, and the chance that seminal ideas will emerge in the process is very good—no matter how limited the institution may have been at the start. This is what the experiences of businesses in general, and the one I know best—AT&T—in particular, have to suggest to the chairperson of seminary trustees who would give leadership to a development that would favor the growth of critical thought—as marked by the emergence of seminal ideas—in the seminary. It may require more acumen from the one in the chair to sustain this urgency in a seminary than in the usual business. But there are only 200 seminaries in the United States, and the nature of the opportunity to serve is such that every seminary should have an exceptional leader to chair its trustees, or the equivalent of that person in seminaries that do not have their own trustees. That urgency will need to be felt at all times if the typical seminary is to move in influence from where it now is to the society-shaping role that it is correctly positioned to carry. Only the chairperson, using tactics that are appropriate for a seminary in these times, is likely to be successful in creating that urgency. If the executive tries to create it, his or her tenure may be short. As I have noted in Chapter I, trustees (including the chairperson) are expendable; administrators are not.

The chairperson need not be able to design the creative steps that will be taken within the seminary to produce the seminal ideas that will inspire and support pastors, nor need he or she be conversant with the curriculum designs that will prepare pastors as significant religious leaders. Both of these are appropriately the professional concern of administrators and faculty. Trustees will want to review and comment on these matters, but they will not be the prime movers in these areas.

Trustees, especially the one in the chair, will need to be clear about the ultimate result of the seminary's work: more religious leaders everywhere and strong, influential, ably led churches; and be able to judge whether, in the carrying out of that mission, the ultimate influence on and support of churches is adequate. Trustees should be aware of and interested in, but stand somewhat aloof from, the effort of administrators and faculty to move the program of the seminary from mission to accomplishment. It is more appropriate for a layperson, than for a credentialed professional, to maintain this detached position. The seminary clearly needs professional strength, although what constitutes optimum, professional strength in a seminary may bear fresh examination—an examination that needs what only wise, lay judgment is likely to bring.

Advantage in the Lay Status of the Chairperson

The issue of strength in lay judgments is a debatable one, but the case for the importance of trustees, particularly the chairperson, in any institution rests upon acceptance of the possibility of that strength being realized. The best example I have of this is drawn from my AT&T experience—an example of the strength in lay judgments in a situation in which *that* was where wisdom resided.

The original National Labor Relations Act (Wagner Act) was en-
acted in 1935. Shortly thereafter, 50 great corporate lawyers met and
agreed that this law would be held unconstitutional and that they
could all advise their client companies to disregard it. When this conclusion was brought back and advocated by our AT&T lawyer who
was present at that meeting, he was promptly and forcefully challenged by my boss, an able and persuasive older man with but a fifth-
grade education. He was not in the upper levels of management, but
he was in a position in which he could be heard. Although his grammar was not impeccable, he was a powerful debater, a strong, honest,
intelligent man, but with no legal training or experience. The gist of
his argument was that this was 1935, not 1905. This was the second
time in as many years that the principle in the Wagner Act had been
legislated (the first was a section of the earlier National Industrial
Recovery Act of 1933 that was declared unconstitutional). It clearly
represented a firm social policy that would prevail. If this present law
was not upheld, new laws would keep coming until one was sustained. Therefore, we should start immediately to bring ourselves
into conformity with it (a state, with largely "company" unions, that
we missed by quite a margin). There was a great verbal battle, but
this boss of mine (20 years my senior) was a tough, formidable man.
After much grumbling, he prevailed and the company started (with
too deliberate speed) toward compliance. If his position had not prevailed, and if AT&T had held to the intransigent position that all of
these lawyers advocated (that the automobile companies and others
did accept and brought on the terrible imbroglio of 1939), AT&T
might have been dismembered then. And if this man's kind of thinking could have been more influential in top management councils in
the years that followed, the breakup might not have occurred.

Part of the strength of this untutored layman's position was that
he was not a lawyer. He was a very conservative man (in the best
sense), and he was able to look at the crisis that confronted the company as a social policy question, not a legal issue. And he believed,
with the comic character of the time—Mr. Dooley—that even the

Supreme Court, given a little time, reads the election returns. The Wagner Act was affirmed by the top court in 1937.

The strength of my old boss in this encounter was not just that he was not a lawyer, although that freed him from the "mind-set" that seems inherent in all credentialed professionals, or that he lacked formal education. Most important, I believe, was that he possessed the priceless gift of seeing things whole and, because of this, his advice was frequently sought by "better educated" people who lacked that gift. Is this not the quality, above all others, that should be sought in the trustee chairperson of a seminary? It is not a common ability, yet it does exist. The 200 seminaries in the United States could find such a person to chair their trustees if they were clear that that is what they need and want. And such are more likely to be found among uncredentialed laypersons.

Such a person in the chair, if otherwise qualified by motives, temperament, and skills, would likely be accepted by fellow trustees and other constituencies of the seminary and could supply the essential ingredient of wisdom regarding the adequacy of the critical thinking that is the heart of the seminary's work. This would be accomplished by watchfulness over the three steps suggested earlier as essential for any institution that achieves greatness as servant.

The Idea of the Seminary

If the seminary answers the question, "Whom and what purpose should this seminary serve" in terms like those suggested earlier in these chapters, the one who chairs the trustees (assuming that that person has the gift of seeing things whole) may ask, "Is this seminary as it now stands—both people, structure, and assumptions—best designed to accomplish that mission? If not, what kind of institution ought it be, and how do we move it prudently from here to there?" Such a question may lead the constituencies of the seminary to search for a creative design for the seminary of the future that, in addition to the present scholarly structure, may accommodate some whose principal qualifications are that they have the gifts of (1) seeing things whole and (2) prophetic communication. They may or may not be scholars.

The Problem of Language

Part of my thinking about language in the field of religion comes from the opportunity I had as a young man in New York to attend services at Riverside Church when Harry Emerson Fosdick preached. These sermons were remarkable for their clarity and simplicity—all in the vocabulary of the ordinary person. I received some insight into his gift many years later when I was privileged to be in the company of a mutual friend to visit Dr. Fosdick in his old age for an afternoon of conversation. In the course of this visit, he told us that as a young man he had had a mental disturbance and had to have help to get himself reoriented. As a consequence he said that, in the years of his ministry, he had reason to believe that he was a good preacher and writer, but that the most rewarding satisfactions in his career were in one-to-one consultations with disturbed people. He felt that he was at his greatest effectiveness here because he could say to his counselee, "I know exactly how you feel because I have been there." The clarity and simplicity of his preaching must have been profoundly influenced by the centrality of personal counseling in his ministry.

However gifted they may be, pastors trained in seminaries need to communicate ideas that give hope and in language that is powerful and beautiful, words that lift the spirit. The chairperson of seminary trustees needs to be concerned that his school wields an influence on its students that favors this result.

The Seminary Chairperson as a Personal Role Model

By giving oversight to the pivotal part of the seminary's mission, critical thought, one has the opportunity to be a role model for those who carry equally important leadership in a local church, the lay leaders of its congregation.

It was argued earlier that seminary trustees and their chairpersons are expendable, but executives and administrators are not. So, in time, lay leaders in churches will come to accept that they are expendable but pastors are not. Expendable persons will take the higher risks of leading.

What Does "Serving the Churches" Mean?

How does a seminary know when it is serving the churches?

A consultant who has worked with several seminaries recently on restudying their missions reports, "One of the observations that comes out of this experience is the propensity of seminaries to give continuity to the safe kinds of ministry they perceive the churches which pay the bills as willing to subsidize." This states the common problem of *all* serving institutions: businesses, schools, churches, governments. What will the constituency, customer, citizen want and be willing to pay for *in the future?* Making this judgment is probably most critical in business.

A few years ago, I found myself seated at a luncheon meeting in New York between the editors of two important magazines that were part of the same group. Plying my trade as I usually do, I engaged them on the question, "How do you make the decision, out of all the stories, articles, and pictures you have available, which ones you will print in your next issue?" Their prompt answer was most illuminating. I will reconstruct it as best I can.

"Most popular magazines make regular reader surveys in which they try to find out what readers liked best in the last issue, what they disliked or were not interested in, and what they would like to see more of in the future. In making the decision on the question you ask, *you do not follow literally what readers tell you.* That is what killed the *Saturday Evening Post*—literally following what readers said they wanted more of. The problem is that readers cannot say what they will want more of in the future. What they will respond to in the next issues when they arrive depends somewhat on what happens in their lives, what public events have caught their attention, in the meantime. What makes magazine editing interesting and challenging is that *planning every issue requires a leap of imagination.* Part of what nourishes that leap is close attention to reader surveys, but only part. The rest of it is vast experience with journalism knowledge about how people evolve and change, and watching closely what is going on in the world. We try to plant in every issue a seed that will grow into a need that we can serve in the future. That is how we editors, with our opportunities, can lead."

A seminary's relationship with churches is not like that of a magazine with its readers, but there is something to be learned from this example. Churches cannot tell seminaries what they will want in the future—and will be willing to pay for. If, as the consultant's observation quoted above suggests, some seminaries assume that churches will continue to want and be willing to pay for what they now receive—a "safe" ministry—providing that may make for a comfortable relationship in the present. But what about the future? What about the future when the present, in terms of church influence and membership, is not good?

This is a question for a seminary chairperson who is disposed to try to influence his or her trustees to *lead*, to go out ahead and show the way and persuade seminary administrators and staff to act now, in the interest of the future soundness of churches. The seminary's prime concern is always for the future of churches. The future of churches will be determined importantly by the ideas, critical thought, that seminaries produce *now*, and persuade churches to consider—*now!*

All true leadership—because it deals with the future—entails risk, and the chairperson who sees things whole will be the first to accept that risk and make the necessary leap of imagination. What supports the seminary chairperson in that risk (as distinguished from the editor of the magazine) is an inspired vision of what the seminary and the churches that depend on it for intellectual and prophetic leadership, might become—greater servants of society.

POSTSCRIPT

The positions taken here regarding the urgency of the need to raise seminaries from the present marginal state of some of them to fully serving institutions rest on beliefs about current America as a low-serving society. Every category of institution I know about, including seminaries and churches, has far too many low-serving elements, when judged by the criterion of what is reasonable and possible with available resources, human and material. Why should anybody in government, business, or education try to do better when seminaries that should be models are not conspicuous for their service to society? If the quality of our total society is to be lifted, seminaries and then churches, one at a time, need to be lifted substantially into a position of preeminent service.

As noted earlier, both the initiative and the sustaining push to achieve this movement will come from trustees who are laypersons and who have a strong determined leader who chairs their effort. If the current chairperson does not feel up to giving this leadership, that person might quietly step aside and help find someone who can and will give that leadership—someone who has the temperament and the staying power for the long, hard struggle that may be required. It could be the supreme achievement of that person's life to learn to lead a seminary effectively and with spirit.

Alongside my convictions about lay influence of trustees in seminaries, I am equally firm about the importance of intellectual power in the seminary—a power that will enable its faculty and other staff to support churches and church institutions at a level of excellence in their performance that, on their own and without the support of the intellectual power of seminaries, might be quite ordinary.

Intellectual power could be said to have two main elements: scholarship and wisdom. What may be needed, first, is a new vision from within seminaries as they now stand, possibly one of those seminaries now labeled as marginal. It is the kind of vision that the King James version of Proverbs suggests is one without which the people perish. Such a vision may simply announce a yearning to be served by being led by a trustee chairperson who has the gift of seeing things whole—a person who is wise and who will give leadership to the end that the seminary comes to be accepted as both scholarly and wise.

And what would a seminary be like (as contrasted with what most are today) when it comes to be known as both scholarly and wise? In my essay "The Servant as Religious Leader" I speculate on what might be the characteristics of a seminary when significant formation of religious leaders takes place there.

- Its priorities will be reversed. Whereas seminaries are now mostly academic and only incidentally formative, formation of religious leaders will be primary and academic teaching will be secondary.

- The staff of the seminaries will contain a strong element of those who have a passion for growing religious leaders—and are good at it. They may or may not be scholars in the usual sense.

- A major mission of the seminary will be to evolve, and maintain, a theology of institutions that deals realistically with the problem of how to recover moribund institutions as vital, effective, caring, and serving. This will not be a theoretical endeavor because it will be forged on the seminary's own experience as it builds itself into—and maintains itself as—the pivotal institution it is determined to become. Seminary students will be deeply involved in this continuous effort to build and maintain this theology. They will not just read and hear lectures about it.

- The primary mission of the seminary will be leading and serving churches and supporting them as strong influential institutions. Most of the learning of seminary students will result from involvement in this effort.

- There will be creative thinkers among its faculty who are developing and articulating a contemporary theology of what makes religious leaders, and the institutions they serve, strong. Students in the seminary will be deeply involved in responding to this with their own thinking.

- Such seminaries will become known as effective nurturers of able religious leaders and they will attract a wide spectrum of strong young people in search of such formative development. Some of these students might find their career opportunities in churches, but the seminary will become a prime source of religious leaders for all segments of society. It will acknowledge that any institution where religious leaders predominate may effectively become a church.

I submit these as achievable goals for a seminary whose constituencies (particularly the faculty that holds the predominant power) accept that new critical thought about both the seminary as an institution and its theology is essential. Further, they accept the leadership of the lay person who chairs their trustees and who is persuasive in helping them to reach those goals.

My Debt to E. B. White

In 1929, when I moved to New York, I was immediately attracted to *The New Yorker* magazine, that was then in its fifth year, and to E. B. White, who had helped make it a remarkable magazine, and who had been on the staff for three years. My debt to Mr. White, after 55 years of living with his writings, stems from two gifts that are rarely possessed by one person: the ability to see things whole, or more whole than most, and the language to tell us ordinary mortals what he sees.

I am not a literary person, but I know that White's writing style is greatly admired among some literary folk. His revision of Strunk's *The Elements of Style* is a widely used text. He is sometimes identified as a humorist, and I find good laughs in his work. He is a fellow who, when the spirit moves him, just naturally breaks into song—so there is quite a bit of poetry. In his later years, there have been stories for children. As a so-called adult, I find them delightful. But his writing style, his humor, his poetry, and his children's stories are not the central focus of what I want to acknowledge here, though, obviously, they are the context within which it is housed.

I have not received from reading E. B. White the solutions to any of life's dilemmas, but for these 55 years, I have had constant assurance that if I will see clearly where I am (and where I and others in similar dilemmas have been), and if my direction is right (uncluttered with zany ideas), I will always better know what to do now. This has been a valuable learning, and I am exceedingly grateful that I received it early. I am not aware that, in the course of my formal education, I heard anything about this. But then, it probably takes an artist to put this over, and for the most part, my teachers were not artists. E. B. White is such an artist.

James Thurber, White's good friend and collaborator from their early days on *The New Yorker*, freely acknowledges White as his mentor on writing. And he seems to have understood White's unique gifts better than White himself understood them. Thurber, writing in 1938 from France, chides White for publishing a piece in *The Saturday Evening Post* (which may have paid better at that time than *The New Yorker*). Thurber, after lamenting the confusion in the world and the crazy things people are doing, says, "It remains for a few people to stand aside and watch them and report what it looks like and sounds like. Among such persons, there isn't anybody better qualified for the job than you—if *you will quit sending pieces to The Saturday Evening Post.*" Thurber goes on to express his concern that White does not understand or appreciate his gift and reminds him that his writing is not simply a response to the writer's *urge* but is a matter of "moral necessity." It is the kind of letter that only a cherished friend would write. In short, Thurber tells White (in my language) to get with it and make the contribution to our times that only he can make.

Thurber seems to be saying to White, "You see things whole, and that is what you should write about—in the only place that is likely to let you do it—*The New Yorker*. Maybe *Harpers*, but not *The Saturday Evening Post*."

Thurber and White as young men shared a small office at *The New Yorker*. In that period, they collaborated on a spoof of psychoanalysis to which they gave the provocative title, "Is Sex Necessary?" It was a best-seller. After Thurber died, White wrote a new introduction for a new edition. In it he said, "You would think that a couple of young fellows trying to get along in the world could have found something better to do."

Elwyn Brooks White was born in the close-in suburb of Mt. Vernon, New York in 1899, the sixth child in a family whose father was a successful piano manufacturer in New York. As a child, he developed a fondness of animals and had pets and kept chickens and pigeons, a disposition that emerged later when he retired to his farm in Maine. About his childhood, White says in the introduction to his collected letters:

> If an unhappy childhood is indispensable for a writer, I am ill-equipped: I missed out on all that and was neither deprived nor unloved. It would be inaccurate, however, to say that my childhood was untroubled. The normal fears and worries of every child were in me developed to a high degree; every day was an awesome prospect. I was uneasy about practically everything: the uncertainty of the future, the dark of the attic, the panoply and discipline of school, the transitoriness of life, the mystery of the church and God, the frailty of the body, the sadness of afternoon, the shadow of sex, the distant challenge of love and marriage, the far-off problem of a livelihood. I brooded about them all, lived with them day by day. Being the youngest in a large family, I was usually in a crowd but often felt lonely and removed. I took to writing early, to

assuage my uneasiness and collect my thoughts, and I was a busy
writer long before I went into long pants.

"In school," he continues, "I contracted a fear of platforms that has
dogged me all of my life and caused me to decline every invitation to
speak in public." When White turned 70 in 1969, a *New York Times*
reporter went up to Maine, where he then lived, to interview him. In
the course of the interview White said, "I was born scared, and at 70
I am still scared." I will come back to this comment later. In that interview, White had some things to say about growing old.

> "How should one adjust to age!" Mr. White was asked, and replied:
> "In principle, one shouldn't adjust. In fact, one does. (Or I do.)
> When my head starts knocking because of my attempt to write, I
> quit writing instead of carrying on as I used to do when I was
> young.
>
> "These are adjustments. But I gaze into the faces of our senior
> citizens in our Southern cities, and they wear a sad look that dis-
> turbs me. I am sorry for all those who have agreed to grow old. I
> haven't agreed yet. Old age is a special problem for me because I've
> never been able to shed the mental image I have of myself—a lad of
> about 19.
>
> "A writer certainly has a special problem with aging. The gen-
> erative process is slowed down, yet the pain and frustration of not
> writing is as acute as ever. I feel frustrated and in pain a good deal
> of the time now; but I try to bear in mind the advice of Hubert
> Humphrey's father. 'Never get sick, Hubert, there isn't time.'"

White attended Cornell University, whose founding president
was one Andrew White. By tradition, every male student to enroll
whose name was White was nicknamed "Andy," and to his close
friends, Elwyn Brooks White has always been *Andy*. At Cornell, he
quickly joined the staff of the campus newspaper and, in his senior
year, he was editor. White was not a scholar at Cornell, but he was
active in a fraternity, and in his senior year, he was its president.

On graduation, he spent a year in New York trying to get a job in journalism, and the best he could do was The American Legion News Service. When a footloose Cornell classmate showed up in New York, they decided to drive to the West Coast in a model T roadster, named Hotspur. They set off early in 1922 and arrived in Louisville, Kentucky, at derby time. White wrote a sonnet on a winning horse which he showed to the editor of the *Louisville Herald*, who asked, "Do you do this for glory or for money?" "For money," White replied. The editor paid him $5 and ran the sonnet on the front page next day.

The trip across the country in Hotspur was eventful. Arriving in Seattle, White got a reporter's job on a Seattle daily which he held for a year, when he was fired. The reason was that when he covered an event, he was so much a perfectionist and took too long to write his story. Frequently, in later life, he acknowledged that he was a failure as a reporter.

Then there was a boat trip to Alaska. Returning to New York after 1½ years in the west, he got a job with an advertising agency where he hated to work—but which was a living, and it gave him an opportunity to write. He says:

> The arrival on the scene of Harold Ross's *New Yorker* on February
> 21, 1925, was a turning point in my life, although I did not know it
> at the time. I bought a copy of the first issue at the newsstand in
> Grand Central, examined Eustace Tilly and his butterfly on the
> cover (every Washington's birthday issue has that cover) and was
> attracted to the newborn magazine, not because it had any great
> merit but because the items were short, relaxed and sometimes
> funny. I was a "short" writer, and I lost no time in submitting
> squibs and poems. In return, I received a few small cheques and the
> satisfaction of seeing myself in print as a pro.

Harold Ross encouraged White to submit more to *The New Yorker* and asked him to drop in. When he did drop in, the editor who greeted him was Katharine Angell. White said, "I noted that she had

a lot of black hair and the knack of making a young contributor feel
at ease. I sat there peacefully gazing at the classic features of my future wife without, as usual, knowing what I was doing." Forty years
later, in an interview, White said of his wife:

> I have never seen an adequate account of Katharine's role with *The
> New Yorker*. She was one of the first editors to be hired, and I can't
> imagine what would have happened to the magazine if she hadn't
> turned up. Ross, though something of a genius, had serious gaps. In
> Katharine he found someone who filled them. No two people were
> more different than Harold and Katharine. What he lacked, she
> had; what she lacked, he had. She was a product of Miss Windsor's
> and Bryn Mawr; Ross was a high school dropout. She had a natural
> refinement of manner and speech; Ross mumbled and bellowed
> and swore. She was patient and quiet; he was impatient and noisy.
> On one thing they usually agreed—what was funny. Katharine was
> soon heading the Fiction Department, sharing the personal woes
> and dilemmas of innumerable contributors and staff people who
> were in trouble or despair, and, in short, accepting the whole un-
> ruly business of a tottering magazine with the warmth and dedica-
> tion of a broody hen.
>
> I had a bird's eye view of all of this, because in the midst of it, I
> became her husband. During the day, I saw her in operation at the
> office. At the end of the day, I watched her bring the whole mess
> home with her in a cheap, bulging portfolio. The light burned late,
> and our bed was lumpy with page proofs, and our home was alive
> with laughter and the pervasive spirit of her dedication and her in-
> dustry. I suspect that one of Ross's luckiest days was the day a
> young woman named Katharine Angell stepped off the elevator, all
> ready to go to work.

I have said that my debt to E. B. White is that he is the person
who alerted me to the gift of seeing things whole, and my attachment
to his writing, beginning when I was 25, encouraged me to cultivate
that gift in myself. My career as an organization man and a bureau-

crat in a huge institution, where I was very much at home, was radically different from White's, who never was an administrator and who had great difficulty keeping regular office hours. Yet, across that great gulf of temperament and experience, he was able to communicate to me his great gift of seeing things whole, and it has proved to be an asset all my life.

What was the man like who was able to do this for me? I have never met E. B. White, and in over 50 years I have exchanged only two or three letters with him. Yet, I feel that I know him very well. His collected letters are interspersed with biographical notes that give quite a complete account of his life. He was a great letter writer and, his letters being literary gems, people saved them. But most of the insight I have about White comes from reading what he has said about other people. There is an old saying, "What Peter says about Paul tells us more about Peter than it does about Paul." This observation seems to be particularly true of White. Let me quote what he has written about three people to whom he was very close: the first, Henry Thoreau, whom White knew only from his writing, and two with whom he worked closely, James Thurber and Harold Ross, whose obituaries he wrote for *The New Yorker*.

On the 100th anniversary of the publication of Thoreau's *Walden* in 1854, White wrote a long piece for *The Yale Review* entitled, "A Slight Sound at Evening." I will note a few excerpts from his essay on Thoreau's *Walden*.

> I think it is of some advantage to encounter the book at a period in one's life when the normal anxieties and enthusiasms and rebellions of youth closely resemble those of Thoreau in that spring of 1845 when he borrowed an ax, went out to the woods, and began to whack down some trees for timber. Received at such a juncture, the book is like an invitation to life's dance, assuring the troubled recipient that no matter what befalls him in the way of success or failure he will always be welcome at the party— that the music is played for him too, if he will but listen and move his feet. . . . It still seems

to me the best youth's companion yet written by an American, for it carries a solemn warning against the loss of one's valuables, it advances a good argument for travelling light and trying new adventures, it rings with the power of positive adoration, it contains religious feeling without religious images, and it steadfastly refuses to record bad news. . . .

When he went to the pond, Thoreau struck an attitude and did so deliberately, but his posturing was not to draw the attention of others to him but rather to draw his own attention more closely to himself. "I learned this at least from my experiment: that if one advances confidently in the direction of his dreams, and endeavors to live the life which he has imagined, he will meet with a success unexpected in common hours." The sentence has the power to resuscitate the youth drowning in his sea of doubt. I recall my exhilaration upon reading it, many years ago, in a time of hesitation and despair. It restored me to health. And now in 1954 when I salute Henry Thoreau on the 100th birthday of his book, I am merely paying off an old score—or an installment on it.

There has been much guessing as to why he went to the pond. To set it down to escapism is, of course, to misconstrue what happened. Henry went forth to battle when he took to the woods, and *Walden* is the report of a man torn by two powerful and opposing drives—the desire to enjoy the world, and the urge to set the world straight. One cannot join these two successfully, but sometimes, in rare cases, something good or even great results from the attempt of the tormented spirit to reconcile them. Henry went forth to battle, and if he set the stage himself, if he fought on his own terms and with his own weapons, it was because it was his nature to do things differently from most men, and to act in a cocky fashion. If the pond and the woods seemed a more plausible site for a house than an in-town location, it was because a cowbell made for him a sweeter sound than a churchbell. *Walden*, the book, makes the sound of a cowbell, more than a churchbell, and proves the point, although both sounds are in it, and both remarkably clear and sweet. He simply preferred his churchbells at a little distance. *[I suspect that White also preferred his churchbells at a little distance]*

I confess that I have not been a Thoreau fan. The first thing I ever read of Thoreau's was his essay on "Civil Disobedience" which he wrote in a fit of pique after spending a night in jail for refusing to pay his Poll Tax. I wrote him off as a wooly anarchist and never read him again. But after rereading White's essay recently, I decided that I had better have a look at *Walden*. So, I read it. And I discovered, to my surprise, that there is more of Thoreau in me than I had been aware of. Such is the fate of one who falls under the spell of one who sees things whole (a trait that White may have acquired from Thoreau since he read Thoreau when he, White, was young and was greatly influenced by him).

Harold Ross, the great founding editor of *The New Yorker*, died December 6, 1951. Writing of him in the December 15th issue, White wrote:

Ross died in Boston, unexpectedly, on the night of December 6th, and we are writing this in New York (unexpectedly) on the morning of December 7th. This is known, in these offices that Ross was so fond of, as a jam. Ross always knew when we were in a jam, and usually went on the phone to offer advice and comfort and support. When our phone rang just now, and in that split second before the mind focuses, we thought, "Good! Here it comes!" But this old connection is broken beyond fixing. The phone has not in its power to explode at the right moment and in the right way.

Actually, things are not going as badly as they might; the sheet of copy paper in the machine is not as hard to face as we feared. Sometimes a love letter writes itself and we loved Ross so, and bear him respect, that these quick notes, which purport to record the sorrow that runs through here and dissolves so many people, cannot possibly seem overstated or silly. Ross, even on this terrible day, is a hard man to keep quiet; he obtrudes—his face, his voice, his manner, even his amused interest in the critical proceedings. If he were accorded the questionable privilege of stopping by here for a few minutes, he would gorge himself on the minor technical problems that a magazine faces when we must do something in a hurry and against all sorts of odds—in this case, emotional ones of almost overpowering weight. He would be far more interested in the grinding of the machinery than in what was being said about him.

All morning, people have wandered in and out of our cell, some tearfully, some guardedly, some boisterously, most of them long-time friends in various stages of repair. We have amused ourself thinking of Ross's reaction to this flow. "Never bother a writer" was one of his strongest principles. He used to love to drop in himself, and sit around, but was uneasy the whole time because of the carking feeling that if only he would get up and go away, we might settle down to work and produce something. To him, a writer at work, whether in the office or anywhere in the outside world, was an extraordinarily interesting, valuable, but fragile object, and he half expected it to fall into a thousand pieces at any moment.

The report of Ross's death came over the telephone in a three-word sentence that somehow managed to embody all the faults that Ross devoted his life to correcting. A grief-stricken friend in Boston, charged with the task of spreading the news but too dazed to talk sensibly, said, "It's all over." He meant that Ross was dead, but the listener took it to mean that the operation was over. Here, in three easy words, were the ambiguity, the euphemistic softness, the verbal infirmity that Harold W. Ross spent his life thrusting at. Ross regarded every sentence as the enemy, and believed that if a man watched closely enough, he would discover the vulnerable spot, the essential weakness. He devoted his life to making the weak strong—a rather specialized form of blood transfusion, to be sure, but one that he believed in with such a consuming passion that his spirit infected others and inspired them, and lifted them. Whatever it was, this contagion, this vapor in these marshes, it spread. None escaped it. Nor is it likely to be dissipated in a hurry.

His ambition was to publish one good magazine, not a string
of successful ones, and he thought of *The New Yorker* as a sort of
movement. He came equipped with not much knowledge and only
two books—Webster's Dictionary and Fowler's *Modern English
Usage.* These books were his history, his geography, his literature,
his art, his music, his everything. Some people found Ross's
scholastic deficiencies quite appalling, and were not sure they had
met the right man. But he was the right man, and the only question
was whether the other fellow was capable of being tuned to Ross's
vibrations. Ross had a thing that is at least as good as, and sometimes better than, knowledge: he had a sort of natural drive in the
right direction, plus a complete respect for the work and ideas and
opinions of others. It took a little while to get on to the fact that
Ross, more violently than almost anybody, was proceeding in a
good direction, and carrying others along with him, under torren-
tial conditions. He was like a boat being driven at the mercy of
some internal squall, a disturbance he himself only half understood,
and of which he was at times suspicious.

In a way, he was a lucky man. For a monument he has the magazine to date—one thousand three hundred and ninety-nine issues,
born in the toil and pain that can be appreciated only by those who
helped in the delivery room. These are his. They stand, unchange-
able and open for inspection. We are, of course, not in a position to
estimate the monument, even if we were in the mood to. But we
are able to state one thing unequivocally: Ross set up a great target
and pounded himself to pieces trying to hit it square in the middle.
His dream was a simple dream; it was pure and had no frills: he
wanted the magazine to be good, to be funny, and to be fair.

We say he was lucky. Some people cordially disliked him.
Some were amused but not impressed. And then, last, there are the
ones we have been seeing today, the ones who loved him and had
him for a friend—people he looked after, and who looked after
him. These last are the ones who worked close enough to him,
and long enough with him, to cross over the barrier reef of noisy

shallows that ringed him, into the lagoon that was Ross himself—a rewarding, and even enchanting, and relatively quiet place, utterly trustworthy as an anchorage. Maybe these people had all the luck. The entrance wasn't always easy to find.

He left a note on our desk one day apropos of something that had pleased him in the magazine. The note simply said, "I am encouraged to go on." That is about the way we feel today, because of his contribution. We are encouraged to go on.

When you took leave of Ross after a calm or stormy meeting, he always ended with the phrase that has become as much a part of the office as the paint on the walls. He would wave his limp hand, gesturing you away. "All right," he would say. "God bless you." Considering Ross's temperament and habits, this was a rather odd expression. He usually took God's name in vain if he took it at all. But when he sent you away with his benediction, which he uttered briskly and affectionately, and in which he and God seemed all scrambled together, it carried a warmth and sincerity that never failed to carry over. The words are so familiar to his helpers and friends here that they provide the only possible way to conclude this hasty notice and to take our leave. We cannot convey his manner. But with much love in our heart, we say, for everybody, "All right Ross, God bless you."

When James Thurber, one of White's closest friends, died on November 2, 1961, White wrote of him in the November 11th *New Yorker.*

I am one of the lucky ones; I knew him before blindness hit him, before fame hit him, and I tend always to think of him as a young artist in a small office in a big city, with all the world still ahead. It was a fine thing to be young and at work in New York for a new magazine when Thurber was young and at work, and I will always be glad that this happened to me.

It was fortunate that we got on well; the office we shared was the size of a hall bedroom. There was just room enough for two

men, two typewriters, and a stack of copy paper. The copy paper
disappeared at a scandalous rate—not because our production was
high (although it was) but because Thurber used copy paper as the
natural receptacle for discarded sorrows, immediate joys, stale
dreams, golden prophecies, and messages of good cheer to the outside world and to fellow-workers. His mind was never at rest, and
his pencil was connected to his mind by the best conductive tissue I
have ever seen in action. The whole world knows what a funny
man he was, but you had to sit next to him day after day to understand the extravagance of his clowning, the wildness and subtlety of
his thinking, and the intensity of his interest in others and his sympathy for their dilemmas—dilemmas that he instantly enlarged, put
in focus, and made immortal, just as he enlarged and made immortal the strange goings on in the Ohio home of his boyhood. His
waking dreams and his sleeping dreams commingled shamelessly
and uproariously. Ohio was never far from his thoughts, and when
he received a medal from his home state in 1953, he wrote, "The
clocks that strike in my dreams are often the clocks of Columbus."
It is a beautiful sentence and a revealing one.

He was both a practitioner of humor and a defender of it. The
day he died, I came on a letter from him, dictated to a secretary and
signed in pencil with his sightless and enormous "Jim." "Every time
is a time for humor," he wrote. "I write humor the way a surgeon
operates, because it is a livelihood, because I have a great urge to
do it, because many interesting challenges are set up, and because I
have the hope it may do some good." Once, I remember, he heard
someone say that humor is a shield, not a sword, and it made him
mad. He wasn't going to have anyone beating his sword into a
shield. That "surgeon," incidentally, is pure Mitty. During his hap-
piest years, Thurber did not write the way a surgeon operates, he
wrote the way a child skips rope, the way a mouse waltzes.

Although he is best known for *Walter Mitty* and *The Male
Animal*, the book of his I like best is *The Last Flower*. In it you will
find his faith in the renewal of life, his feeling for the beauty and

fragility of life on earth. Like all good writers, he fashioned his own best obituary notice. Nobody else can add to the record, much as he might like to. And of all the flowers, real and figurative, that will find their way to Thurber's last resting place, the one that will remain fresh and wiltproof is the little flower he himself drew, on the last page of that lovely book.

⚜

Etched in my memory when my wife Esther and I were living as young people in New York in the 1930s and following the contemporary art scene is the incident of the Rivera mural in the new Rockefeller Center. Nelson Rockefeller, then a young man, was interested in contemporary art and was in charge of building the Center. He had commissioned Diego Rivera, the radical Mexican artist, to paint a mural in the entrance hall of the main building just above the skating rink. The work was done in fresco in which a plasterer lays up the surface just ahead of the painter who uses water-soluble pigments that penetrate the wet plaster—so when the plaster dries, it is really on there. When Rivera arrived at the lower-right corner when he would normally sign, he introduced a large head of Lenin and the hammer and sickle, signed his name and was through. There was a great uproar and the mural was ultimately destroyed— chipped off the wall. White wrote a poem about it in *The New Yorker*.

I Paint What I See
(A Ballad of Artistic Integrity, on the Occasion of the Removal of Some Rather Expensive Murals from the RCA Building in the Year 1933)

"What do you paint, when you paint on a wall?"
Said John D.'s grandson Nelson.
"Do you paint just anything there at all?
"Will there be any doves, or a tree in fall?

"Or a hunting scene, like an English hall?"
"I paint what I see," said Rivera.
"What are the colors you use when you paint?"
Said John D.'s grandson Nelson.
"Do you use any red in the beard of a saint?
"If you do, is it terribly red, or faint?
"Do you use any blue! Is it Prussian?"
"I paint what I paint," said Rivera.
"Whose is that head that I see on my wall?"
Said John D.'s grandson Nelson.
"Is it anyone's head whom we know, at all?
"A Rensselaer, or a Saltonstall?
"Is it Franklin D.? Is it Mordaunt Hall?
"Or is it the head of a Russian?"
"I paint what I think," said Rivera.
"I paint what I paint, I paint what I see,
"I paint what I think," said Rivera,
"And the thing that is dearest in life to me
"In a bourgeois hall is Integrity;
"However . . .
"I'll take out a couple of people drinkin'
"And put in a picture of Abraham Lincoln;
"I could even give you McCormick's reaper
"And still not make my art much cheaper.
"But the head of Lenin has got to stay
"Or my friends will give me the bird today,
"The bird, the bird, forever."
"It's not good taste in a man like me,"
Said John D.'s grandson Nelson,
"To question an artist's integrity
"Or mention a practical thing like a fee,
"But I know what I like to a large degree,
"Though art I hate to hamper;
"For twenty-one thousand conservative bucks

> "You painted a radical. I say shucks,
> "I never could rent the offices —
> "The capitalistic offices.
> "For this, as you know, is a public hall
> "And people want doves, or a tree in fall,
> "And although your art I dislike to hamper,
> "I owe a little to God and Gramper,
> "And after all,
> "it's my wall . . . "
> "We'll see if it is," said Rivera.

Rivera was born 50 years too soon, because I understand that New York now has a law that gives the artist some control over how his work is shown. They might have some trouble getting rid of that mural today. A replica of Rivera's Rockefeller Center mural is now on the wall of a museum in Mexico City. It pleases me to think that some day ours will become a mature enough society that that mural will return to New York, head of Lenin and all, and be given an appropriate spot so that people can judge its artistic merit. When and if that happens, it may be that this poem of E. B. White's, which is widely anthologized, will have helped keep alive the idea that there is some unfinished business from the 1930s.

When White was about 40, he and his wife moved from New York to a farm on the coast of Maine. They both continued to work for *The New Yorker* with occasional trips to New York. Katharine, who was the older, died in 1977. Mr. White died October 1, 1985.

White, as we know from his comments on his childhood, confirmed in several letters, has lived all his life in a state of anxiety with several long illnesses. A friend commented on his leaving New York, "Andy moved to Maine to save his life." Living in Maine in a small community and close to farm animals was a necessary condition for his existence, and much of his later writing has been about life on his farm and among small-town people in whom he found much-treasured wisdom.

Despite his lifelong anxiety, White was a very social guy. He and his wife, Katharine, had many friends, spent much enjoyable time with them, and carried on a lively correspondence.

My most interesting, and perhaps my most significant experience with White's writing came in 1969. After retiring from AT&T in 1964, I spent some active years in consulting work. Two of my clients in that period were universities during the traumatic years of student unrest. Time has healed some of the scars, but I have vivid memories of that period, particularly talks with the radical students. It was a wild time, and I was right in the thick of it.

In September of 1969, my alma mater, Carleton College, did an interesting thing. As a smaller college of 1500 students, they were not as threatened by the unrest as were large universities, but they were disturbed enough to convene, for two weeks ahead of the opening of school that year, all of the student leaders. This included class officers, team captains, editors of paper and year book, etc., plus three or four faculty and the college chaplain who presided. Their purpose was to just have a leisurely talk about the problems of operating the college under these disturbing conditions. I was invited to meet with them for two days as a resource person (since I had been up to my ears in this confusion in other places).

Near the end of my two days with them, I read them E. B. White's essay "The Second Tree from the Corner." Before reading it, I told them a little about White and reminded them of White's statement to the reporter, "I was born scared and at 70 I am still scared." I asked them to bear this in mind because I suspected that the essay was somewhat autobiographical. Some years later when White's letters came out, I confirmed that it was written after a session with his psychiatrist in New York.

The essay, "The Second Tree from The Corner," concerns a man named Trexler in a routine session with his psychiatrist, and what Trexler thinks about as he walks down the street after the session. The interview deals with Trexler's fears and a question that the doctor repeatedly pressed, "What do *you* want!" In the course of the

session, Trexler turns the question on the doctor, "What do *you*
want!" And the doctor, caught short, stammers, "I want a new wing
on my house on Long Island."

When I finished reading, I commented to the students that I
thought that White, in this essay, had a literary strategy somewhat
similar to that of Camus' when he wrote *The Stranger* (which I knew
they had all read in freshman English). Camus takes 100 or so pages
to describe a situation, a murder, and the trial and conviction of the
murderer to set the stage, it seems to me, for three or four pages at
the end which tell of the conversation between a priest and the con-
victed man on the eve of the latter's execution. I believe that the content of this interview was what Camus really wanted to get across to
us. White, more devoted to economy of language than Camus, takes
five pages to describe this session with the psychiatrist to set the stage
for two paragraphs at the end where, it seems to me, he tells us what
he really wants us to get. And I reread those two paragraphs.

> It was an evening of clearing weather, the Park showing green and
> desirable in the distance, the last daylight applying a high lacquer
> to the brick and brownstone walls and giving the street scene a lu-
> minous and intoxicating splendor. Trexler meditated, as he walked,
> on what he wanted. "What do you want!" he heard again. Trexler
> knew what he wanted, and what, in general, all men wanted; and he
> was glad, in a way, that it was both inexpressible and unattainable,
> and that it wasn't a wing. He was satisfied to remember that it was
> deep, formless, enduring, and impossible of fulfillment, and that it
> made men sick, and that when you sauntered along Third Avenue
> and looked through the doorways into the dim saloons, you could
> sometimes pick out from the unregenerate ranks the ones who had
> not forgotten, gazing steadily into the bottoms of the glasses on the
> long chance that they could get another little peek at it. Trexler
> found himself renewed by the remembrance that what he wanted
> was at once great and microscopic, and that although it borrowed
> from the nature of large deeds and of youthful love and of old

songs and early intimations, it was not any one of these things, and that it had not been isolated or pinned down, and that a man who attempted to define it in the privacy of a doctor's office would fall flat on his face.

Trexler felt invigorated. Suddenly his sickness seemed health, his dizziness stability. A small tree, rising between him and the light, stood there saturated with the evening, each gilt-edged leaf perfectly drunk with excellence and delicacy. Trexler's spine registered an ever so slight tremor as it picked up this natural disturbance in the lovely scene. "I want the second tree from the corner, just as it stands," he said, answering to an imaginary question from an imaginary physician. And he felt a slow pride in realizing that what he wanted none could bestow, and that what he had none could take away. He felt content to be sick, unembarrassed at being afraid; and in the jungle of his fear he glimpsed (as he had so often glimpsed them before) the flashy tail feathers of the bird courage.

There were a few moments of silence after I finished, and the students took off and talked for two hours. I didn't say another word—just listened. Condensing two hours of discussion into one sentence: they ultimately identified the problem of the students of their generation as a sort of mental illness, and, like White, they would only recover their poise when they accepted their illness as health—and got on with their work. It was the most fascinating two hours of discussion I ever listened to.

The sequel to his session came several weeks later when Professor Maitland, the Chaplain, sent me a copy of the first issue of the college newspaper in which this two-week session was reported. The report concluded with the announcement that the group had agreed to continue to meet during the school year and that they had named their group *The Second Tree from the Corner*. That was over 15 years ago, and I still hear the occasional reverberation from that meeting. Such is the influence of thinking that sees things whole, and of language that tells us what one sees that is powerful and beautiful.

One of the things one discovers by reading White's letters is that, in the early days of *The New Yorker*, he was the handyman. He did everything. He wrote essays, poems, newsbreaks, reported events, and wrote the opening "Talk of the Town." He even drew one cover, *and* he wrote captions for cartoons. My favorite quote from an early issue of *The New Yorker* is the caption on a full-page cartoon. As I remember it, there is a rich kid of 8 or 9 seated alone at dinner in a big posh dining room, being served by maid and butler, and with his governess standing behind him saying, "Oswald dear, please eat your nice *broccoli*." Says Oswald, "I say it's spinach, and I say the hell with it." I have found that line appropriate on several occasions over the years. And I discovered in the letters that it is pure E. B. White.

White was not a "cause" man—with two exceptions. During the war, he became interested in world government and wrote extensively on that subject with one of the loveliest pieces on that theme entitled, "The Wild Flag." But then, after the war, he covered the founding meeting of the United Nations for *The New Yorker* and concluded that world government was not a realistic expectation in our times. In a letter to a niece explaining his position, he said, "I think the most precious thing in the world is not the concept of world federation but the concept of justice—that is, justice as it has developed in the Western world. The only sort of one-world I would settle for is a one-world firmly based on that type of justice."

The other cause, long standing and still much alive in White as an old man, is the cause of integrity in journalism. Over the years, there have been three major public manifestations of this concern. Some years ago, White discovered the practice of *Reader's Digest* commissioning and paying for articles, giving them to other publications to print, and then condensing them in *Reader's Digest*. He strongly condemned this practice in the pages of *The New Yorker*, others joined in, and there was quite a stir about it. It didn't deter the *Digest*. But it did result in a *New Yorker* policy not to permit the *Digest* to take any of their stuff.

Then when a fellow *New Yorker* writer, Alexander Woolcott, gave

a testimonial for a beer ad, White took out after him—in the pages of
The New Yorker. Maybe okay for a movie actor, he said, but not for a
journalist. This created something of a stir, but I doubt that it influenced Woolcott.

In 1974, when White was old, he learned of the arrangement
wherein Harrison Salisbury, retired associate editor of the *New York
Times*, accepted a substantial fee from Xerox Corporation to write an
article that would appear in *Esquire* Magazine with a full-page Xerox
ad before and after it. White took pen in hand and wrote a letter to
the editor of the *The Ellsworth (Maine) American* describing the details of the arrangement and taking sharp exception to it.

In due course, White received a letter from Xerox outlining their
ground rules for sponsoring articles and asking, "With these ground
rules, do you still see something sinister in the sponsoring?" White's
reply of January 30, 1976, said unequivocally, "Yes, I do," and he
went on to support that judgment with careful reasoning. This is
what he wrote:

Letter to Mr. W. B. Jones
Director, Communications Operations
Xerox Corp.
January 30, 1976

Dear Mr. Jones,

In extending my remarks on sponsorship, published in *The
Ellsworth American*, I want to limit the discussion to the press—that
is, to newspapers and magazines. I'll not speculate about television,
as television is outside my experience, and I have no ready opinion
about sponsorship in that medium.

In your recent letter to me, you ask whether having studied
your ground rules for proper conduct in sponsoring a magazine
piece, I still see something sinister in the sponsorship. Yes, I do.
Sinister may not be the right word, but I see something ominous
and unhealthy when a corporation underwrites an article in a

magazine of general circulation. This is not, essentially, the old familiar question of an advertiser trying to influence editorial content: almost everyone is acquainted with that common phenomenon. Readers are aware that it is always present but usually in a rather subdued or nonthreatening form. Xerox's sponsoring of a specific writer on a specific occasion for a specific article is something quite different. No one, as far as I know, accuses Xerox of trying to influence editorial opinion. But many people are wondering why a large corporation placed so much money on a magazine piece, why the writer of the piece was willing to get paid in so unusual a fashion, and why *Esquire* was ready and willing to have an outsider pick up the tab. These are reasonable questions.

The press in our free country is reliable and useful not because of its good character but because of its great diversity. As long as there are many owners, each pursuing his own brand of truth, we the people have the opportunity to arrive at the truth and to dwell in the light. The multiplicity of ownership is crucial. It's only when there are few owners, or as in a government-controlled press, one owner, that the truth becomes elusive and the light fails. For a citizen in our free society, it is an enormous privilege and a wonderful protection to have access to hundreds of periodicals, each peddling its own belief. There is safety in numbers: the papers expose each other's follies and peccadillos, correct each other's mistakes, and cancel out each other's biases. The reader is free to range around in the whole editorial bouillabaisse and explore it for the one clam that matters—the truth.

When a large corporation or a rich individual underwrites an article in a magazine, the picture changes: the ownership of that magazine has been diminished, the outline of the magazine has been blurred. In the case of the Salisbury piece, it was as though *Esquire* had gone on relief, was accepting its first welfare payment, and was not its own man any more. The editor protests that he accepts full responsibility for the text and that Xerox had nothing to do with the whole business. But the fact remains that, despite his full acceptance of responsibility, he somehow did not get around to paying the bill. This is unsettling and I think unhealthy. Whenever money changes hands, something goes along with it—an intangible something that varies with the circumstances. It would be hard to resist the suspicion that *Esquire* feels indebted to Xerox, that Mr. Salisbury feels indebted to both, and that the ownership, or sovereignty, of *Esquire* has been nibbled all around the edges.

Sponsorship in the press is an invitation to corruption and abuse. The temptations are great, and there is an opportunist behind every bush. A funded article is a tempting morsel for any publication—particularly for one that is having a hard time making ends meet. A funded assignment is a tempting dish for a writer, who may pick up a much larger fee than he is accustomed to getting, and sponsorship is attractive to the sponsor himself, who, for one reason or another, feels an urge to penetrate the editorial columns after being so long pent up in the advertising pages. These temptations are real, and if the barriers were to be let down, I believe corruption and abuse would soon follow. Not all corporations would approach subsidy in the immaculate way Xerox did or in the same spirit of benefaction. There are a thousand reasons for someone's wishing to buy his way into print, many of them unpalatable, all of them to some degree self-serving. Buying and selling space in news columns could become a serious disease of the press. If it reached epidemic proportions, it could destroy the press. I don't want IBM or the National Rifle Association providing me with a funded spectacular when I open my paper. I want to read what the editor and the publisher have managed to dig up on their own— and paid for out of the till.

My affection for the free press in a democracy goes back a long way. My love for it was my first and greatest love. If I felt a shock at the news of the Salisbury-Xerox-*Esquire* arrangement, it was because the sponsorship principle seemed to challenge and threaten everything I believed in: that the press must not only be free, it must be fiercely independent—to survive and to serve. Not all papers are fiercely independent, God knows, but there are always enough of them around to provide a core of integrity and an example that others feel obligated to steer by. The funded article is not in itself evil, but it is the beginning of evil, and it is an invitation to evil. I hope the invitation will not again be extended, and, if extended, I hope it will be declined.

About a hundred and fifty years ago, de Tocqueville wrote: "The journalists of the United States are generally in a very humble position, with a scanty education and a vulgar turn of mind." Today, we chuckle at this antique characterization. But about fifty years ago, when I was a young journalist, I had the good fortune to encounter an editor who fitted the description quite closely. Harold Ross, who founded *The New Yorker*, was deficient in education and had—at least to all outward appearances—a vulgar turn of mind. What he did possess, though, was the ferocity of independence. He was having a tough time finding money to keep his floundering little sheet alive, yet he was determined that neither money nor influence would ever corrupt his dream or deflower his text. His boiling point was so low as to be comical. The faintest suggestion of the shadow of advertising in his news and editorial columns would cause him to erupt. He would explode in anger, the building would reverberate with his wrath, and his terrible swift sword would go flashing up and down the corridors. For a young man, it was an impressive sight and a memorable one. Fifty years have not dimmed for me either the spectacle of Ross's ferocity or my own early convictions—which were identical with his. He has come to my mind often while I've been composing this reply to your inquiry.

I hope I've clarified by a little bit my feelings about the autonomy of the press and the dangers of sponsorship of articles. Thanks for giving me the chance to speak my piece.

Sincerely,

E. B. White

Xerox thanked White for "telling us what we didn't want to hear." A few months later, they wrote saying that Xerox had decided not to underwrite any more articles and that they were convinced that it was "the right decision."

The Journalism Review of the Columbia University School of Journalism printed this entire exchange of letters under the title of, "What E. B. White Told Xerox—or How a Solitary Man of Letters Talked a Corporation Out of Funding Magazine Articles—and Helped to Define a Free Press."

I hazard the prophecy that in the long test of history, this one letter will establish E. B. White as one who sees things whole and who has the gift of language to tell us ordinary mortals what he sees.

I want to close with a brief reference to the three children's stories.

The first, *Stuart Little*, is about a mouse by that name. The book seems to lack an ending. It just stops. When I first read it, I thought a bunch of pages were missing from my copy. And White received letters complaining about this.

To one of them he replied, "I think many readers find the end inconclusive, but I have always found life inconclusive, and I guess it shows up in my work."

To another he replied, "Quite a number of children have written to ask me about Stuart. They want to know whether he got back home and whether he found Margalo (the bird he was hunting for). They are good questions, but I did not answer them because, in a way, Stuart's journey symbolizes the continuing journey that everybody undertakes—in search for what is perfect and unattainable. This is perhaps too elusive an idea to put in a book for children, but I put it in anyway."

And to a girl named Jill, he writes, "*Stuart Little* is the story of a quest or search. Much of life is questing and searching, and I was writing about that. If the book ends while the search is still going on, that's because I wanted it that way. As you grow older, you will realize

that many of us in this world go through life looking for something
that is beautiful and good—often something we can't quite name. In
Stuart's case, he was searching for the bird Margalo, who was his
ideal of beauty and goodness. Whether he ever found her or not, or
whether he got home or not, is less important than the adventure itself. If the book made you cry, that's because you are aware of the sad-
ness and richness of life's involvement and the quest for beauty.
Cheer up—Stuart may yet find his bird. He may even get home
again. Meantime, he is headed in the right direction, and I am sure
you are."

"The right direction," which White also attributed to Harold
Ross in his obituary, is central to White's concept of wholeness. One
often does not know the precise goal, but one must always be certain
of one's direction. The goal will reveal itself in due course.

It seems fitting, in view of White's closeness to animals, that in
his later years he should turn to writing children's stories about animals. In this period, in a letter to a friend, he wrote that mice and
spiders have been around for millions of years without damaging the
environment. But, in the few thousand years that so-called civilized
man has been around, he has nearly destroyed it.

In another letter he wrote, "if it were not for spiders, the insects
would take over the earth."

Let me note the concluding paragraphs in *Charlotte's Web* and
The Trumpet of the Swan.

Charlotte, the spider, has woven messages in her web that saved
Wilbur, the pig, from being butchered and made him famous. The
story concludes:

> Mr. Zuckerman took fine care of Wilbur all the rest of his days, and
> the pig was often visited by friends and admirers, for nobody ever
> forgot the year of his triumph and the miracle of the web. Life in
> the barn was very good—night and day, winter and summer, spring
> and fall, dull days and bright days. It was the best place to be,
> thought Wilbur, this warm delicious cellar, with the garrulous
> geese, the changing seasons, the heat of the sun, the passage of

swallows, the nearness of rats, the sameness of sheep, the love of spiders, the smell of manure and the glory of everything.

Louis the swan, from a genus of swans that make a trumpeting sound, was named after Louis Armstrong. Louis was born without a voice and acquired a trumpet that he learned to play. Sam, the boy who helped him learn to play it, says at the end:

> Tonight I heard Louis' horn. My father heard it, too. The wind was right, and I could hear the notes of taps, just as darkness fell. There is nothing in all the world I like better than the trumpet of the swan. . . .
>
> On the pond where the swans were, Louis put his trumpet away. The cygnets crept under their mother's wing. Darkness settled on woods and fields and marsh. A loon called its wild night cry. As Louis relaxed and prepared for sleep, all his thoughts were on how lucky he was to inhabit such a beautiful earth, how lucky he had been to solve his problems with music, and how pleasant it was to look forward to another night of sleep and another day tomorrow, and the fresh morning, and the light that returns with the day.

In the preface to his recent collected book of poems, E. B. White wrote:

> To me, poetry is what is memorable, and a poet is a fellow or a girl who lets drop a line that gets remembered in the morning. Poetry turns up in unexpected places, in unguarded moments. I have yet to encounter the line from the song in *Oklahoma*, "All the sounds of the earth are like music," without being brought to the edge of tears.

The interview with E. B. White on his 70th birthday ends with the question of what he cherished most in life. "When my wife's Aunt Caroline was in her '90s," he replied, "she lived with us and she once remarked, 'Remembrance is sufficient of the beauty we have seen.' I cherish the remembrance of the beauty I have seen. I cherish the grave compulsive world."

8

Old Age: The Ultimate Test of Spirit

An Essay on Preparation

Spirit! What are we talking about? The unabridged dictionary I consulted begins a full page of definitions with "The breath of life." But dictionaries can do little more than summarize common usage; and it seems clear to me, after reading the full page of definitions, that there is no well-accepted meaning for this much used and important word.

I conclude, then, that I cannot give a concise definition for *spirit*, for which old age seems to me to be the ultimate test. The meaning of that word, as I use it, lies beyond the barrier that separates mystery from what we call reality. Yet I have a sharp awareness of spirit when it is present, in myself and others, and I have a depressing feeling of loss when it is absent, in myself and others, at times when it is urgently needed.

I have come to connect spirit, the kind I would like to see more of, to a concept of *serve* as I see it in the consequences on those being served: do those being served grow as persons? Do they, while being served, become stronger, wiser, freer, more at peace with themselves, more likely themselves to become servants? And, what will be the effect on the least privileged in society? Will she or he benefit, or at least not be further deprived? The quality of a society will be judged by what the least privileged in it achieves. My hope for the future rests on the belief that among the legions of deprived and unsophisticated people are many true servants, and that most people can be helped to discriminate among those who presume to serve them, and identify, and respond only to those who are true servants.

Spirit can be said to be the driving force behind the motive to serve. And the ultimate test for spirit in one's old age is, I believe, can one look back at one's active life and achieve serenity from the knowledge that one has, according to one's lights, served? And can one regard one's present state, no matter how limited by age and health, as one of continuing to serve? One of my deeply etched memories is the view of an old man of 95 sitting by the window of his fisherman's house on the far out coast of Maine quietly knitting nets for lobster traps which the active fisherman in the family would use. He was still serving with what he could do best at his age.

Much of my present perspective on old age comes from having watched my father grow old. I was very close to him. He was an intelligent and good man but with a fifth-grade education, and he lived a life of limited opportunity. But by a prudent use of his life, he managed to leave a little corner of the world a bit better than he found it. He stands tall in my memory as a model of the true servant. One of my treasured memories as a small boy is attending occasional evening meetings when he was a member of the city council. I would stay awake as long as I could because the meetings were sometimes exciting—tumultuous is a better word—and father was generally in the thick of the action. Then I would curl up in his overcoat behind his chair and go to sleep, to be carried home at the close of the meeting.

Father lived to be 80 and achieved a remarkable serenity in his last years. A couple of years before he died, he told me that he realized that he was in his twilight years and that he had concluded that he should read some of the Bible since he had not read it at all. Then he added plaintively, "I tried, but I quickly gave it up because it made no sense."

When I was about 13, I recall listening to a conversation with a committee from our church that had come to try and persuade father to raise his quite nominal contribution. Father listened patiently and then said, "No." He thought his contribution was about right. He was glad the church was there, but as an instrument for doing good in the world he rated it well below both his labor union and his political party. The committee left in a huff.

In his old age, father once commented to me, "The tragedy of our town is that it once had a great people but it no longer has them." In his judgment the "status" people of our town—bankers, industrialists, merchants, professional people—were all mediocre. In the heat of one of father's political battles, the town's leading citizen, in money and prestige, tried to buy him off.

There is a much greater story to tell about my father but I will take another occasion for that. I have given enough of that story here to suggest that my early formative years when I was very close to him have shaped the way my life unfolded in important ways. I have given this much to suggest that watching my father grow old was a very special kind of experience, and it alerted me to watch my own aging so that I came into my old age with my eyes open—and aware.

I also feel it important to note that I did not grow up in a church-identified home. Consequently, I found it necessary to think my own way through a spiritual orientation for my life. There was much in the model of my father to guide me and it overshadowed what I got from the little exposure I had to churches. I am not recommending mine as the best way to grow up. I am simply noting what it was because it had a great deal to do with the adventure in preparation on which I have been embarked.

At 50, father suffered a health setback from which he recovered, but he dropped out of politics. In his old age, he told me that this was a wise move. "All of my old political cronies my age are gone. If I had won my last contest for office, that would have put me into the big money and I probably would not be here today. I am lucky that I lost." What he did not say, but I would observe, is he would have missed the joy of the serenity of his old age.

I have now gone past 80 and I have entered a new phase of life that I will comment on later, and I have frequent occasion to reflect on the quality of my father's old age, at a time when the Bible made no sense, and after an active life in which he rated churches in a quite inferior position. And I have concluded that, with all of this, he was a deeply religious man; and, he would be seen as religious in any peace-loving culture. I see his basic religious feeling as the root of his serenity, and I think of him now as one who was sustained by great human spirit all of his life.

My father and his father had lived their whole lives in the town where I was born and lived until I was 20, and father was deeply disappointed that I did not choose to make my home there. At age 22, I had made my career decision and I would go wherever it led me. Ultimately, it led to New York where I lived for 40 years. My roots, however, are in my father's tradition in Terre Haute, Indiana. These roots are still very much a part of me in my older years, even though the more than 60 years since I left Terre Haute have been in a very different world from the one my father lived in. Those 20 years with him in Terre Haute were the years of my formation, and they have stayed with me. I am sorry about people who reach old age without being aware of their roots.

Malcolm Cowley's little book, *The View From Eighty*, makes the point that rings true to my experience: that most of the literature about aging is written by younger people who have not been there, and that until one passes through that magic number that makes one old, one really cannot appreciate what old age is like. I could not have anticipated the view of life that I now have. And I may not be able to describe it in a way that is meaningful to younger people, perhaps not even to my own age group because I suspect that we oldsters are just as different, one from the other, as we have been at earlier stages in life. Each of us in our old age may be at the point of summing up our own unique experience and examining, and relating to, the very different roots from which we spring: roots that have shaped our whole existence.

I have long pondered those lines with which Robert Browning opens his poem "Rabbi Ben Ezra":

> Grow old along with me!
> The best is yet to be;
> The last of life for which the first was made.

A friend my age who is crippled with arthritis recently wrote quoting those lines and concluding with, "Bah!" I suppose that if I were wracked with pain my response might be the same. In the absence of that pain I keep wondering what is that "best" that Browning was talking about, or did he know what he was talking about?

I have long been a meditator, and as I have grown older, meditation has become more central to my existence and takes much more of the typical day. I have taken training in both transcendental and Buddhist meditation, but my current meditation practices are pretty much my own. I have arrived at a point where I prefer my own private meditation to any formal religious service. As I have grown older, I have come to value solitude more and more. I doubt that I would ever want to be a hermit and live in complete isolation, but I definitely limit my contact with people and this tendency is growing. My wife and I, without talking about it, have evolved a relationship in which there is very little conversation. We enjoy being together and we appreciate our solitude together. Neither of us feels the need to be entertained, nor do we yearn to be young again.

I read some, but much less than I once did—although my vision is still good. Much of what I do read is rereading what I have read before, and I continue to find fresh meaning.

At age 75 I stopped making speeches, though I was still active. At 80 I stopped going to meetings, and I no longer travel at all. I use an automobile for local shopping only, and I will soon give that up.

At age 73, my wife and I entered a lifecare retirement community. I don't believe it is a good idea to segregate old people this way and thus limit their interaction with younger people. Both the old and the young lose by it. Someday, when we are a more civilized people and have come to live in and appreciate community, I suspect places like the one I now live in will be abandoned. We chose to come here because it was the best option available to us. If we were making the choice today, we would come to the same place we now live. The conscientious Quakers who run the place we live in do a good job of managing the services on which we depend. We are served by caring and sensitive people, and the trustees keep the place solvent, which is more than can be said for some places like this. I am deeply grateful to the dedicated trustees who maintain the integrity of the place where I will spend my last years.

We try to be friendly with fellow residents, and there are a few with whom we occasionally share meals. But my wife and I stay clear away from the frenetic activity, the game playing, and the traveling to exotic places that occupy so much of people's time. Most of my interaction with people is with younger people in active careers elsewhere. I share their joys and sorrows and I believe I give them something of value from my relative detachment and my more meditative life. And they give much to me. I know that at age 83 I am lucky to have these relationships with younger active people, and I appreciate them.

Occasionally I am asked what it is like to be old; and there is some conversation about it. I am not sure I can put it down in black and white, but I will try.

As I see it now, my most interesting and productive years were from 60 to 75. This was not so much that I was a late bloomer, but because from 40 to 60 I made conscious preparation (more on that later) for a second career, and I had a really good one. Also, that new career that started at age 60 rested on 38 years as a disciplined organization man in a huge bureaucracy. A disciplined life can be lived in many ways, but the kind I had in my early work was absolutely essential for a good second career. People who have managed their lives without experiencing that kind of sustained discipline, both the bitter and the sweet, seem to me to have missed something important.

I have never been a "high energy" person, and at 75 there were definite signals that I should slow down. I welcomed the change of pace. I stopped traveling altogether, something I had done a great deal of. In a way, this may be seen as the start of a third career, a very low-key one. Now, at age 83, I write some, reflect a lot, see a few people, and occasionally write a letter to someone in active life suggesting some line of thought or action. I do not miss the more active life I used to lead.

There may have been a special impact of the big round number 80 that I passed three years ago. Our children put on a big party for my wife and me so we could not overlook the fact that something important had happened. A different view of life gradually emerged. I always knew that I was not immortal but as I passed 80 I became aware that I was in a "countdown" era. It was not that the signs of death were imminent, but I slowly became more detached. This has been a new and different phase, an even more radical break than I made at age 60 when I retired from my main career and started a second career; or, at 75 when I stopped traveling, except that this time there was not a precise point of change. I had come to realize that I could no longer serve by carrying an active role in the world. I would only get in the way if I tried. Now, I came to accept, I can best serve by being. It was not a new career, like it could have been seen at age 75 when the major change I made was to stop traveling and making speeches. Now, no mountains to climb. I may continue to do some things, mostly writing; but it is no longer "production." Whether I get it done or not is no longer important, as it used to be.

I scan the daily newspaper but I rarely listen to radio or TV news—because they cannot be scanned. I prefer to meditate, and I have come to view my meditating as serving. Somehow the quiet and peace of anyone's meditation communicates and enriches the culture. I feel the fruits of other people's meditation.

Reviewing or summing up my life is not a preoccupation. Occasionally I call up something out of the past as a help in clearing my thought about where I now am—and I hope to remain sharply aware of where I am. I do not brood on the past. There have been errors, failures, and hurts but they were in that other existence from which I am now quite separated, and I look back on it with detachment, as if it were the record of another's life.

The main difference between this present past-80 period and my earlier old age when I still felt myself to be in a career, of having a work, may be that up to recently there has always been a future that would ultimately be connected with the present as the past. Now there is no future and there is really no past. There is only a history that may as well be another's past. There is only now. Maybe this is the "best" that Robert Browning assured us of: finally to achieve living wholly in the present moment, unencumbered with the record of one's past and oblivious to the future, and accepting of the loss of energy and the passions of youth. I believe this is what my father achieved in his old age. He bound over to me a sense of rest and being at peace with himself and the world, and I recognized this state when I arrived at 80, 34 years after my father's death. I find this chapter of my life as rewarding as any previous one. And I feel a greater sense of continuity with my father's life than I ever felt before.

Let me hasten to add to what I have just said: these recent changes have not put me in a state of euphoria, although I feel okay most of the time. I have withdrawn from active participation in society and live in a lifecare community. Consequently, the usual frustrations and irritations of life have been substantially reduced. But when these do occur, as on occasion they still do, my reaction is little different from what it has always been.

I have noted that my father in his 80th and most serene year, could lament the tragedy of our town because of the paucity of great people in it. So I, in my 83rd year and with a much larger view of the world than my father had, now lament what seems the small number among those who see themselves as able, conscientious, and dedicated, and who are disposed to respond to a vision of the larger roles they might play and the much greater service to society that the institutions they influence might render. We have plenty of people with the ability and the stamina to build and lead a much more serving society and I believe they would lead fuller lives, if they would rise to their opportunities. What they seem to lack is spirit, and I wonder what they will be like when they grow old. Will they find it the "best" that is yet to be? I said at the outset that I cannot define spirit. But I have tried in what I have said to give human spirit a meaning that is beyond rational definition.

Earlier I noted, as I look back now, my years from 60 to 75 were in some ways my most interesting and productive because, in part, from age 40 to 60 I made conscious preparation for my old age. When I was about 40, I had the good fortune to read an article by a radio commentator of that day, Elmer Davis. Davis had a coronary attack when he was past 60 that slowed him down and made him more reflective. Out of his reflection came an essay entitled, "The Uses of Old People." In it he made the point that old people can be particularly useful, not just for the reason that they are more seasoned and experienced, but because there are important things to be done that are best done by old people, either because they do not fit well into a career or they are too risky for younger people to undertake. Furthermore, he advised that young people should look forward to, and prepare for old age as a time of potentially great usefulness rather than as a time when one is put out to pasture when one wears out. This message came through to me loud and clear, and I resolved that I would then begin to prepare for a second career at age 60 when I could elect my pension where I worked.

I had been reasonably successful in my work and my volunteer activity up to age 40, but I realized that I was not a person of great talents or highly specialized abilities, and that I would not emerge at age 60 as a much sought after professional. Without a specific second career in mind, what would I prepare for?

Making plans for my life has never been a preoccupation. I left college with the aim of entering a big business and with the expectation that my career would evolve as opportunities presented themselves and as the spirit moved me. This strategy had served well up to age 40, and I saw no reason to change it. I simply had my eye on age 60 when I would start a second career (if I was still around), and in those intervening years I would continue to evolve, but with the aim that I was preparing for something that I could not then define. I had no idea what my old age would be like or what I would do with it. "Take it as it comes" was my motto as it had been up to that point. I do not recall that I thought in these terms, but I seemed to set out to favor and accelerate the kind of evolutionary development that had taken place up to age 40. I did not awake each morning with the question, "What will I do today to prepare for my old age?" In fact, once I embarked on this course, I rarely gave it a thought. It simply became a way of life, and there was a good deal of chance in it. What was different was that I became more venturesome and experimental in doing things that would widen my horizons and enlarge my self-understanding. All that I am now sure of is that I arrived at age 60 well prepared to be useful, and that interesting and challenging opportunities that I could not have anticipated at age 40 were numerous; more than I could take on.

I am quite a "private" person and I shared this thinking only with my wife, who understood and approved. I am sure, however, that I was considered "odd" by my friends and associates because I did unconventional things. It is also clear that my superiors in my company were at times a bit puzzled about what to do with me. I know they regarded me as valuable because they paid me well. But valuable for what? They resolved their puzzlement when I was 50 by appointing me director of Management Research, providing me with sufficient budget to hire a professional staff, and giving me a broad charter to research and advise regarding the management of this huge company, especially how its top structure functioned (or failed to function). My last ten years with my company were excellent preparation for my old age, better than any other executive post I know about. I have often wondered how the choices I made in using my optional time, both inside and outside the company, contributed to how my final role there evolved. However, it was not a bed of roses. While I had the charter and the responsibility and the budget, the bureaucracy did not understand it, and I was in collision with the establishment all over the place. This too was good preparation for living with ambiguity and served me well in my second career. When I retired, the position disappeared. I could not train a successor. That person would have to prepare himself or herself as I did. And no one did.

In writing about my experience now, I hope to encourage others to resolve in their own ways to prepare for their old age, to prepare to face uncertainty. Such preparation, if wisely done, may not only favor a fruitful old age but it may, as with me, make the years of preparation more productive and enjoyable. I recall that once a colleague my age, one who was obviously not preparing, came into my office one morning, seated himself before my desk, puffed violently on his cigarette for several seconds, and then said, "I am leading a life of quiet desperation!" Later, when we had both retired, he called my wife one morning and asked her advice on how he could get into the kind of work I was doing. Shortly after I had announced my retirement, a close friend who was president of one of our subsidiaries, a very successful man as measured by income and prestige, lunched with me and asked how, when he retired in a couple of years, could he get into the kind of work I would be doing. I had to say, as gently as I could tell him, "No way!" If one will settle for a retirement of golf and fishing and simple civic chores, no preparation may be needed. But if one wants one's life to ascend creatively and in new ways, as long as one has one's wits, then my experience would suggest that one is well advised to prepare.

In my later years in my company, I did some lecturing in business schools. When I described my role in my company some of the students' eyes would brighten and someone would say, "That is the kind of job I would like to have." To which I would reply, "I should tell you that it took me 25 years to get into a position to do this work." And the response would likely be, "Oh no! Maybe 6 months, but not 25 years" (as much as most of them had already lived). And I would say, "Maybe you could do it in less; but you would have to take the time to build the trust that this kind of unstructured role requires. I have the charter because the company has some needs and feels some pains that no one can define with precision. For those in charge, trust that I will search for and carry out actions that will do more good than harm. That trust needs to be high and one does not earn it quickly. Whatever your career, if you would like to evolve into a position of great trust, then you will need to use your opportunities in a way that constitutes preparation for being given that trust." Young people have a hard time grappling with that idea, but it is of the very essence.

A detailed account of my 40 to 60 preparation would not be useful to another. Everyone should chart her or his own course. I will give a brief summary of mine just to suggest the range of opportunities that may be available if one opens one's imagination and is alert to opportunities, which the two colleagues noted above seemed unwilling, perhaps lacked the courage, to do.

I made the decision to prepare for my old age near the end of WWII, when commercial air travel was just resuming. I made the firm resolve that I would not fly in connection with my work. I did not want to be speeded up. The trains were still good and I enjoyed train travel. But mostly I valued the meditative intervals that train travel afforded. I do not recall that I thought this through at the time but, in retrospect, meditative intervals have been very important to me—both long ones and short ones. It has sometimes been crucial, in the heat of controversy, to withdraw into the silence for just a few seconds so that the creative processes can function. For a big idea to evolve, I have found that a big chunk of meditative time is required, and train riding was sometimes the best way for me to get those big chunks.

I have seldom gotten an important learning from reading. I am slow and it is hard work. Most of my learning in this 40 to 60 period was in conversation with people. I got as much out of organizing my thoughts as I did from listening, and listening was important. I found my way to people interested in sharing (and I had much to share, especially in those last ten years) with people whose perspectives were different from mine and who made me stretch.

Two years were spent in weekly sessions with Jungian analysts (one year with a woman, one with a man) on the analysis of my dreams. These sessions greatly enlarged my awareness of my inner life, and I believe my creativity was quickened.

I developed a really close relationship with several quite different institutions: The Menninger (psychiatric) Foundation, The U.S. Air Force, and the National Council of Churches, along with several large businesses. I accepted my first teaching position in a university-related school for managers with which I worked for parts of seven summers.

Most important in all of this was my relationship with people. In the last part of my AT&T career, I became interested in the ethics of the company (to the discomfort of some well-placed people), which led me to establish a relationship with professors of ethics in Catholic, Jewish, and Protestant seminaries. Some close friendships developed, especially my friendship with Rabbi Abraham J. Heschel.

I am not a scholar, and little of my work in this period was centered on reading, with two exceptions. I made quite an in-depth study of the history of AT&T. Because of being in the corporate office, I had access to the archives. I made a determined, but unsuccessful, effort to interest the executives of the company in that rich history, by knowledge of which officers and directors might have saved the company from dissolution in 1984. The other study in this period was to read extensively in the history of the Religious Society of Friends. This was useful in my retirement years when I wrote regularly for an outstanding Quaker magazine, *Friends Journal*. Both of these excursions into the history of institutions with which I was very familiar confirm what a noted historian once said, "The main thing we learn from history is that we do not learn from history." Both of these depth interests in the history of institutions I was involved with were important parts of my years of preparation, and both were enjoyable activities while I engaged in them.

I noted above two of my AT&T colleagues who were my age and who retired and found themselves rudderless. Both had the same opportunity to prepare for their old age that I had, and the preparation I experienced would have made a more enjoyable existence while they did it. Both were better scholars than I, one Phi Beta Kappa, but neither apparently heard the same signal that I did at age 40. Perhaps they were not listening for signals as I was, all of the time—and still am. Neither of them lived long after retirement.

In giving some details of my own preparation I am not suggesting that what I did would be appropriate or possible for anyone else. But of this I am quite sure: anyone who thinks of his or her old age as an event to be prepared for is more likely to have a more fruitful old age than one who has not thought that way, regardless of what his or her preparation consists of. Whether one's gifts and opportunities are great or small, my advice would be—prepare!

The temptation to be resisted by highly gifted people, I believe, is the hope (if they think about it at all) that they will be able to exploit their gifts to the end. Some may make it through life on that assumption (charitable friends may assure them they are making it when an objective appraisal might tell them that they are not). I have just finished a new biography of a leading theologian of a generation past, a man of exceptional gifts. He had a health setback as he approached old age, and he spent miserable years fretting that he could no longer exploit his gifts as he once did. He was unprepared.

What would adequate preparation have meant to such a person? I can only speculate. It seems to me that one of the signs of emerging maturity is an acceptance of life's fragility and acceptance of new conditions, whatever they may be, plus recognition of G. K. Chesterton's admonition that (life's) "wildness lies in wait." It is not an obsessive preoccupation that makes one sick or fearful. It is alertness, readiness to respond when it is appropriate to respond. As one attains maturity, one learns to live peacefully and sleep well with a submerged awareness of constant danger. The most important part of preparation for old age may be awareness, while one is young, that a time will come when one steps aside from one's main career and life will be different. If one looks forward to a second career in which appropriate old age involvements are at the center, then it seems important that one make that change—if one has the option—while one still has the energy to undertake it, and that one prepare for that change.

Old age may be one of those conditions that everyone knows about but for which some do not prepare. The benefit of preparing may be that no matter what impairments one suffers, one can make a good life of it as long as one has one's wits. (When one's wits are gone, it doesn't matter.) It may be that what deters some people from preparing for such a contingency as old age is want of courage, what Paul Tillich called "The Courage to Be"—the courage to be aware and to live comfortably with the constant threat of adversity, pain and anxiety. I suspect that what results from such want of courage is a false security that may betray one when one faces old age and finds that one lacks what Fosdick called "The Power to See Life Through." Thus, serenity may not be what one achieves in old age; it may be one of the fruits of what one has learned by preparing while one is young.

There are many signals all of the time that will cue one to the ideas that will make life more rewarding, at all stages. But one is likely to hear those signals only if one is alert to signals, all of the time. The problem is that there is a baffling number of signals if one is alert to them, and one must choose which of them one will heed. At this point meditation will serve, at all stages of life. Not only do our rational reflective processes sometimes function better in meditation, but one may develop sensitivity to intimations from beyond the barrier that separates what we call reality from mystery. Jung might say that in meditation we may tap the collective unconscious. What appears in meditation is sometimes the same as what appears in dreams. Then, in one's conscious logic, one can always ask, "Is the originator of this signal really acting in the spirit of my servant?"

When, at age 40, I heard the signal from Elmer Davis, "prepare now for your old age," I judged him to be a true servant and heeded his advice. In the perspective of 43 years' experience, I find that earlier judgment confirmed. I am grateful to Elmer Davis, and to my father, and many other true servants for the gifts of spirit, by both advice and example, that have sustained me. Old age *is* the ultimate test of spirit.

Surviving from my Boy Scout experience 70 years ago is the motto: *Be prepared*. I am eternally grateful for it.

And I am grateful to E. B. White for "Sufficient is the remembrance of the beauty I have seen." That remembrance is always with me, and I do not have to see it again.

Afterword

JAMES P. SHANNON

Students of Robert K. Greenleaf should find the publication of this select collection of essays from his most productive years both timely and useful. Timely, because the number of his followers has grown geometrically in the last two decades; and useful, because this growing company of students is currently very much in need of a single source book that brings together the best of Greenleaf's separate essays, now available in print only in several discrete publications.

As a young man, Greenleaf was fascinated by his father's ability to "get things done." Greenleaf's father was an engineer and a tinkerer in Terre Haute, Indiana. Through the rest of his life Robert would be searching for those persons who could emulate his father's ability to actualize their own potentialities by helping other persons learn how to "get things done."

Armed with his B.A. degree from Carleton College in 1926, and motivated by the counsel of his sociology professor, Oscar Helming, to seek employment in a company large enough to prepare its employees to become leaders in a society increasingly in need of leaders with vision, he sought and got his first job, with Ohio Bell Telephone, a subsidiary of the giant AT&T.

His first assignment at Ohio Bell was digging postholes for telephone poles. It is a tribute to his supervisors there that they soon made him a teacher to train other entry-level construction workers how to become foremen. In this role, between 1927 and 1929, he once said, he spent "the most formative years" of his life. It was here that he found his life's work: to identify people of talent and to help them obtain the skills they need to move into leadership positions. During the next three decades, Greenleaf and AT&T prospered jointly by his remarkable success in identifying and developing generations of promising employees who would come to be known in his vocabulary as "servant-leaders."

In essence, Greenleaf was AT&T's in-house talent scout. The "comers" he spotted tended to be persons who were motivated primarily by a creative desire to be effective in doing whatever had to be done to make their organization work. They also tended to be persons who were generous with their time, their talent, and their training. They tended to be nonjudgmental and benevolently disposed toward their co-workers. They also tended to be good listeners who favored collegial decision making, who knew themselves well, respected themselves, and had those qualities Greenleaf considered essential: sound values, personal strength, intuition, and spirit.

Throughout his life, Greenleaf would insist that his theses on leadership were based on empirical evidence in the workplace, not on deductive corollaries from some abstruse philosophical or theological premises. Even though he would spend his life as a teacher, he continued to have an innate suspicion of "education with a capital E."

The epitaph he chose for his tombstone reflects both his modesty and his commitment to grass-roots learning. It reads, "Potentially a good plumber, ruined by a sophisticated education."

Readers of this book should bear in mind that AT&T and Greenleaf were consciously motivated by their mutual desire to find, train, and empower young people who would be able one day to lead that enormous company to new heights of success and profitability. To achieve such results, all parties to this joint venture had to agree that wanting to become a leader and being a leader are good and wholesome, human objectives. They are not signs of hubris or self-seeking. John W. Gardner, in one of his earliest and best-known essays, warned that the egalitarian and democratic thrust of our educational system, left to itself, will inevitably inoculate our children with what he calls the "anti-leadership vaccine." To counteract this predictable perversion of democracy, we must teach our children that it is good mental hygiene for them to want to become leaders and that our healthy society eventually depends on our continuing ability to raise up generations of visionary and energetic leaders in every sector of our national life.

An essential element in this educational process, according to Greenleaf, is our ability to teach our children that true leadership ultimately depends on the legitimacy of one's appointment, election, or promotion to a position of authority and on one's subsequent ability to validate or confirm this role by the quality of one's performance, called "the authority of service."

The authority of service is that additional level of legitimacy or validation that is earned after one is elected mayor, appointed chief of police, or elevated to the rank of bishop. These two levels of authority can exist separately; but ideally they co-exist, with each level giving added legitimacy to the other. The authority of service is that added distinction that good parents, good teachers, and good pastors enjoy by reason of their dependable performance over time, and which beginners in any career envy and covet. This kind of authority is built slowly and depends on one's ability to do one's homework, to treat others fairly, to meet one's deadlines, to get the job done right, and to tell the truth habitually.

Leaders who see their strength only in their alleged "power" are understandably reluctant to share that strength. Leaders who see their strength in the quality of their performance are eager to share it, and, in so doing, to multiply it.

In Herman Hesse's novel *Journey to the East*, the servant Leo is the person who has the greatest legitimacy as a leader because he has earned the authority of service by his performance. Reading this novel helped Greenleaf crystallize his own thinking that true leadership is always a result of performance. In the Greenleaf economy, power shared is power multiplied, not lessened. This kind of generous participation in the workplace turns followers into peers and peers into new leaders and builds new levels of trust among persons mutually committed to the pursuit of desirable shared objectives.

Management consultants who diagnose corporate strengths and weaknesses typically focus their studies on customers, products, or shareholders. Robert Greenleaf opted to focus his analyses on employees, the persons he considered the neglected stakeholders, the persons whose goodwill, energy, and loyalty are too often taken for granted. In his view, if employees received the care, training, and attention they deserve, shareholder and customer satisfaction would inevitably follow.

One reason that Greenleaf's essays are in such demand today is that modern corporate restructuring has indeed tended to take the employees for granted. In Greenleaf's value system, if the human persons who do the work of the company are neglected, shareholders and customers will suffer; and conversely, employees who are carefully selected, well trained, and appreciated will give shareholder and customer satisfaction higher priority.

Entirely apart from his appeal to business leaders today is Greenleaf's attractiveness as an advocate of humane values across the spectrum in all human relations. To the extent that we could practice his style of servant-leadership, we would not only be better employees; we would be better parents, better spouses, better friends, better human persons. We would be more civil, more courteous, more thoughtful, more gracious, more generous. One need not be a professional anthropologist to realize that these attractive human qualities are in short supply in our frenetic society. Nor need one be a psychologist or psychiatrist to see why so many thoughtful persons see Greenleaf as a welcome voice for our time.

One of Greenleaf's favorite aphorisms was, "Organization kills spirit." If he were with us today, I would bet that he would be a fan of the "Dilbert" cartoon. When he took early retirement from AT&T to work as an independent consultant, he was intrigued by the irreverence of the college students of the sixties. He regularly prowled campus book stores to find out what the students were reading and singing. He saw himself as a dedicated change agent, and he saw the young people of that age as his likely allies in this pursuit.

In my decade as director of the General Mills Foundation, I became a practitioner and a true believer in the teachings of Robert Greenleaf. In that period, our company decided to restructure. The downside of that process for me was that my staff was cut from 6½ persons to 4 persons. The upside was that our corporate profits rose dramatically and my grants budget doubled, from $4.5 million to $9 million. But in our office we had to cut back on "site visits" to the local turf of our grant applicants because we lacked the personnel to do it. There is one school of thought in the field of philanthropy which holds that site visits are the single best indicator of the quality of any grant-making program, and our ability to make site visits was slipping away.

Taking a page from Greenleaf, I made quiet personal visits to about a dozen persons in our company, none of whom reported to me, to ask whether they had any interest or desire to volunteer some of their free time to help our staff make up for our loss of personnel. Wonder of wonders, they were eager to help us! Sometimes on holidays, sometimes on weekends, sometimes in the evening after work, these generous fellow employees pitched in to help us do our work.

They were truly servant-leaders. Their only reward was the psychic satisfaction they got from helping our small staff maintain some of the community outreach we needed so desperately and that was slipping away from us.

Please bear in mind that I had no mandate from management to use Greenleaf's ideas or to recruit in-house volunteers. I neither sought nor asked permission from above. The point here is that Greenleaf's ideas are portable and can be productively used by anyone, anywhere—in a family, in a school, in a church congregation, in a soccer team. All it takes is a decision by two or more persons to explore ways to help one another actualize more of their individual potential.

There is an expression among pilots who fly float planes off the lakes in my native Minnesota: When a plane is at rest in the water, the surface tension of the water "holds" the plane. Prior to take-off from water, the pilot must take enough time and generate enough speed so that the water loses its "grip" on the floats and the plane gets "up on the step"—that is, out of the water but not yet in the air—before the pilot can actually take the plane airborne.

In my view the organization that Robert K. Greenleaf founded in 1964—now called The Greenleaf Center—is "up on the step." It is poised for take-off to new heights. This book itself is a graphic illustration that the center and its energetic director Larry Spears are responding to the growing need in our society for the ideas of Robert Greenleaf and to the growing number of students of Greenleaf who need and want a single source compendium like this welcome volume.

References and Permissions

The Foreword is an original essay created for this collection by Peter Vaill. Copyright © 1998 Peter Vaill. Printed with permission of the author.

The Introduction is adapted from previous writings by Larry C. Spears, especially the Introduction to *Insights on Leadership*, published by John Wiley & Sons. Copyright © 1998 by Larry C. Spears.

Chapter 1: **Servant: Retrospect and Prospect** was originally published in 1980. Copyright © 1998 The Greenleaf Center.

Chapter 2 : **Education and Maturity** was originally published in 1962. Copyright © 1998 The Greenleaf Center.

Copyright permissions from *Complete Poems of Robert Frost*. Copyright 1916, 1921 by Holt, Rinehart and Winston, Inc. Copyright renewed by Robert Frost. Reprinted by permission of Holt, Rinehart and Winston, Inc.

Copyright permissions from *The Hollow Men* in "Collected Poems" 1909–35, by T. S. Eliot. Copyright by Harcourt, Brace & World, Inc. Reprinted by permission of Harcourt, Brace & World, Inc.

Chapter 3: **The Leadership Crisis** was originally published in Volume XIV, Number 3, November, 1978 of *HUMANITAS: Journal of the Institute of Man*, Duquesne University. Copyright © 1998 The Greenleaf Center.

Chapter 4: **Have You a Dream Deferred?** was originally published in 1967. Copyright © 1998 The Greenleaf Center.

Chapter 5: **The Servant as Religious Leader** was originally published in 1982. Copyright © 1998 The Greenleaf Center.

Chapter 6: **Seminary as Servant** was originally published in 1981. Copyright © 1998 The Greenleaf Center.

Chapter 7: **My Debt to E. B. White** was originally published in 1987. Copyright © 1998 The Greenleaf Center.

Reprinted by permission of Harper & Row, Publishers, Inc.: From *Letters of E. B. White*, copyright 1976 by E. B. White; from "A Slight Sound at Evening" in *Essays of E. B. White*, copyright 1954 by E. B. White; "I Paint What I See" from *Poems & Sketches of E. B. White*, copyright 1933 by E. B. White; from "The Second Tree from the Corner" in *The Second Tree from the Corner* by E. B. White; from *Charlotte's Web* by E. B. White, copyright 1952, 1980 by E. B. White; from *The Trumpet of the Swan* by E. B. White, copyright 1970; from "Preface" in *Poems & Sketches of E. B. White*, copyright 1981 by E. B. White.

Reprinted by permission of the *New York Times*: From "E. B. White: Notes and Comment by Author," by Israel Shenker, of July 11, 1969.

Reprinted by permission, copyright 1951, 1961, 1979, *The New Yorker Magazine*, Inc.: From *Poems & Sketches of E. B. White* (Harper & Row), copyright 1933, 1961 by E. B. White. Originally in *The New Yorker*; From *The Second Tree from the Corner* (Harper & Bros.), copyright 1947, 1975 by E. B. White. Originally in *The New Yorker*.

Chapter 8: **Old Age: The Ultimate Test of Spirit** was originally published in 1987. Copyright © 1998 The Greenleaf Center.

The Afterword is an original essay created for this collection by James P. Shannon. Copyright © 1998 James P. Shannon. Printed with permission of the author.

Greenleaf Bibliography

Greenleaf, Robert K. "Abraham Joshua Heschel: Build a Life Like a Work of Art," *Friends Journal*, 1973, 19(15), 459-460.

—. *Advices to Servants*. Indianapolis: The Greenleaf Center, 1991.

—. "The Art of Knowing." *Friends Journal*, 1974, 20(17).

—. "Business Ethics—Everybody's Problem." *New Catholic World*, 1980, 223, 275-278.

—. "Choose the Nobler Belief." *AA Grapevine*, 1966, 23(5), 27-31.

—. "Choosing Greatness." *AA Grapevine*, 1966, 23(4), 26-30.

—. "Choosing to be Aware." *AA Grapevine*, 1966, 23(1), 26-28.

—. "Choosing to Grow." *AA Grapevine*, 1966, 23(2), 11-13.

—. "Community as Servant and Nurturer of the Human Spirit." *Resources for Community-Based Economic Development*, 1986, 4, 9-11.

—. *Education and Maturity*. Indianapolis: The Greenleaf Center, 1988.

—. *Have You a Dream Deferred?* Indianapolis: The Greenleaf Center, 1988.

—. *The Institution as Servant*. Indianapolis: The Greenleaf Center, 1976.

—. *The Leadership Crisis*. Indianapolis: The Greenleaf Center, 1978.

—. *Life's Choices and Markers*. Indianapolis: The Greenleaf Center, 1986.

—. *Mission in a Seminary: A Prime Trustee Concern*. Indianapolis: The Greenleaf Center, 1981.

—. *My Debt to E. B. White*. Indianapolis: The Greenleaf Center, 1987.

—. *Old Age: The Ultimate Test of Spirit*. Indianapolis: The Greenleaf Center, 1987.

—. *On Becoming a Servant Leader*. San Francisco: Jossey-Bass, 1996.

—. "Overcome Evil with Good." *Friends Journal*, 1977, 23(10), 292-302.

—. *Robert Frost's "Directive" and the Spiritual Journey*. Boston: Nimrod Press, 1963.

—. *Seeker and Servant*. San Francisco: Jossey-Bass, 1996.

—. *Seminary as Servant*. Indianapolis: The Greenleaf Center, 1988.

—. *Servant Leadership*. New York: Paulist Press, 1977.

—. *The Servant as Leader*. Indianapolis: The Greenleaf Center, 1991.

—. "The Servant as Leader." *Journal of Religion and the Applied Behavioral Sciences*, Winter 1982, 3, 7-10.

—. *The Servant as Religious Leader*. Indianapolis: The Greenleaf Center, 1983.

—. *Servant: Retrospect and Prospect*. Indianapolis: The Greenleaf Center, 1980.

—. *Spirituality as Leadership*. Indianapolis: The Greenleaf Center, 1988.

—. *Teacher as Servant: A Parable*. Indianapolis: The Greenleaf Center, 1987.

—. "The Trustee and the Risks of Persuasive Leadership," *Hospital Progress*, 1978, pp. 50-52, 88.

—. Trustee Traditions and Expectations." In *The Good Steward: A Guide to Theological School Trusteeship*. Washington, D.C.: Association of Governing Boards of Universities and Colleges, n.d.

—. *Trustees as Servants*. Indianapolis: The Greenleaf Center, 1990.

—. "Two More Choices." *AA Grapevine*, 1966, 23(3), 22-23.

Index

289

About the Editor
and The Greenleaf Center
for Servant-Leadership

Larry Spears is the editor of two acclaimed collections of essays on servant-leadership—*Insights on Leadership: Service, Stewardship, Spirit, and Servant-Leadership* (1998) and *Reflections on Leadership: How Robert K. Greenleaf's Theory of Servant-Leadership Influenced Today's Top Management Thinkers* (1995)—both published by John Wiley & Sons. Spears has previously co-edited two books by Robert K. Greenleaf, *On Becoming a Servant Leader* (1996) and *Seeker and Servant* (1996)—both published by Jossey-Bass Publishers. He is also a contributing author to *Stone Soup for the World* (1998) and *Leadership in a New Era* (1994). Since 1970, Spears has published many articles, essays, and book reviews. Among his more recent articles are "Reflections on Robert K. Greenleaf and Servant-Leadership" and "Being a Servant-Leader."

Spears was named CEO of the Robert K. Greenleaf Center for Servant-Leadership in 1990, shortly before Robert Greenleaf died. Under his leadership, The Greenleaf Center has experienced tremendous growth and influence. As a manager and leader, Spears has been noted for his successes in applying entrepreneurial methodologies to nonprofit organizations. He also speaks on the topic of servant-leadership. The titles of several of his addresses include "Servant-Leadership and the Honoring of Excellence" and "Understanding Robert K. Greenleaf and Servant-Leadership."

In addition to his involvement with the Center, Spears is a member of the National Society of Fund Raising Executives, the World Futures Society, and the American Society of Association Executives. Like Robert Greenleaf, Larry Spears is a Quaker. In the 1980s, Spears worked on the staff of the Quaker magazine, *Friends Journal.* From 1988–98, Spears has served as a board trustee for *Friends Journal* where he chairs its advancement committee. Prior to joining The Greenleaf Center, he served as Managing Director of The Greater Philadelphia Philosophy Consortium, and as a staff member with the Great Lakes Colleges Association's Philadelphia Center.

The Greenleaf Center for Servant-Leadership, headquartered in Indianapolis, Indiana, is an international, nonprofit, educational organization that seeks to encourage the understanding and practice of servant-leadership. The center's mission is to improve the caring and quality of all institutions through a new approach to leadership, structure, and decision making.

The Greenleaf Center's programs include the worldwide sale of books, essays, and videotapes on servant-leadership and the preparation and presentation of workshops, seminars, institutes, retreats, an annual international conference, a partnership program, and consultation.

Through the dissemination of Robert Greenleaf's idea about servant-leadership, a number of institutions and individuals have been changed. Servant-leadership is now used as an institutional model, as the basis for educating and training board trustees and community leaders, as the foundation of college and university courses and corporate training programs, and as a vehicle for personal growth and transformation.

For further information about the resources for study and programming available from the Center, contact:

The Greenleaf Center for Servant-Leadership
921 East Eighty-Sixth Street, Suite 200
Indianapolis, IN 46240
Phone (317) 259-1241; Fax (317) 259-0560
E-mail: greenleaf@iquest.net
Visit us at http://www.greenleaf.org

Other leading-edge business books from Berrett-Koehler Publishers

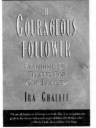

Berrett-Koehler Publishers

BERRETT-KOEHLER is an independent publisher of books, periodicals, and other publications at the leading edge of new thinking and innovative practice on work, business, management, leadership, stewardship, career development, human resources, entrepreneurship, and global sustainability.

Since the company's founding in 1992, we have been committed to supporting the movement toward a more enlightened world of work by publishing books, periodicals, and other publications that help us to integrate our values with our work and work lives, and to create more humane and effective organizations.

We have chosen to focus on the areas of work, business, and organizations, because these are central elements in many people's lives today. Furthermore, the work world is going through tumultuous changes, from the decline of job security to the rise of new structures for organizing people and work. We believe that change is needed at all levels—individual, organizational, community, and global— and our publications address each of these levels.

We seek to create new lenses for understanding organizations, to legitimize topics that people care deeply about but that current business orthodoxy censors or considers secondary to bottom-line concerns, and to uncover new meaning, means, and ends for our work and work lives.

See next page for other books from Berrett-Koehler Publishers

A Higher Standard of Leadership
Lessons from the Life of Gandhi

Keshavan Nair

THIS IS THE FIRST BOOK to apply lessons from Gandhi's life to the practical tasks faced by today's leaders. Through examples from Gandhi's life and writings, Nair identifies commitments—to conscience, openness, service, values, and reduced personal attachments—and describes the courage and determination necessary to lead by them.

Hardcover, 174 pages, 10/94 • ISBN 1-881052-58-3 CIP
Item no. 52583-270 $24.95

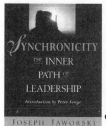

Making the Grass Greener on Your Side
A CEO's Journey to Leading by Serving

Ken Melrose

THIS IS THE STORY of how Ken Melrose, CEO of The Toro Company, adopted a philosophy of leading by serving and made it work in a real-world—and often challenging—situation. His mission at Toro has been to build an environment that not only serves the needs of the corporation, but also provides a climate for its constituents—the employees—to grow and develop as human beings. Readers will learn how to cultivate an environment for individual growth and create a win-win situation.

Hardcover, 250 pages, 9/95 • ISBN 1-881052-21-4 CIP
Item no. 52214-270 $24.95

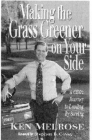

Synchronicity
The Inner Path of Leadership

Joseph Jaworski

JOSEPH JAWORSKI tells the remarkable story of his journey to an understanding of the deep issues of leadership. It is a personal journey that encourages and enlightens all of us wrestling with the profound changes required in public and institutional leadership, and in our individual lives, for the 21st century. Jaworski offers a new definition of leadership that applies to all types of leaders: community, regional, international, corporate, political.

Hardcover, 228 pages, 6/96 • ISBN 1-881052-94-X CIP
Item no. 5294X-270 $24.95

Audiotape, 2 cassettes/3 hours • ISBN 1-57453-044-5
Item no. 30445-270 $17.95

Available at your favorite bookstore, or call (800) 929-2929

Leadership and the New Science

Learning about Organization from an Orderly Universe

Margaret J. Wheatley

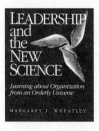

Our UNDERSTANDING of the universe is being radically altered by the "New Science"—the revolutionary discoveries in quantum physics, chaos theory, and evolutionary biology that are overturning the prevailing models of science. Now, in this pioneering book, Wheatley shows how the new science provides equally powerful insights for changing how we design, lead, manage, and view organizations.

Paperback, 172 pages, 3/94 • ISBN 1-881052-44-3 CIP
Item no. 52443-270 $15.95

Hardcover, 9/92 • ISBN 1-881052-01-X CIP • **Item no. 5201X-270 $24.95**

Audiotape, 2 cassettes/3 hours • ISBN 1-57453-017-8
Item no. 30178-270 $16.95

A Simpler Way

Margaret J. Wheatley and Myron Kellner-Rogers

Margaret Wheatley and Myron Kellner-Rogers explore the primary question, "How could we organize human endeavor if we developed different understandings of how life organizes itself?" They draw on the work of scientists, philosophers, poets, novelists, spiritual teachers, colleagues, audiences, and their own experiences in search of new ways of understanding life and how organizing activities occur.

Hardcover, 168 pages, 9/96 • ISBN 1-881052-95-8
Item no. 52958-270 $27.95

Audiotape, 2 cassettes/3 hours • ISBN 1-57453-053-4
Item no. 30534-270 $176.95

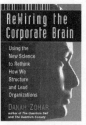

Rewiring the Corporate Brain

Using the New Science to Rethink How We Structure and Lead Organizations Danah Zohar

Drawing on a solid background in the contemporary sciences, Zohar shows how organizational structures mirror the organization of the human brain and how to utilize the capacity of the whole corporate brain. She presents a fundamentally new conceptual model for deep transformational change to the structure and leadership of organizations.

Hardcover, 250 pages, 11/97 • ISBN 1-57675-022-1 CIP
Item no. 50221-270 $27.95

Available at your favorite bookstore, or call (800) 929-2929